Jay Wiseman's
Erotic Bondage Handbook

By Jay Wiseman

greenery press

Cover photograph by Todd Friedman Photography, www.TFPhoto.com.

Illustrations by Jack Cleveland.

Published in the United States by Greenery Press, 1447 Park Ave., Emeryville, CA 94608.

www.greenerypress.com

ISBN 1-890159-13-1

TABLE OF CONTENTS

ACKNOWLEDGMENTS

This book is dedicated to one of my oldest and dearest friends, and a first-rate SM educator in her own right, Karen Mendelsohn of QSM in San Francisco. Thank you very much, Karen, for your years of friendship, for our many hours of wonderful conversation, and for suggesting that I write this book.

Many, many people helped me, in one way or another, to create this book, and expressing the proper degree of thanks is always somewhat tricky. Undoubtedly, some people are going to (correctly) perceive that they are not being shown proper gratitude here, or were even forgotten entirely. Allow me to apologize for that right now. Please contact me and I'll fix that shortcoming in future printings.

While an author ultimately works alone, they rarely work in complete isolation. The following people, listed alphabetically, served as advisors, consultants, crash test dummies (technique testers), baby sitters (monitoring me to make sure that I was working on the book while at the computer instead of spending time on the Internet or playing a computer game), and sources of inspiration. Some served in more than one capacity. While I take responsibility for any mistakes, flaws, and shortcomings in this book, these people share any praise.

First of all, my loving thanks to Lynn, who has given me so much, in so many ways. You have been such a joy and a comfort to me.

Next, my loving thanks to Baraka, who has also given me so much, in so many ways. You have been wonderful as a baby sitter, a crash test dummy, a confidante, a sounding board, and a general co-conspirator.

The following people, listed alphabetically, have also provided wonderful assistance in terms of baby sitting, crash testing, and so forth: KJ, Katy B., Lane, Linda K., Lori A., Pat.

The following people, also listed alphabetically, provided excellent assistance in terms of manuscript reading, idea polishing, reality checking, and helping me think my way through the trickier parts of this book: Beth, Dr. Charles Moser, Eddie T., John Warren, Joseph Bean, Lolita Wolf, Mark B., Rachel S., Tom Burns, and Vicki.

The writings, demonstrations, and other teachings of the following people contributed to my own development as a bondage practitioner: David El, Lana White, Loreli, Lou Duff, Molly Devon, Race Bannon, Robin Roberts, Tammad, Takeshi Nagaike, Wolf G.

Finally, of course, my deepest and most loving thanks to Janet. This book owes its existence to her love, patience, and unflagging support. Thank you so much. I love you.

A NOTE TO MY READER

Hello there, Dear Reader. How are you? Fine, I hope. Hey, before we go any further, let's you and I have a little chat. There are some fairly important matters regarding this topic that I want to make sure you understand.

First of all, while I forget who originally said it, there is a saying that goes something like "Those who do not hear the music think that those who dance are insane." This saying is very relevant to bondage (and other aspects of sadomasochism).

The appeal of erotic bondage is very personal, and can arise from a very deep place. While it can be appealing in an intellectual sense, the real sense of attraction is usually much more visceral, more primordial. The urge to tie someone up during sex, or to be tied up during sex, comes from a deep place, perhaps a subrational place, within the mind. Thus, trying to understand the desire in rational terms can be very difficult.

At one end of the spectrum are people who find such urges deeply attractive and wish to explore them. At the other end of the spectrum are people who find such urges deeply repellent and want nothing whatsoever to do with them. There are, of course, a large number of people who are somewhere in the middle.

I am, of course, one of those people who "hear" this particular type of "music" and thus find the idea of engaging in the "dance" of erotic bondage highly attractive. However, let me make it clear that I certainly don't feel that this activity is for everybody (actually, I don't think it's for most people, as I will explain later). Furthermore, if the idea of engaging in erotic bondage deeply repels you, I certainly have no problem with that and I am not inclined to spend a lot of time urging you to reconsider.

(The one exception I might make to that would be for you to make sure that you have a reasonable idea of what is actually involved regarding how most of us engage in erotic bondage. After all, before we can have reasonable debate or discussion about a particular topic, we must first make sure that we are in acceptably close agreement regarding our terms before we go too much further. Otherwise, we're unlikely to communicate effectively .)

So, if you're fairly certain that you have a reasonable idea of what's involved in erotic bondage as I've outlined it in this book, and you nonetheless find the idea of doing this in any way deeply repellent, then I urge you, in a genuinely friendly and cordial way, to seek your erotic satisfaction elsewhere. I certainly understand that not everybody is aroused by the same things and, in a way, I'm actually glad that is the case. As the wise old grandpa once told his grandson, "Tommy, if everybody in this world wanted the same thing, the whole world would be after your grandma."

On the other hand, if you feel drawn to explore the dance of erotic bondage, then I believe this book will be helpful to you.

WARNING AND DISCLAIMER

Whenever an imbalance of power exists, the potential for abuse also exists.

This imbalance of power can take many different forms: raw physical power, economic power, the power to persuade or emotionally manipulate, and so forth. I'm sure you can think of other examples.

So whenever an imbalance of power exists, the potential for abuse necessarily and unavoidably also exists. Such abuse doesn't always actually occur, and in fact it's my experience that in the huge majority of cases it doesn't occur, but it could. It most definitely could. That's worth keeping in mind.

In what I will call BDSM (more commonly known, if not accurately understood, by the average citizen as "sadomasochism"), we intentionally, consensually create such an imbalance of power because we find it rewarding to explore the unique, intense energy that exists whenever such an imbalance of power exists. Most of the time such explorations go pretty well. In fact, at least within the BDSM community, reports of people abusing this imbalance are very rare. Not entirely nonexistent, you understand, but nonetheless still very rare.

The main purpose of this book is to teach techniques that will allow one person to physically restrain another person in a reasonably safe, consensual manner. Some of the techniques in this book, when applied as directed, will restrain the bound person so that they are reduced (for lack of a better word) to a level of helplessness and vulnerability about equal to that of an infant. A very substantial imbalance of raw physical power is thus created between the bound person and the unbound person. Even a very small person can, if they choose, nonconsensually abuse a much larger person, if that larger person is effectively bound. That's a very sobering reality to contemplate.

I confess that I feel a bit nervous regarding writing this book. I can fill the book with safety warnings (and I have done so, and done so to the point where I'm certain that some readers will become annoyed with the frequency of such warnings). However, I cannot ultimately control who reads this book or what use they make of the information herein. That worries me.

Of course, perhaps I worry overmuch. After all, people create and distribute material all the time on topics whose abuse potential is much higher than that of this book. There are literally thousands of books, magazines, and videos (and information available through other venues, especially the internet) on subjects such as various martial arts techniques, knife fighting, gun fighting, how to make bombs, how to make booby traps, "real" torture methods, and so forth. There's even at least one military manual on hand-to-hand combat put out by the United States government, that depicts "prisoner tying" techniques far harsher than many of the techniques that I've included in this book, and that is available to civilians.

Furthermore, mainstream films and television shows routinely show bondage and torture techniques. For example, when someone gets restrained in such a film or television show by the use of duct tape, as I recently saw on an episode of "South Park," this "bondage lesson" is seen by millions of viewers of all ages. Yet I don't see anybody going after the producers of such major films or shows and accusing them of irresponsibly dispensing such information.

Additionally, the producers of such shows certainly don't seem to feel any responsibility (or, more importantly, liability) if someone watches what they produced and then goes out and nonconsensually does it to another person.

So if such rich, important, and powerful "bigwigs" don't worry overly much about the misuse of material that they presented in their movies and television shows, why should "little old me" worry about it? Well, I do, that's all. I just do. The idea that somebody might end up being nonconsensually tortured because of something that the assailant learned in this book bothers me a very great deal.

So what can or should I do about that? Well, let's see, what are my options?

At one extreme, I could choose to not write or publish the book at all. Taking that option would entirely eliminate the possibility that any information I might communicate could be abused – because I wouldn't be communicating any information! This is a harsh, but 100% abuse-proof approach.

At the other extreme, I could take the "hey, it's not my problem, it's not my responsibility, and it's most certainly not my liability" approach. (As I mentioned, this seems to be the approach taken by most mainstream producers of material that depict bondage techniques.) Somebody misused what's in here? That's none of my concern.

A third approach would be the "going through the motions of giving safety warnings" approach. I could give lip service to the various safety matters, and then go on to present a number of highly dangerous techniques. They misused what's in this book? Hey, I warned them, didn't I?

How about a fourth approach? Let's try a very sober, clear look at the material in this book.

Dear Reader, I strongly suggest that you consider what you are holding in your hand to be a very large, sharp, double-edged sword. More correctly, you are holding in your hand informational material that will allow you to create and use such a sword. Remember, this sword is, by its nature, unavoidably double-edged. A rope, like many other everyday items such as a car, a kitchen knife, a hammer, or a match, has great potential for positive, constructive use, and also great potential for negative, destructive use.

A rope is intrinsically neutral. It is a common, everyday item that has no specific purpose. A rope can be used for both good and for evil, for both consensual, erotic play and for nonconsensual, horrible torture.

How are people injured by bondage? By intentional misuse, and by ignorant misuse.

My experience has led me to believe that far more injuries are due to ignorant misuse than are due to intentional abuse. So by writing this book I can do good by reducing the number of injuries due to ignorance. I can also reduce the number of injuries caused by intentional misuse by reducing the number of people who are vulnerable to such abuse. I do this by teaching potential victims how to avoid putting themselves into such vulnerable positions – thus depriving the predator of victims, and enabling the victims to recognize the predator much earlier than they otherwise would – and to warn others.

So, while a small number of predators may gain some small advantage, I strongly believe that the overall effect of writing this book will be to greatly reduce the number of victims available to such predators and to reduce the harm caused by non-malicious bondage.

Furthermore, this is certainly not the only place where a predator could learn. In fact, I want predators to feel distinctly uneasy that this book exists, because it will make life harder on them. This book will reduce the number of potential victims available to them. It will also enable their potential victims to recognize the predator much earlier in the process of dealing with them, and to take effective counter-measures.

I strongly advise you to acknowledge that bondage is an inherently risky activity. Like driving a car, there are always risks associated with engaging in bondage. These include risks to your physical well being, your emotional well being, the relationship you have with your bondage partner, and even your legal situation. These risks can be reduced, but never entirely eliminated. Fortunately, if you follow the safety recommendations in this book, you should reduce the risks you face to a very low level.

You are the primary person responsible for keeping yourself safe, and you have the right to take reasonable measures to ensure your well being. If your potential partner is uncomfortable with your taking such measures, it may be a very good idea to consider whether or not doing bondage with them at all is a good idea.

My book "SM 101: A Realistic Introduction" includes the statement, "You almost never get into serious trouble by going too slowly." To this I would now add "especially at the beginning." Almost all problems make themselves known fairly early. If you take things slowly, especially at first, and pay attention, you should almost always spot potential trouble while it is still manageable.

There is a test for potential bondage partners, particularly if you are going to be the one getting tied up, that I call the "NTA test." To perform this test, you ask yourself how you think you would feel if you were "Naked, Tied up, and Alone" with this person (and with nobody else knowing about your situation). If your feelings about this scenario – a scenario which, of course, could very well come to pass – are other than strongly and warmly positive, then I suggest you act accordingly.

We can never predict the future with perfect accuracy. When doing bondage, most people take safety precautions of one sort of another – and many of these safety precautions are very effective – but whether or not the precautions taken will actually be adequate if a situation should arise is always something of a matter of guesswork. To help ensure that the safety precautions taken will actually be adequate in the event of an emergency, I suggest that bondage practitioners "overprepare" just a bit.

I have a saying that I believe will help in this regard: "Take one more precaution than you think you need to."

Let's face it, bondage is often a sexual activity, and people faced with the prospect of imminent sexual activity are often not at their most rational. So please give yourself just a bit more of a safety margin than you at first think you're going to need. This "take one more precaution than you think you need to" approach can take a number of forms. It might involve making one more phone call to tell a friend where and with whom you're going to be. It might involve making sure that one more item of safety gear, such as a flashlight or pair of scissors, is handy. It might involve quickly summarizing the points of pre-bondage negotiations one last time before starting to play. Fortunately, this can almost always be done without spoiling the mood.

So that's it. Truth be told, just as with driving a car, most of the time things actually go pretty well, especially if you learn and follow "the rules of the road." While it's not for everybody, exploring erotic bondage can be incredibly satisfying and fulfilling. It has the potential to enrich your life, enrich your relationship, and can even be a means of profound personal growth.

Just remember: Take one more precaution than you think you need to.

Best wishes,

Jay Wiseman

San Francisco, California

January, 2000

"Power without wisdom is terrifying. Wisdom without power is pathetic." – Jay Wiseman

ABOUT THE QUOTES

Throughout this book, in attempt to convey a taste of what it's like to do bondage, I have included a number of quips, remarks, and other comments I've heard over the years. None of the people felt, as far as I know, that they were making a significant comment at the time they spoke. These are just passing comments, and therefore more revealing.

PLEASE ALLOW ME TO INTRODUCE MYSELF

Q uestion: Why should you, the reader, pay any special attention to what I, Jay Wiseman, have to say about bondage?

An excellent question! Let me attempt to answer it.

There is a very good chance that you are reading this book, and quite possibly have paid money for this book, because you believe that there is likely to be information in here on the subject of bondage that you (a) don't already know and (b) are likely to find useful. Let us both hope that this is the case.

However, before we go any further, it's only reasonable to ask why you should give any credence to, or even pay attention to, what I have to say on the subject. What is it about me that makes what I have to say about this matter more useful than, say, someone you would stop at random on the street? How do I justify representing to you that I am some kind of expert on this distinctly unusual topic?

Let us please assume, for the purposes of discussion, that bondage is one aspect of a broader subject called erotic power play, BDSM, leathersex, SM and/or sadomasochism. There are a lot of people out there who are doing, and/or studying, and/or teaching SM. However, at this time there is no such organization as the International Association for the Advancement of the Study and Practice of Sadomasochism. There is no widely accepted training program. There are no formal licensing requirements, credentialing procedures, review board, continuing education requirements, or malpractice insurance.

Thus, any idiot can step forward and claim to be an "expert" on bondage or any other aspect of BDSM (and a fair number of idiots have done exactly that, some in a very high-profile manner), and it is difficult to refute their claim of expertise.

So what makes me some sort of expert? Well, how is the word "expert" defined? My dictionary has a concise definition of the term. *Expert: (adjective) having, involving, or displaying special skill or knowledge derived from training or experience. (noun) one who has acquired special skill in or knowledge of a particular subject.*

So what sort of education, training, and experience do I have regarding bondage? Please let me present you with a somewhat abbreviated version of my "bondage credentials."

I started fantasizing about bondage in 1970, and it has remained a very central aspect of my sexuality ever since then. I started doing bondage (in a very untrained way; thank goodness there were no major mishaps) in 1971. I have continued doing bondage with my lovers on a regular basis pretty much ever since then, and I have spent a large amount of time both "outside the ropes" and "inside the ropes."

In 1972 I read an excellent article called "Bishop on Bondage" in an SM adult publication. This article was a good introductory essay on the basic principles of bondage. Additionally in 1972, I had a chance to read the book "Kill or Get Killed" by Rex Applegate. This is a book on military hand-to-hand combat techniques, and it includes a chapter on prisoner tying that I found very interesting reading.

In 1974, I purchased "The Joy of Sex" and repeatedly read over the "bondage" and the "discipline" chapters in that book. (Yes, I also read the rest of it – just not quite so closely.)

In 1975, I joined an SM education and support organization in the San Francisco Bay Area called "Backdrop" and attended many of their educational programs – including, of course, every one I could get to on the subject of bondage. It was during this time that I acquired my "basic training in SM" and learned in a formal sort of way – or, at least, as formal as things usually get in the SM community – many of the core teachings of the SM world. (There will be more on those teachings, as appropriate, later in this book.)

It was also at this time that I started to meet people who knew a lot more about bondage than I did, including the director of Backdrop, Robin

Roberts, and a professional dominatrix named Mistress Lana White. I learned everything I could from these people. Additionally, Backdrop had a large "SM library" and I thus had a chance to look through numerous books and magazines that dealt with bondage (and other aspect of SM).

In 1977, I joined another SM education and support organization in the San Francisco Bay Area called the Society of Janus and, again, attended many of their programs, including, of course, programs on bondage. I remain a Janus member to this day.

During this time, I was also learning about bondage-related practices in an entirely different context. I was an ambulance crewman for many years, and one of the things I routinely did was to put patients into restraints. (Before anybody gets too alarmed here, let me add that such restraints had to be pre-authorized by either a police officer or a physician. Let me add very clearly and unequivocally that I never mixed business with pleasure in this regard. Of course, those of you who have spent some time in the emergency services yourselves will know that people who need to be restrained are usually, shall we say, not very erotically appealing at that moment in their lives. Thus I'm sure that many of you, especially those who have been there yourselves, will understand entirely when I say that I cannot recall so much as a single instance of feeling even vaguely tempted to do any such mixing.)

Given that I was also working closely with many people in law enforcement during this time, I had a chance to learn about, and sometimes use, various handcuffing techniques. I carried handcuffs, and routinely used them, while working for a couple of different ambulance services.

In 1978 or thereabouts, I was becoming known as a bondage aficionado and was therefore asked to give a presentation on the subject to the members of the Society of Janus. The presentation was well received. I made a number of similar presentations over the next ten or so years to various groups.

In 1992, after working on it for years, I self-published the first edition of my book "SM 101: A Realistic Introduction." I'm proud to say that this book has sold a very large number of copies and has become one of the most widely recommended books in the field. In 1996, an updated second edition of "SM 101" was published by Greenery Press. The publication of the book also most definitely changed the course of my life.

Since "SM 101" was first published, I have been widely in demand as an SM-related speaker and author. I have given more talks, and written more articles and essays, than I can remember. I have given presentations about SM in (among other places) San Francisco, New York, Los Angeles, Boston, San Jose, Chicago, Sacramento, Las Vegas, Oakland, Portland, San Diego, and Seattle.

> "I want to make sure that I really know how to tie you up."

I have been consulted regarding the realities of SM by people from many different parts of life, including physicians, police officers, paramedics, researchers, mental health workers, coroners, attorneys, students, teachers, sex workers, journalists, therapists of many different kinds, and, of course, lots of average citizens.

I have continued to be very active in the SM community at both the local and national level. I've been a speaker at three national conventions (more properly called the "Living in Leather" conferences) put on by the National Leather Association. I don't know the total number of SM-related events I have attended in the last quarter of a century, but if you add up the number of educational programs, parties, social events, and other types of gatherings, it is easily well over one thousand.

During all this time, I have continued to practice and study the SM activity that is my personal favorite: bondage – especially rope bondage.

I first became seriously interested in writing this book about a year ago, after a dear friend of mine who is also an SM bookseller (Karen Mendelsohn of QSM, San Francisco), told me that there was significant interest in a book devoted pretty much exclusively to bondage.

In this last year, a great deal of research has gone into the creation of this book. In many ways, it was an interesting and unusual experience to "learn a lot about something that I already knew a lot about." In conducting research for this book, I have gone over hospital restraint policies, police prisoner-control techniques, martial-arts-related tying techniques, and, of course, erotic bondage techniques. I've lurked in various types of libraries and bookstores. I have read and re-read many books on knots and ropecraft. I've also, of course, had a large number of in-depth conversations with various people who shared my interest in bondage. These conversations were an especially useful source of information and perspective for this book, and I thank those people for their contributions.

I put out a call for bondage-related information at several places on the Internet. In particular, I asked people to share with me their experiences of what I called "Type One Incidents" (in which there was an unexpectedly bad outcome) and "Type Two Incidents" (in which there was an unexpectedly good outcome). I got dozens of replies, and that feedback did a lot towards helping me to make the various recommendations in this book more reality-based.

I also repeatedly visited and bought items from hardware stores, variety stores, boating supply houses, medical supply companies, police equipment stores, and mountaineering equipment companies.

My research for this book got an additional, unexpected boost from another source. After being out of "the medical game" for a few years, I decided to take a few re-entry courses at a local college, including courses in anatomy, physiology, and microbiology. I wonder if my anatomy teacher ever speculated about why I seemed so especially interested in the anatomy of the wrists and ankles.

During the research and writing of this book, Janet's and my living quarters turned into something resembling "The San Francisco Bondage Research Institute," with various types of rope, webbing, scarves, tape, bandages, restraints, gags, blindfolds, earplugs, locks, chains, and other bondage-related paraphernalia strewn all over the place. Load after load after load of laundry was done to determine how well various types and arrangements of materials stood up to being washed. Of course, a great deal of "bondage beta testing" went on during this time, and I owe a particular debt of gratitude to my "bondage crash test dummies."

So here the book is. A very great deal of time, effort, care, experience, research, thought, discussion, scholarship, fact checking, and experimentation went into its creation. I hope that all concerned benefit by it.

Bondage Research Difficulties

One of the more difficult aspects of researching and developing the material in this book has been the distinct difficulty of finding usable information.

One of the most obvious uses of rope, familiar to any child, is that it can be used to tie someone up. And yet when you look into almost every book on rope and knotcraft, there is very little, if any, mention of this practice. (In a way, I suppose that is good news for me personally, otherwise there would have been no need for me to write this book.)

In any event, when looking through almost all of the existing works, it is clear that people-binding is a topic the "rope and knot people" consider "the cousin we don't talk about." There is clearly an element of fear, shame, and embarrassment over this aspect of rope work.

Indeed, so far the only serious published works on how to do rope bondage that I have found have been in SM-related erotica, military hand-to-hand combat manuals, and in descriptions of the Japanese martial art of prisoner-tying known as hojo-jitsu. Good examples of any of these are fairly difficult to find.

Furthermore, when examining various historical records of how bondage was used, good examples of bondage techniques (at least, good examples of bondage techniques that we could use in our practice of erotic bondage) are also very difficult to find.

In much "real world" bondage, security or inescapability is the primary concern. There is also a very good chance that the bound person will be in this bondage for the rest of their life – a period which will not be all that long. It is further clear that, in those circumstances, there is little or no concern that the bondage be non-damaging. In fact, if there is "bad blood" between the person doing the tying and the person being tied, the person doing the tying may consider that bondage which is itself painful, or even tortuous, is all the better.

Thus, discovering bondage techniques that are effective but not damaging is very difficult – particularly bondage techniques which use everyday items such as rope as opposed to more formal bondage gear such as handcuffs or leather restraints. This is clearly knowledge that "respectable" people are supposed to neither need nor, especially, want to know.

This belief is reinforced by the fact that many vendors of "formal" bondage gear, such as handcuffs or institutional restraints, refuse to sell them to the general public. After all, no decent person would want or need such materials, therefore any "civilian" who wants to buy them must clearly have some indecent purpose in mind, and it would thus be better to refuse them. (Indeed, if the person were not intending to use these materials for consensual, BDSM-related purposes, I can see that this vendor might have a point.)

A NOTE TO EXPERIENCED SADOMASOCHISTS

Writing this book has posed a number of challenges. As part of writing this book, I gave presentations on bondage to a number of BDSM groups. While doing this was fun, I knew that I was, in some respects, "preaching to the choir." Most of the people who showed up for my presentations already strongly self-identified as being interested in some aspect of BDSM, and likely some interest in bondage in particular.

Also, such people were likely to be "SM veterans" to at least some degree (and some were very seasoned veterans indeed). In any event, I could be pretty sure that most of the members of my audience had already been through "basic training in BDSM" and were familiar with such fundamental SM concepts such as safewords, limits, consent, negotiation, low-risk practices versus high-risk practices, and so forth. I cannot make such an assumption regarding the readers of this book.

I was a bit surprised when my old friend, SM educator Karen Mendelsohn of QSM in San Francisco, strongly urged me to write a book that dealt mainly with bondage. After all, there were already some books out on the market that did a pretty good job of covering the basics of bondage. "Screw the Roses, Send Me the Thorns" and my earlier book "SM 101: A Realistic Introduction" both covered the topic in some detail, along with the more fundamental information on matters such as safewords. Furthermore, there was good basic information in some of the other "intro to SM" books. However, Karen was quite clear and firm in her views.

Given that she runs the largest SM bookstore in the world and is in very close touch with the wants and needs of people who buy SM-related books, I have learned over the years that in matters such as this it is best to listen to her carefully, so I did. This book is the result.

Additionally, there were several pretty good websites that also presented good, basic bondage information, and some more advanced information, for free. Given that reality, a book on bondage was going to have to be very worthwhile indeed. (The increasing availability of good information for free online is a challenge to those who make our living doing education in any area.)

Finally, there would be very little point to creating this book if all it did was repeat the existing knowledge associated with the practice of bondage. To help it be worthwhile, this book should move the body of knowledge forward.

Thus, four of the major challenges of this book were:

1. To provide at least minimal education about the general, fundamentally important, aspects of SM without writing yet another overall "Introduction to SM" book.

2. To be significantly better than the resources, both commercial and free, currently available.

3. To provide enough information regarding bondage theory and practice to get my readers "well and truly launched" into their explorations, and yet not provide so much information that the book turned into something of an encyclopedia. (For example: experienced bondage practitioners will note that not every single known bondage technique is described, although the more commonly used ones are almost all represented.)

4. To deepen, broaden, clarify, and update the body of knowledge regarding bondage, and the teachings that derive therefrom.

There are a number of "standard" bondage-related teachings of the "never do this" and "always do that" variety. While researching and writing this book, I tried to re-examine these standard teachings with what I hoped was some degree of intellectual rigor. I re-examined the evidence in support of and against the various teachings. In some cases, I found that the available evidence did support the standard teaching. In other cases, I found that the available evidence did not necessarily either support or not support the standard teaching. In yet other cases, I found that the available evidence did not support the standard teaching. In these latter cases, I did my best to frame a new teaching that the available evidence did support.

I imagine that some of these "new teachings" will generate some degree of discussion and even controversy. Those who know me know that I am not particularly afraid of discussion and controversy; however, I do hope that any which result will be evidence-based. Rather than merely trading personal opinions and value judgments, let us do our best to cite our evidence in support of our conclusions.

I don't believe this is asking too much. For example, the long-running, very vigorous debate on the Internet regarding the relative risk level of what is called "breath control play" (basically, suffocation or strangulation done in an erotic context) has become nearly saturated with references from medical journals, forensic pathology textbooks, legal citations, and so forth. This is, in my opinion, a very good thing, and I hope to see a similarly high level of evidence-based debate regarding other SM-related matters, particularly as they relate to bondage.

In preparing the recommendations of this book, I spent many hours in places such as medical school libraries, pulling dozens of journal articles relating to matters such as positional asphyxia, restraint-related injuries, and similar matters. In making my conclusions and recommendations, I studied these articles carefully, compared them to my own experience of about 30 years, and discussed the topic with many knowledgeable others. Thus, these conclusions were reached after a very diligent analysis of the available data, and lengthy, detailed discussion with other knowledgeable practitioners. They represent carefully considered conclusions on my part. I hope you find these conclusions useful, and I look forward to receiving your feedback.

BONDAGE AND EROTIC POWER PLAY

hile bondage can be regarded in a number of ways, I have found that one of the more useful viewpoints is to consider it as one of a group of behaviors commonly categorized as erotic power play, BDSM, SM, D/S, leathersex, kink and/or sadomasochism. I recognize that these words are frightening to many readers, and so I ask you to bear with me as I explain my reasoning.

Bondage is, in and of itself, a way of shifting the power dynamic between the person on the outside of the ropes and the person on the inside, and thus qualifies under at least the broader definitions of sadomasochism. Furthermore, bondage is frequently combined with other behaviors that can also be considered part of sadomasochism, such as spanking, whipping, using clamps, "slave training," and so forth. Therefore, before we get too much further involved with specifically with bondage, let's look over the broader aspects of what's often called sadomasochism.

Note: If you're interested in a much broader, more detailed introduction regarding sadomasochism, please allow me to refer you to my book "SM 101: A Realistic Introduction." You will find information on that book and on many other excellent introductory texts at the end of this book.

OK, so what is sadomasochism (SM, for short)? Good question. Unfortunately, there is no one universal, widely agreed-upon answer. There is also no such organization as the National Sadomasochistic Board of Standards and Practices which issues rulings from on high which all must follow (or, if you like, which all must be bound by), regarding what is and what is not sadomasochism. So, to a certain extent, each of us is left on our own to define the term.

This lack of universal agreement can sometimes be a problem, particularly when attempting to evaluate the knowledge, judgment, and skill of a potential dominant partner. Right now, there is no approved training program that someone must complete before they proclaim themselves to be a Master, Mistress, Dominatrix, and so forth. There is no licensing board, no continuing education requirements, no formal peer review, and certainly no malpractice insurance.

Still, a surprisingly large degree of agreement exists regarding SM – so much agreement that a large and growing SM community has appeared, with clubs in essentially all major cities and many smaller ones. There is also enough agreement that detailed discussions of the finer points can proceed with remarkable clarity. There are even national conventions. (I've been a speaker at a few of them.)

In a way, it's not surprising that there is such a large degree of agreement. I've discovered that the challenges of engaging in enjoyable sadomasochism are fairly universal, so people who are exploring in isolation often work out what tend to be comparable solutions. (Either that, or they have a history of repeatedly running into the same problems.)

SM can be compared to mountain climbing in this regard. (We even use some of the same equipment!) Mountain climbers in the Swiss Alps, the Himalayas, and the Rocky Mountains all face a similar set of problems. Thus, it's not really all that surprising that they would have worked out a similar or comparable set of solutions.

Therefore, people who have a markedly different definition from that used by the rest of the SM community would have the burden of proof regarding why their definition should be considered a good one. Indeed, one of the most important things a novice to SM can do is to seek opinions and advice from a wide variety of unrelated sources. This sort of cross-checking is one of the most valuable things that an uninformed novice can do to protect themselves from predators.

Let's start by asking: Where does the urge to engage in sadomasochistic behavior come from? Well, if we look at "regular" sexual activity, we see that even the most conventional erotic behavior often involves elements of aggression, submission, and so forth. For example, long before I developed an interest in sadomasochism, I more than occasionally would have a lover say something to me during a passionate moment such as "take me!" or even "rape me!"

(I confess that, young fellow that I was, I found these "rape me!" requests to be somewhat confusing and even a bit alarming. I knew at least something about how horrible and traumatic rape could be, and I certainly had no desire to do something like that to anybody, much less a woman that I cared about. What strange things my lovers sometimes asked for!)

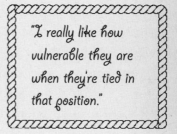

"I really like how vulnerable they are when they're tied in that position."

I also noticed, in my pre-sadomasochism days, that a significant percentage of my lovers (yes, I had considerably more than one; I was fortunate enough to participate in the "sexual revolution" of the late '60s and early '70s) seemed to like it when I assumed a sort of take-charge attitude during our lovemaking. Sometimes they would even encourage or "provoke" me into doing so. As one woman put it, "I like it when you take over."

Other women wanted to be more in charge of our sex. For example, one woman used to look at me very directly and say "lie face-up on the bed, stretch your arms and legs out towards the four corners, and don't move until I tell you to." She would then proceed to use her hands, mouth, and other parts of her body upon me for a very long time. These were intensely erotic experiences for me, and I remember gasping out at the time, "My God, you could torture someone this way!" (Little did I know then exactly how correct I was!)

So we can see that, even for "normal" people, there are frequently elements of aggression and submission associated with sexual desires and behaviors. In one Kinsey study ("Sexual Behavior in the Human Female" by Kinsey, Pomeroy, and Martin) while only 11% of those studied stated that they had specifically sadomasochistic desires, about 50% reported being aroused by activities that included causing mild pain (biting, scratching, and so forth) or by activities that included dominant or submissive types of behavior.

Sadomasochism can be, and often is, a way of taking the implicit aspects of domination and submission that often accompany sex and making these aspects more explicit. Sadomasochism "names the game" and, furthermore, even gives this "game" rules of conduct so that the "players" (within the SM community, to engage in SM with someone is frequently called to "play" with them; getting together with someone is frequently called a "play date") can play with a very high degree of intensity and yet a relatively small degree of actual physical and/or emotional risk. Thus, if I had to define SM in the briefest possible way, I'd define it as "ritualized sexual aggression."

A more formal definition can be found in my book "SM 101: A Realistic Introduction." The section "SM defined in one sentence" reads: "SM is the use of psychological dominance and submission, and/or physical bondage, and/or pain, and/or related practices in a safe, legal, consensual manner in order for the participants to experience erotic arousal and/or personal growth."

THE ELEMENTS OF SM

While the exact techniques and styles of SM play vary tremendously, there are certain almost universally agreed-upon elements. Some of those elements are:

Consent. This is the big one. All SM play is, by definition, consensual. While some advanced practitioners play at the outer edges of consent, and while great debate can and does take place regarding the nuances and subtle aspects of what constitutes adequate consent, at its heart SM is a consensual activity. The basic nature of this consent is relatively straightforward and easily understood by the average person. It is very comparable to the type of consent that one person needs to give in order for another person to legally have sex with them.

SM play should only be done by people who are adequately informed of the nature of what they are doing and who are mentally competent to decide for themselves whether or not this is something that they want to do. That being the case, SM should not be engaged in by people who are too emotionally immature, senile, intoxicated, mentally retarded, or uninformed to understand the basic nature of the activity. (In fact, engaging in SM with such a person could get you charged with rape.) Also, it is not ethical to "manufacture consent" by manipulating or exerting any undue influence upon another person to get them to engage in SM.

In summary, it usually works best to engage in SM with people who do not merely consent, but rather with people who give their informed, enthusiastic consent. In other words, the person is most definitely of sound mind, they most definitely have an adequate understanding of what is and is not involved, and they most definitely want to do this of their own free will, without having been coerced or manipulated.

Use of a "safeword." Because SM play can sometimes become very intense, both physically and emotionally, and because people sometimes like to role-play SM scenes in which they are "forced" to do things "against their will," it is very common in SM for the players to agree upon some type of real-world signal to indicate to their partner that the activity has reached a point that they are no longer comfortable with. Typically, a specific word, commonly called a "safeword," is used to fulfill this function. For example, the two people might agree ahead of time that they will role-play something like rapist and victim, in which the victim will be "captured" and tied up while struggling (somewhat) against their captor, perhaps even crying out "no" or "stop" as part of the role-play. But if the "victim" (or the "rapist" for that matter) calls out the word "carrot," it signals that they really need to have some issue addressed and that it's not part of the game.

Note: I have met a fair number of people within the SM community who solemnly claim that they play without safewords, but when I look closely at what they actually do with their partners I almost always discover that they have the functional equivalent of a safeword in place. Sometimes I find that they don't play with safewords, but they are so careful to keep their play within the "acceptability zone" of their partners that the need for one essentially never arises unless something unexpected occurs.

On those very few occasions that I discover that the person really isn't using a safeword, I usually find that they have a history of having a way-above-average number of their SM scenes ending with hurt bodies and/or hurt feelings, and with very few of their former partners being willing to either play with them again or to recommend them to others. I also usually find that these no-safeword players have a history of relatively short relationships.

Negotiation and limits. Discussing and agreeing ahead of time regarding what will take place during an SM play date (and, perhaps more importantly, what will not take place

"She asked me about the handcuff key on my keychain."

during this play date) is a very important part of obtaining adequate consent. While people who are highly experienced at playing with each other may need very little or no negotiation before playing, people who are just getting to know each other usually need to do a significant amount of discussion and negotiation beforehand. (I usually allow up to an hour for pre-play negotiations with a new partner.)

"Reality" is kept out of it. SM play is almost always never a good place to attempt to resolve any "real world" negative feelings you have towards another person. It is not a good idea (and in fact it is often outright courting disaster) to do something along the lines of tie someone up and spank them because you are mad at them because they got a parking ticket, failed to take out the garbage, or forgot your birthday. Issues like those get handled in "straight time" and outside of your SM play.

There are occasional exceptions to this (there are occasional exceptions to almost everything about sadomasochism) but those exceptions usually occur within the context of ongoing, highly developed SM relationships in which one person has freely agreed that the other person has the right to punish them in this way. In other words, if this right isn't freely agreed upon well ahead of time, it's almost always better to not introduce punishment for real-world misconduct into your SM play.

Insignificant damage. SM play often involves significant amounts of pain, and often a certain amount of damage to the body, but there is an upper limit. The basic default upper limit is that the dominant partner will not intentionally do anything to the submissive partner beyond the submissive's ability to self-heal. (This is true even if the submissive might consent to such damage or even, in the heat of passion, actively encourage the dominant to inflict it.) Thus, in the aftermath of an intense SM play date, the submissive partner may have welts, bruises, and such, but they will not have large deep lacerations, fractures, and so forth. Neither will they be deeply emotionally traumatized or damaged. (They will also, as I hope I don't really need to point out, still be alive.)

The major subdivisions of sadomasochism. As I mentioned, there is no such thing as an official, all-encompassing definition of sadomasochism. However, a very great deal of what happens during most sadomasochistic play falls into one of three major subdivisions, and it is very common for the play to involve two or even all three of them.

The main subdivisions of sadomasochism are bondage play, sensation play, and domination/submission play. Let me talk briefly about each.

Bondage play is, of course, what this book is about, so we'll be going over it in much greater detail later. Basically, it usually involves applying rope or some other material to the submissive partner's body in order to limit their ability to move.

Sensation play is frequently, but not always, synonymous with pain play. Sensation play would typically include such practices as spanking, whipping, applying clamps, using ice cubes, dripping hot wax, and so forth. However, please note well that not all SM-related sensation play is related to pain. Sometimes pleasant sensations can be involved such as rubbing a piece of velvet or fur over a person's skin, or sexually stimulating them.

(Note: a fairly large number of people are into spanking as a form of erotic or semi-erotic play, but some of them deny that what they are into is a subdivision of SM. They see spanking as a stand-alone activity in its own right and sometimes speak of themselves as members of the "spanking community" as opposed to the "SM community." While this matter is subject to debate, I can see their point.)

Domination and submission play (sometimes abbreviated as D&S play or D&s play) has to do with the general idea of one person making themselves subservient to the will and commands of another person to a greater or lesser degree. In this form of SM play, one person gives orders and the other obeys them, within whatever boundaries the two of them have negotiated.

SM play can also involve a number of activities that can be thought of as "related practices," in that many people who are into SM are also into these practices and sometimes combine them with their SM play. These are separate practices and not by definition part of SM itself. Cross-dressing (particularly a man dressing in women's clothing) would be a typical example. While a dominant woman might "force" a man to cross-dress as a woman as a way of "humiliating" him, it is certainly possible to be interested in SM without being interested in cross-dressing and it is certainly possible to be interested in cross-dressing without being interested in SM.

A few other examples of related practices would include age play (in which an adult role-plays that they are a child or an infant), enema play, corsetry, and foot fetishism.

MEET THE PLAYERS

With the exception of things like self-bondage practices, you need (a minimum of) two people to engage in bondage. To help you follow what I'm saying in this book, I need an easy way for you to tell those two people apart.

There are various words used regarding sadomasochistic practices to describe who is "doing the doing" and who is "getting done to." The dominant partner is commonly referred to by a number of terms, including Dominant, Master, Mistress, Goddess, Top, Owner, and Sadist. The submissive partner is frequently referred to as the Submissive, Slave, Property, Bottom, or Masochist. People who enjoy both roles are commonly referred to as switches. There is a great deal of debate within the SM community regarding which is the proper term for whom. (Actually, there is a great deal of debate within the SM community about virtually everything.)

There is something of a trend to refer to the person in the position of psychological dominance and command as the "dominant" and to refer to the person in the position of psychological submission and obedience as the "submissive." There is also something of a trend to refer to the person who enjoys giving the pain as the "sadist" and to refer to the person who enjoys receiving the pain as the "masochist."

In the '70s and '80s, there was a tendency to refer to someone who enjoyed both psychologically dominating and giving pain to their partner as a "top" and to refer to someone who enjoyed both being psychologically dominated and receiving pain as a "bottom." In the '90s, something of a semantic drift occurred in language usage within the SM community. Now it seems to be more common for those who enjoy the more psychological/emotional/etc. aspects of SM play to be referred to as "dominants" and "submissives" and for those who enjoy giving and receiving pain (and other forms of sensation) to be referred to as "tops" and "bottoms."

There is also a trend for people who are in the owner role of an ongoing SM relationship to be referred to as "Master" or "Mistress" and for those who are in the owned role in such relationships to be referred to as "slaves." Thus, these terms are frequently used in a way much like such terms as "husband," "wife," or "boyfriend" – as indicators of an ongoing relationship and the nature of that relationship.

Exceptions exist to all of the above-described trends. Some SM people will be happy to discuss those exceptions with you at great length and in extreme detail – especially over the Internet.

SM is nonspecific regarding gender and sexual orientation. Indeed, one can have a fine old debate regarding whether or not SM is itself a sexual orientation. (This is not idle discussion. SM people can face serious discrimination regarding matters like child custody, and the laws that prohibit discrimination on the basis of sexual orientation have not, as of this writing, been explicitly extended to include SM.)

Anyway, to describe who is doing what to whom in this book, I will use the gender-neutral term of "top" to refer to the person who is doing the tying and ends up on the outside of the ropes. I will also use the gender-neutral term of "bottom" to refer to the person who is getting tied up and ends up on the inside of the ropes. Furthermore, please note that I am referring to bondage play that involves two people (and only two people) unless I specify otherwise.

THE SCOPE OF THIS BOOK

ost of the bondage techniques in this book would likely be considered by many people in the BDSM community to fall into the basic-to-intermediate range in terms of difficulty, complexity, and risk. There is no universal standard by which bondage techniques are judged, so this is something of a guess on my part, but I'd like to think it's an educated guess.

Anyway, this book covers basic to intermediate techniques, according to the best of my ability to judge them. It generally does not cover techniques that many bondage fans would consider more advanced. In particular...

1.   This book does not cover what are commonly thought of as "suspension bondage" techniques, in which the bottom is partially or completely suspended off the ground. In fact, I decided not to include any techniques in this book which involved a rope that was under strain, load, or tension when running from an overhead attachment point to the bottom. The whole subject of "vertical ropes under tension" can be a very complex one, and I have heard of more incidents than I can remember of bottoms suffering injury after mishaps such as "securely mounted" screw eyes pulling loose from their overhead mountings. Thus, I decided to leave that whole area alone.

2.   This book does not cover (in great detail) the highly stylized procedures commonly referred to as "Japanese bondage" techniques. Those are bondage techniques commonly depicted in Japanese erotica, but they are distinctly different from the Japanese martial arts techniques of

prisoner-tying commonly called hojo-jitsu. (This book also does not cover hojo-jitsu techniques in great detail.)

3.   This book does not cover the techniques and challenges associated with doing what are sometimes called "prolonged bondage" techniques. Among other things, unless special precautions are taken, engaging in prolonged, highly immobilizing bondage can lead to muscle cramps, pressure sores, and (in a worst-case situation) the formation of potentially life-threatening blood clots. All bondage techniques in this book are presented with the understanding that the bottom will be bound for not longer than two hours at a time. (Two hours of being in bondage can seem like forever under some circumstances.) After being in bondage for two hours, I recommend that the bottom be released entirely – or, at least, released to the point where they have full range of motion in their body – for at least ten minutes so that they may use the bathroom, stretch out their body, and so forth.

4.   This book does not cover the special techniques that are used to bind someone while they are trying to physically resist being bound (one type of what is sometimes called "resistance play"). The bondage techniques presented in this book are presented with the assumption that the bottom is voluntarily complying with instructions to position their body in a certain way, to remain still, etc.

Also…

5.   This book is written under the assumption that, once the bottom is in bondage, only conventional sex acts such as intercourse, oral sex, and so forth will occur. If the top plans to use other items of SM equipment, such as whips, paddles, and clamps, it is very important for the health and well being of all concerned, and for the health and well being of their relationship, that the top first get adequate instruction in how such equipment is used. Please note that this book does not provide such instruction. For more information on how to use such equipment, please consult the book "SM 101" or other educational writings on such matters. If at all possible, try to get personal instruction in how to use such items of equipment from a few different experienced SM practitioners.

WHO? WHAT? WHEN? WHERE? WHY?

WHAT? Before we go much further into the "who," "where," "when," "why," and especially before we go much further into the "how" of erotic bondage, let's make sure that we agree on the "what" of what we are talking about. In other words, let's define our terms. When I use the term "erotic bondage" what do I mean by that term?

Well, let's see. That phrase contains two words: "erotic" and "bondage." Let's look at each one in turn.

My dictionary defines "erotic" as "of, devoted to, or tending to arouse sexual love or desire."

My dictionary also defines "bondage" as "a state of being bound" or "subjugation to a controlling person or force."

Looking around a bit more in my dictionary, I find the following:

My dictionary defines the word "restrain" as "to limit, restrict, or keep under control."

"To bind" is defined as "to make secure by tying" and "to confine, restrain, or restrict with bonds."

So we could broadly define erotic bondage as "to confine, restrain, or restrict with bonds in a way intended to arouse sexual desire."

I will not be referring in this book to other ways to restrain one's erotic partner, such as confining them to a cage (although I have friends who are very much into that practice). Nor will I refer to the use of arm locks and other restraining holds to restrict another person's movement.

To bind someone is, usually, to apply materials to their body with the intention of limiting their ability to move. (I will outline some other reasons for bondage in the "why" section.)

There are various reasons why people are bound. Police officers bind their prisoners (usually by using handcuffs). Criminals bind their victims. Medical personnel sometimes bind patients to prevent them from hurting themselves and/or others. Ordinary people occasionally bind criminals as part of making a citizen's arrest. People are sometimes placed into bondage as a way of exploring alternative forms of consciousness. This is sometimes called "shamanic" bondage.

So what do I mean, in this book, by "erotic bondage"? To put it very simply, in this book I will refer to erotic bondage as the practice of one person's applying restraining materials to the body of a consenting partner with the intention of increasing the erotic arousal level of at least one of the two people involved. (Hopefully, of course, both people involved will have their erotic arousal level increased, but I would say that the "minimal acceptable condition" is that both people consent and that at least one of them is being aroused.)

Note: Henceforth in this book, when I refer to bondage, please understand that I am referring specifically to erotic bondage.

Why? One of the most basic questions regarding erotic bondage is "why should anyone want to do it in the first place?" After all, the very idea of tying up your partner as part of your sex life, or of having them tie you up, can seem pretty weird, and even dangerous, to a large number of people – possibly even to the majority of people. So why should we want to do it?

This is not the place to go into a detailed analysis of the psychology of bondage, or to discuss the role of parts of the human brain such as the limbic system (see "SM 101" and related books for more on that), so let us simply note in passing that there is no reason to believe that such urges are necessarily, or even usually, pathological. Legions of people who are quite mentally healthy want to engage in bondage or some other aspect of SM in one way or another.

Let us also note that there can a distinct element of aggression and submission associated with a great deal of healthy sexual desire and healthy sexual behavior. Even the most "vanilla" person may sometimes say something to their spouse like "I'm going to fuck your brains out" or "take me." A great deal of sadomasochism in general, and of bondage in particular, is associated with consensually enhancing and enjoying the aggressive and submissive feelings that often accompany sexual arousal.

The submissive aspect of sexuality often involves assuming a state of being that may be described with words like receptiveness, openness, submitting, passivity, bottoming, surrender, letting go of control, "bottom space," and vulnerability. (Within the SM community, the nuances of such terms can be, and are, debated at great length. Please let me make it clear, particularly to the "SM purists" reading this, that I'm using terms such as "submissive" in a very generalized, generic way.)

So, to put it another way, what is the purpose of erotic bondage? Erotic bondage can be done for a number of purposes, either separately or in combination. Some of the more common purposes for putting a consenting partner in bondage include bondage for vulnerability, bondage for decoration, and bondage for sensation.

• *Bondage for vulnerability.* Probably the most common reason that bondage is applied to a consenting partner is to restrict, in one way or another, their ability to move. This is significant because if a person's ability to move is limited, then their ability to run away, fight off their "attacker," cover vulnerable parts of their body, and so forth is also limited. In short, they are more vulnerable when they are bound than they are when they are not bound.

One could identify sub-aspects of bondage done to increase vulnerability. For example, one could think of "bondage for control," "bondage for immobilization," and "bondage for exposure."

In the first example, that of bondage for control, the bottom might be simply bound with their hands behind their back, but nothing more. This type of bondage is very similar to the bondage that police officers put suspects in upon arresting them.

In bondage for control, the bottom's ability to "fight off their attacker" is lessened and their ability to run away is hampered (and their body may be somewhat exposed). Thus, although the bottom may still be able to move about fairly freely, and to assume a large number of positions, the top can still control their movements relatively easily. (Of course, if the bottom is significantly larger and/or stronger than the top, the bondage will have to be more extensive. Exactly how much bondage it is necessary for the top to apply in order to accomplish this control can take some planning – and can be a fun game for the top and the bottom to play.)

In an example of bondage for immobilization, the bottom might be tied nude in a face-up, spread-eagled position on a bed. In this position, their ability to fight anybody off is very greatly lessened. Their ability to run away is essentially eliminated, and the entire front half of their body is exposed. (If the bottom is a woman, the fact that her legs are tied apart and that she is unable to close them may have a particularly strong emotional impact.)

One somewhat unusual example of bondage for immobilization is what can be thought of as "tether bondage." In an example of such bondage, the person might be chained by one ankle to something relatively immobile such as a bed. Within the limits of their tether, the person has almost complete freedom of movement, but they much stay within its limits. (In practice, such tethers are often long enough to reach places like the nearest bathroom.)

In bondage for exposure, the bottom is often tied in such a way that either as much of their body as possible, or a part of their body in particular, is held in place and especially revealed and accessible to the top. The body parts involved are frequently their breasts, genitals, or buttocks.

• *Bondage for decoration.* Bondage is sometimes done mostly for its decorative effect, often in a way that signals a kind of availability for and/or "vulnerability" to sex. (I put vulnerable in quotes here because it is frequently the case that the person in question is quite heartily consenting to sex. If you're not sure, ask.) In such a case, rope or other materials may be applied to the bound person's body in such a way as to call attention to their breasts, genitals, or some other part of them. People may wear "rope dresses," "body harnesses," and similar arrangements that may do so little to actually limit their mobility that they could run a marathon while wearing them. Still, such outfits can look very hot.

There is a type of bondage-for-decoration that can be thought of as "symbolic" bondage. In this type of bondage, the bound person's ability to move is often not limited to any significant degree – and sometimes not at all. Rather, in such cases it is more typical that the bondage signals that the person wearing it is in a state of servitude or submission, usually to a specific person. One typical example of symbolic bondage would be of one person to have their hands linked together in front of them with a very wide length of chain or rope. In such bondage, the person could do almost everything (including participate almost normally in sex) but it would be a symbol of their state.

One specific type of symbolic bondage is the applying of some sort of bondage to a special part of the bottom's body to indicate that the body part in question is "owned" by someone else. For example, a man who is in a submissive relationship to another person, male or female, might agree to wear a short chain that has been locked around his genitals (and he does not have a key to this lock) in order to symbolize that his genitals are "owned" by someone that he might refer to as his Master or his Mistress. Obviously, this person has to do a bit of special planning when he is scheduled to do things like walk through an airport metal detector.

Probably the most common "symbolic bondage" within the SM community is the collar. While the meaning of a collar can vary widely – from meaningless fashion accessory to a symbol of a relationship as deep and committed as any marriage – in practice it is very common for a person who is in some type of submissive relationship to another person to wear that person's collar. Thus, if you meet someone at an SM-type event and they are wearing a collar

> "You're easier to get along with when you're tied up."

around their neck, do not be surprised if you learn that there is someone in their life that they refer to as their Master, their Mistress, their Owner, or by some similar term.

Another type of symbolic bondage is a length of relatively thin "body chain" jewelry worn around the person's waist. While there is no intrinsic meaning to wearing such a chain (sometimes jewelry is just jewelry) such a chain can sometimes have a symbolic meaning identical to that associated with wearing a collar.

- *Bondage for sensation.* Bondage may be applied to the bottom's body for the sensations that such bondage creates. Typically this is done in either a specific location or in a more generalized way.

  Examples of bondage applied to a specific location for sensation enhancement would be bondage applied to the bottom's breasts or genitals. Breast and genitals, especially male genitals, that have been bound can become swollen and more sensitive to being touched. Bondage applied in a more general way for the sensation it creates may have a more overall effect. For example, it's very common for bottoms to report that ropes wrapped entirely around their body, perhaps particularly ropes that have been wrapped several times around their upper torso, have a kind of calming effect. This calming effect is frequently compared to the calming effect that applying swaddling clothes has on infants.

  While the details are beyond the scope of this book, let me note that bondage which covers almost as much of the bottom's body as it is possible to cover – a technique sometimes called "mummification bondage" – is frequently associated with the bottom's entering into altered states of consciousness. Altered states of consciousness also sometimes occur if a bottom wears a hood that covers the entire head except for a few breathing holes.

Who? One of the very first questions that comes up regarding bondage is "Who should I let tie me up?" Obviously, this is a critically important question. A bound person can be reduced to an infant-like level of helplessness and vulnerability. It's only reasonable that you should consider very carefully to whom you should make yourself this vulnerable.

There is a way of thinking about this issue that I have found useful. I call it the "NTA Test." Long before there is any chance that you might let this person tie you up, ask yourself how you would feel about being "naked, tied up, and alone" with this person. Indeed, it can be a useful question about how you feel about them in general.

Another useful approach is what I call the "ninety, nine, and one" rule. It's useful to assume that, out of one hundred people, ninety of them will be basically safe enough to let yourself be tied up by. They may not know much in the way of technique, and they may have some unrealistic ideas of what is and what is not involved, but those shortcomings can be remedied by having them acquire adequate basic education (which, hopefully, this book will help provide). Once they've been educated, they are basically safe to play with.

The remaining ten people are emotionally unsuited for the role of either binder or bindee. For a number of reasons, they are simply not emotionally stable enough to do this, particularly in the role of binder.

Of those ten people, there is one – one person out of your original group of one hundred – who is genuinely dangerous, and capable of treating you with real malice if they get you in a vulnerable position. Indeed, if you find yourself naked, tied up, and alone with this person, you could be at very real risk of being slowly, agonizingly tortured to death. (Fortunately, accountability has a way of strongly deterring these people. If you make a point of never compromising on matters such as setting up a silent alarm – to be described later in this chapter – they will probably, rather quickly, decide that they want nothing to do with you.)

So, given the above, how do you determine which of the three groups your prospective bondage partner belongs to?

The basic answer: give it time.

As a good, overall, basic rule, you should only let yourself be tied up by people that you know well and are on good terms with. Letting yourself be tied up by strangers, or by people with whom you are having interpersonal difficulties – even if you have known them for a long time – can be asking for serious trouble.

When? There are two general aspects to the "when should you engage in bondage with someone?" question. The first part of the question deals with your relationship your potential partner. I think that I adequately addressed this matter in the "Who" section.

So, OK, you know this person well enough for it to be appropriate for you to consider doing bondage with them, now the question emerges of when should you do it.

> "I like to tie him up and then clean the house."

I think it can help to clarify the question if we look at it from a reverse point of view. In other words, when should you *not* do bondage with this person?

I suggest that you do *not* engage in bondage with someone if…

- *You do not (yet) know them well enough.* As I mentioned earlier, you want to make sure that you know this person pretty well. Do they pass the NTA test?

- *Either of you is significantly intoxicated.* I have heard more case reports than I can remember of SM scenes that "crashed and burned." In many such reports, it is very clear that the use of intoxicants was an essential co-factor in what happened. If intoxicant usage had not been involved, it is very reasonable to conclude that the crash would not have happened.

- *Either of you is physically tired.* Trying to do bondage at the end of a long day, when either of you is exhausted, can be asking for trouble. I know of numerous "SM disasters" that can be traced to trying to play while tired.

- *Either of you is significantly depressed, angry, sad, or otherwise emotionally upset.* Erotic bondage can be a very emotional experience for both parties. If they are already near their emotional overload point because of other stresses, doing bondage can push them over the edge.

- *Either of you doesn't feel well.* Bondage and illness, even mild illness like a headache or upset stomach, are a bad mixture. The potential for the discomfort to get worse during the bondage session is significant.

Also, I've found that a partner who isn't feeling well when the session begins is far likelier to have an emotional upset during the session.

- *Your relationship is significantly troubled.* Bondage involves significant degrees of trust, vulnerability, and so forth. If your relationship is currently not of a type that makes creating this degree of vulnerability a good idea, it's best to hold off for a while.

- *There is not adequate privacy.* You should only do bondage in private or in the presence of consenting others. Doing bondage, or any other aspect of SM play, in the presence of people who do not understand it and/or who have not consented to see it is asking for trouble.

- *You lack suitable materials,* either in terms of bondage gear or safety gear. Many crashes can be traced to trying to bondage with inadequate equipment, or to the lack of adequate safety gear. (More on this topic on "On Tying Up and Being Untied," later in the book.)

- *Either you or your partner is not adequately educated* regarding how to do bondage with at least a baseline degree of safety. Uneducated people can have wildly unrealistic impressions of what is and what is not involved in bondage. Lack of education can also lead to serious injuries.

- *Either of you is dehydrated, has low blood sugar, etc.* It can be a very good idea to make sure that you have had enough to eat and drink just prior to playing. This type of play can use up a lot of energy and water. More than one scene has come to a bad end because of something like a thirst level that was too high or a blood sugar level that was too low. (On a related note, it's a very good idea for both partners, and particularly the bottom, to empty their bladder and possibly their bowels before beginning a bondage session.)

- *Your bondage scene has not been adequately pre-negotiated.* It is my experience, after talking to many, many people over a period of more than two decades, that the single most common cause of a bondage scene, or other type of SM scene, ending badly is rushed or otherwise inadequate pre-scene negotiations. I've found that you can tell a lot about the suitability of a potential SM partner by how carefully they conduct their pre-scene negotiations. As one part of these negotiations with a relatively new partner, you should set up a silent alarm and make sure your potential partner knows you have done so.

- *You don't feel like it.* This seems almost too obvious to mention – but you're doing this for fun. If one of you isn't in the mood, the chances that you're going to have fun are not too good.

Bondage as "near edge" play. One type of SM play is frequently called "edge play." While there is no widely agreed upon definition of this term, it frequently involves activities where the degree of physical risk involved is much greater than the degree of risk involved in more routine types of play.

I mention this because, while most bondage does not qualify as edge play, I do believe that it is riskier than many people perceive it to be. On many occasions, I've heard remarks like "I'm not interested in doing any edge play or anything really heavy. How about if I just tie you up a little bit?" This suggestion always makes me nervous, particularly when I hear it from someone that I don't know all that well.

The problem with this remark is that it fails to address the reality of how dangerous bondage can be. Most bondage is not highly dangerous in and of itself, but it does create a potentially very dangerous degree of vulnerability. Once you are tied up, you are at that other person's mercy. If, after they've put you into "just a little bondage" they turn out to be not all that sane or friendly or sober, you could find yourself in a nightmarish situation.

Most bondage does not qualify as edge play, but it can create enough vulnerability to qualify it as "near-edge" play.

Where? Where should you do bondage? Only in the presence of informed, consenting, supportive others.

This being the case, most of the time your bondage adventures will involve only you and your lover, playing alone in private. Please take a few minutes to make sure that you are not likely to be inappropriately seen or heard by others. If you have kids in the house, make sure that, as with all other aspects of your sex life, they will not be aware of what is going on. Also, your housemates, neighbors, and so forth really don't need to be aware of what you're doing. Trying to do such practices in more public, uncontrolled environments such as a city park is asking for trouble in many different ways.

Attending an SM club's events can be an excellent place to do bondage in the presence of supportive others. They can be great events to share what you know, learn from others, and see some really hot bondage techniques "in the flesh."

While some people in the SM community insist that it is their perfect right to put their bottom into bondage and lead them down the street on a leash, or to tie their bottom to a streetlight while they go into a restaurant to eat a meal, I think that such activities are only asking for trouble. On the other hand, leading your bound bottom on a leash while being part of the SM contingent of your annual Gay/Lesbian/Bisexual/Transgender/Etc. Freedom Day Parade can be very, very big fun.

If you decide to play outside, take extra precautions to make sure that you won't be discovered by passers-by. Keep in mind that there is the potential for genuine disaster to occur if such a passer-by attempts to "rescue" the bottom from the top. (Furthermore, not every passer-by may have such noble intent. Some may have much more malicious inclinations.) Also please keep in mind that "incriminating" sounds can carry much further outdoors than you might appreciate, especially at night. Finally, remember to bring along some sunscreen and some water to drink.

I know that some people think it's fun to tie their partner up and then drive them around in a car, sometimes even with the bound person in the trunk of the car, but the risks associated with this practice seem too numerous and severe for me to feel comfortable recommending it.

THE SILENT ALARM

Let's take a moment to look directly at what has the potential to be a very stark reality. When we talk about doing erotic bondage, we are frequently talking about a situation in which two people are alone together, and one of them is very securely tied up. The potential for Bad Things to happen in this situation is obvious.

With the understanding that we can never entirely eliminate the chances of Bad Things happening in such a situation, it's only reasonable for us to ask what we can do to reduce the chances of their happening.

It's my belief that, for the most part, people don't do Bad Things for one of two reasons:

The first reason, and by far the more common reason, is that most people, most of the time, are basically good, decent people. If you make allowances for an occasional moment of human weakness (and I find that I am becoming more tolerant and forgiving on that point than I used to be, possibly in part because I have had so many weak moments myself) most people are good people most of the time. They don't lie, steal, or harm someone else, even if they could get away with it. In other words, they don't do Bad Things because they aren't Bad People.

OK, fine, but there certainly are Bad People in this world. Why don't Bad People do Bad Things? My point of view is that a Bad Person will do a Bad Thing unless they think that they're gonna get caught. A more formal way of saying this is to say that after-the-fact accountability deters unwanted behavior.

A key teaching in criminal justice is that you don't decrease the frequency of a specific crime by increasing the punishment for that crime. (The politicians regularly try to sell this nonsense to the voters by passing laws that increase such penalties. This approach allows them to look like they're working on the problem without doing much actual, real work on it.) Rather, you decrease the frequency of a given criminal behavior by increasing the probability of getting caught.

In other words, if a Bad Person believes that he'll get caught if he tries to do a certain Bad Thing, the chances that he will actually try to commit the crime in question drop way down. Again, accountability (or, at least, the belief that there will be accountability) deters unwanted behavior.

In the SM world, we use this "accountability aspect" to protect ourselves, particularly when playing in private with a new partner, by setting up what is called a "silent alarm." (It's also sometimes called a "safe call.")

The basic way it works is pretty simple. Before going out on an in-private play date with a new partner, Person A simply tells a Trusted Friend where they will be, who they will be with (Person B), what they will be doing, and approximately how long they will be there. The agreement is that if Person A doesn't check in by that deadline time (and, often, do so in a particular way; more on that later), the Trusted Friend is to assume that Person A is in very serious trouble and needs to be rescued from Person B, usually by the police. Person A then tells Person B ahead of time (diplomatically and courteously) that such a "silent alarm" will be in place when they play. This last step is actually the most important one, yet it is also the most often skipped.

Of course, it's also only prudent that Person B take the same precaution regarding Person A. In particular, please understand that "silent alarms" are definitely not only for people who will be taking the bottom role.

A refinement to setting up the silent alarm is the inclusion of an "all clear" word or phrase. This phrase, which is never uttered in the play partner's presence, signals that the person is genuinely free and clear and is not deactivating their silent alarm under duress. The "all clear word" is frequently a word that is rather unusual and would have no place in a routine "the play date is over and I had a great time" conversation. Mentioning a dinosaur might be a good example. (One could also use something like a planet, a color, an astrological sign, the make of a car, a sports team – the list is endless.)

For example, if you're acting as a "silent alarm baby-sitter" and your Person A calls in telling you that she "had a great time with the new guy and he's really a great top" but she fails to mention the word "Brontosaurus" during the conversation, you then know that she's in trouble no matter what else she says. (Human fallibility and forgetfulness being what they are, you might try to subtly prompt your friend, remembering that you might be overheard, if she seems fine but is forgetting to mention her all-clear signal. For example, you might ask her, "Hmmm, sounds great. Did he remind you of any particular animal?")

Setting up a silent alarm may seem cumbersome at first, but after a while it becomes a routine and ordinary precaution.

It's worth keeping in mind that the primary purpose of a silent alarm is deterrence, not after-the-fact accountability. Therefore, the most important part of using a silent alarm is to make it clear to your potential play partner that a silent alarm will be in place when the two of you play and that this is non-negotiable. As I said, be firm on this point, but also be polite about it. It's likewise good form to suggest that your partner also set one up. While a novice might have some questions about this practice, they should have no major problems with it once its purpose has been explained to them. On the other hand, a real predator will be genuinely unhappy with this news and will either choose another partner or try really hard to talk you out of the idea. Obviously, anybody who strongly tries to talk you out of using a silent alarm is sending a major warning signal about their suitability as a potential partner by this act alone.

I've listened to a large number of "horror stories" during my years in the SM community involving people who were tied up by partners who seemed just fine and then went on to do terrible, nonconsensual things to them after they got them tied up. I've taken to asking "If that other person had been certain that a third person knew where you were and who you were with, do you think that those Bad Things would have happened?" In every single case so far, the reply has been "no."

THE IMPORTANCE OF STAYING IN THE HERE AND NOW

This book is, unavoidably, something of a collection of generalizations. I have engaged in erotic bondage, both as a top and as a bottom, fairly frequently for more than 25 years, with many different partners. I have also spoken with hundreds of other bondage fans about their experiences. Over time, my explorations and interactions have led me to a number of recommendations. I have done my best to share the most useful of these recommendations with you in this book.

However, it is crucial that you understand the following: Every situation is unique. Every person's body and/or mind is unique. Even the same person's body and/or mind may (and eventually will) change significantly, sometimes within a very short period of time. What worked yesterday may not work today. The likes and dislikes that a person had a week ago may be very different from the likes and dislikes that they have today. Occasionally, what was once a hard limit for somebody may eventually become their preferred activity. On the other hand, what was once their preferred activity may become something that they now find utterly repulsive, and a hard limit.

I believe that this book presents a great deal of generally useful material, and can help provide you with a much more informed view. However, you must understand that the information within this book absolutely cannot be a substitute for your paying close, ongoing attention to what is happening in the immediate moment during your SM play, and to how well things are working, or not working, for both people. I believe that it is especially important for the top to stay in the here and now during an SM session.

I have seen bottoms get very "spacey" from being in bondage (and from other SM experiences). Indeed, the ability of bondage to induce various types of altered states of consciousness in the bound person is one of its major points of appeal. This being in a spaced-out state of mind can be intense, pleasurable, and a great deal of fun, for the bottom. However, a spaced-out top is a potentially very dangerous top.

Because the bottom may enter something of a spaced-out altered level of consciousness, it is important for the top to realize that they may find themselves "paying attention for two" during the bondage session. Therefore, it is very important for the top to remain sharply focused. As you can see, anything that detracts from the top's ability to pay sharp attention to the situation can cause problems for, and even endanger, the bottom (or the top, or even both people).

"I just love a man with rope in his hands."

So what are some of the more common factors that can impair a top's ability to stay in the here and now and "pay attention for two"?

Obviously, intoxicant usage of any kind has significant potential to pull the top out of the here and now. While I'm not going to talk down to you by telling you to never use any intoxicants under any circumstances while you engage in bondage, you should understand that using even small amounts of intoxicants has the very real potential to dramatically increase the risk level. Please also understand that the amount of risk increase may be far greater than it seems to be. In a very large percentage of the many SM disasters that I have heard about over the years, it is quite reasonable to conclude that the aforementioned "crash and burns" would never have happened if intoxicants had not been involved.

Other things that can take the top out of "the here and now" include:

- Trying to play while excessively tired. A sleepy or exhausted top will find it essentially impossible to remain properly alert.

- Trying to play with someone while you still have significant unresolved personal difficulties with them. If you are noticeably angry or otherwise upset with someone, it's probably better to hold off doing bondage with them until those issues are resolved.

- Trying to play with someone while there is some major issue in your life that is consuming all of your thoughts. You can't stay "on station" as a top if your thoughts keep drifting away to some work-related issue, some financial difficulty, a personal problem, or some similar thought-consuming matter.

Note: Some people find that they can "turn off their brains" by bottoming in one way or another, so they may want to be tied up as a way of taking their minds off of some thought-consuming issue for a while. This can be reasonably safe, provided that the bottom remains "present" enough to monitor their own basic well-being.

In summary, bottoms can "drift away" while in bondage, and this is not at all necessarily a bad thing provided that they don't drift so far away that they become unable to monitor their basic well-being. Tops, on the other hand, must stay in the here and now during an SM session, "paying attention for two" while the play is in progress. The top, assisted as appropriate by the bottom, has to stay in tune with what is working, and what isn't working, for those two people at that particular time, and to adjust or even stop the activity as indicated. Anything that interferes with the top's ability to pay such close attention endangers not only the bottom, but also the top, and the relationship between them.

ON BEING TIED UP AND BEING UNTIED

*M*ONITORING. How closely should the top keep an eye on a bottom that they've put into bondage? To use a more formal term, how closely should the top "monitor" the bottom?

Obviously, that depends upon a number of factors, including how immobilizing the bondage is, whether or not the bottom is gagged, the bottom's underlying health, and so forth.

I've found that there are three basic levels of bondage monitoring: closely monitored bondage, loosely monitored bondage, and unmonitored bondage.

Closely monitored bondage. In this situation, the top is keeping a very close, constant watch on the bottom. The top is awake, unintoxicated, physically near enough to the bottom to both hear and see them quite easily, and within "lunge distance" to allow them to reach the bottom very quickly in the event of an emergency. (Some police departments define maximum "lunge distance" as twenty feet). In a close monitoring situation, the top only rarely leaves the bottom, and then only when necessary (such as to urinate or get a quick drink of water) and for only the shortest of periods – typically less than two minutes. This is the most common type of bondage monitoring.

Loosely monitored bondage. Bottoms who are placed in somewhat prolonged erotic bondage often end up being "loosely monitored." This can basically be compared to how closely a parent might monitor a sleeping infant. For example, the top might tie the bottom to the bed and then go into the living room to study or watch TV.

The top may not be within "lunge distance" but will be within "yelling distance" of the bottom. This means that the top will be able to hear the bottom if the bottom yells for help and will be able to return to the bottom fairly promptly – in less than thirty seconds – without the top having to having to move at a pace faster than a brisk walk.

By the way, I can cover about sixty yards in thirty seconds while walking at such a brisk pace on level, unobstructed ground, so I'm inclined to believe that the farthest a top can be from a bottom and still be considered to be within "loose monitoring" distance is sixty yards.

Note: If the bottom is gagged while in loosely monitored bondage (a practice that significantly increases the risk level), they should be provided with an alternative, very reliable, means of signaling for help, supplemented with electronic monitoring equipment such as a nursery monitor (more on this later).

When a parent is caring for a sleeping infant, they look in on the sleeping infant from time to time. Similarly, in a "loose monitoring" situation, the top should similarly look in on the bottom from time to time. Precisely how often this should be done is a judgment call, but I notice that prisoners on "suicide watch" in jail cells are often observed by the deputies about every fifteen minutes, so I recommend that the top check on the bottom at least that often. This check-in requires that the top move close enough so that they can actually both see and hear the bottom. The mere fact that the bottom has not yelled for help since the last check-in is *not* to be taken as adequate assurance that everything is OK.

Here are a few additional hints regarding loosely monitored bondage.

Running back to the bottom greatly increases the chances that you will stumble and injure yourself or your bottom, or otherwise make the situation worse. If you feel that you must quickly return to your bottom's side, try to do so at no faster than a brisk walk.

Running downstairs can be particularly risky. If you must return to your bottom's side quickly, and moving downstairs is necessary, please be extra-careful while on the stairs.

Be very careful of putting any lockable door between you and your bottom. There have been several incidents of a top being locked out of the room in which the bottom has been bound. If such a door is present, make very sure that you have an additional key to it and/or block it open.

Unmonitored bondage. In this situation, the bottom is essentially tied up and abandoned. The top cannot see or hear the bottom, and is neither within lunge distance or yelling distance of them. If any sort of problem develops, the bottom cannot depend upon the top (or any other person) to come to their aid.

While the degree of risk in a loosely monitored situation is somewhat increased over the degree of risk in a closely monitored situation, both degrees of risk are *much* less than the level of risk associated with an unmonitored situation. Just as there are many cases of infants who have been badly harmed or even killed after being left alone (as in "alone in the house or apartment"), there are also many  reports of people being badly injured or even killed after being left alone for long periods of time while in bondage.

The degree of risk involved in erotic bondage sharply increases when no one is available to monitor the bottom while they are in bondage, and the more immobilizing and stringent the bondage, the more the risk increases. It should be noted that the degree of risk to a bound, unmonitored person takes a significant additional jump if they are also gagged. One of the reasons for this is that gags can slowly work their way into the back of a bottom's mouth and into their throat, thus closing off their airway and suffocating them; this is a frequent cause of death during the commission of a crime, and appears often in forensic pathology reports.

Unfortunately, almost all self-bondage that is immobilizing to any significant degree falls into the "unmonitored" category and, sure enough, I have heard of numerous case reports of self-bondage injuries, and even several case reports of self-bondage fatalities. (See p. 63.)

It should be noted that a bottom who is bound by an intoxicated top, or by a top who becomes intoxicated after binding the bottom, is, in essence, an unmonitored bottom. I have at least one case report in my files of an intoxicated top who tied up a bottom and then passed out. The bottom was unable to reawaken the top, and therefore had to endure several very unpleasant hours in bondage before they were able to free themselves.

The crucial importance of a monitor. The more I worked on this book, and the more I researched the whys and wherefores of erotic bondage, the more the presence of a monitor for the bound person grew in importance. This monitor is usually also the top – although it may in some cases be a designated third party – and that's usually OK.

There are more hazards, problems, and annoyances related to erotic bondage than I can possibly describe in this book. (I did try to cover the most important ones and the most common ones.) However, the presence of a sane, competent, and sympathetic monitor can mitigate almost all of them.

A very large proportion of bondage-related problems do not appear instantly and demand immediate attention, but rather tend to develop over a period of minutes or even hours. A monitor can usually alleviate them with relatively little difficulty while still maintaining the erotic energy of the scene.

Thus, while I have worked hard to provide you with useful information and general guidelines, please understand very clearly that nothing can take the place of good, clear communication between the bound person and the monitor regarding what is and what is not working for both of them at that particular time.

ON BEING UNTIED

There are several useful things to know about being untied.

Probably the most important guideline is that bottoms who are being untied should resist the urge to struggle and pull free of bondage as it is being removed. For one thing, such movement may actually slow down the untying process by hindering what the top is doing. For another thing, body parts that have been bound for a while may have lost a bit of muscle tone, and sudden, strong movements may strain muscles or even sprain tendons and ligaments. Finally, given that muscle tone may have decreased and given that the bottom may not be able to predict how their body will move, strong movements can put the bottom at increased risk of falling. As a general rule, I recommend that the bottom remain still until the top specifically tells them, "You may move." (It's wise to cover this point in pre-play negotiations.)

Upon being given permission to move, it is often wise for the bottom to begin moving their body very slowly, thus allowing muscle tone and balance to return at an easy-to-tolerate rate. Because muscles which have been relatively motionless for some time can develop very painful cramps if suddenly stretched, I recommend that the bottom try modest movements before attempting an all-out stretch.

Because muscle tone may be especially low in the upper arms, it is not uncommon to see freshly untied bottoms do things such as use their fingers to "spider walk" (like in the old "Let Your Fingers Do the Walking" TV commercials) their arms out from behind their backs. Similar movements can sometimes be seen when the bottom uses small movements of their feet and ankles to move their upper legs.

Well-meaning tops often make the following two mistakes:

- *Moving a part of the bottom's body for them.* While this can seem like a kind thing to do, moving a body part before it has had time to re-establish adequate muscle tone can actually increase the chances of a strain or sprain. As a rule, it's usually better to wait and allow the bottom to move their own body unless they request your assistance.

- *Rubbing freshly unbound tissue.* "Rope tracks" in freshly unbound tissue may look a bit scary, but unless the bondage was applied with unusually high pressure, such tracks will usually go away by themselves within a few hours – as in, "they'll be gone in the morning." Well-meaning tops sometimes attempt to help the bottom by rubbing the tracked area. In general, this does no actual good and may even be mildly harmful. Remember that this is compressed tissue: Further compression is unlikely to do it any good and may actually be harmful. It's usually better to simply let the tissue re-expand at its own rate.

If a numb body area such as an arm or leg gets a "pins and needles" feeling to it as the bondage is removed, it may indicate that the bondage was applied so tightly that it compressed a nerve or interfered with blood flow into the limb. In such a case, the bottom may find it helpful to have some light, general massage in that area. As always, get feedback as appropriate.

Blindfold removal. Eyes that have been blindfolded may have lost a bit of muscle tone and thus be unable to comfortably accommodate sudden exposure to light. While I have never heard of a bottom suffering an actual injury from a sudden blindfold removal, it can certainly be an unpleasant experience. I don't think a top should do something like that unless they are intentionally trying to be sadistic. One fairly considerate approach can be to unbind the bottom's arms and let them remove the blindfold at their own pace. Keeping the light in the playroom at a low level during this process is also a kindness.

POST-BONDAGE EMOTIONAL ASPECTS

People vary in how much post-bondage "aftercare" they need. Some are quite robust and almost immediately ready to move on to something else. Others may be in a very physically and mentally delicate place. Both tops and bottoms need to keep in mind that both they and their partner are likely to be in an at least somewhat tender place, both physically and emotionally, and to treat both themselves and each other accordingly.

Freshly untied bottoms often feel spacey and non-verbal afterwards. (Tops may feel a bit spacey too.) This feeling is sometimes called "the afterglow" and may last for several hours. Thus, this is often not a good time for detailed conversation about what worked and what didn't, when and if the two of you are going to play again, and so forth. (Bringing up negative subjects, whether related to the play or not, can be especially unpleasant and jarring.) Save such conversations for later – as in the next day.

Note: If, for some reason, you absolutely must talk about what happened during the session fairly soon afterwards, try to allow at least the better part of an hour to elapse first. Also, if the players really must "turn their brains back on," it often works better if you go to a significantly different environment – for example, going to a local restaurant for a light meal.

Also, both bottoms and tops may be feeling a bit nervous about how good a partner they were. Thus, a few words of reassurance such as "thank you, that was very nice" or "you were very pleasing" may be more deeply appreciated than is apparent. In general, it's a good idea to limit immediate post-play communication to a general "I'm basically OK; are you basically OK?" emotional check-in.

Bottoms may feel very tired afterwards, and they are often easily chilled. Thus, the opportunity to take a brief, warm nap may be very welcome. They may also appreciate having something to eat or something to drink afterwards. (One person I know especially likes cold milk to drink after a scene. Others have their own preferred foods and drinks.) One sign of a skillful player is that they will make sure as part of their pre-play planning that the things they are likely to need for aftercare – food, drinks, blankets, etc. – will be readily available.

IN CASE OF EMERGENCY

Because we can never predict the future with complete certainty, all BDSM play, including all bondage play, must necessarily involve a certain degree of what the attorneys call "assumption of risk." Emergencies will sometimes occur, thus it's only reasonable to have an at least minimally adequate "Plan B" in place.

In the case of bondage play, this will often mean having the ability to release the bottom very quickly. While we can, and should, make good usage of slipknots and other quick-release mechanisms, bondage tops should always keep in the back of their mind that there may come a moment when the only prudent thing to do is to cut the bottom free. This means that the top will need to keep some kind of cutting implement handy.

I've occasionally seen various specialty items recommended for emergency quick release from bondage, such as rescue-type seat belt cutters. While these can work well, they are relatively hard to find, somewhat expensive, and not very versatile. Therefore the two basic kinds of cutting implements that can be used for quick release are various types of knives and scissors. Let's look at each one.

While knives can be used to good effect in BDSM play, they may not be a good first choice as a piece of emergency release equipment. Keep in mind that people under stress lose fine motor control. (Ever raced up to a door and fumbled to get the key in the keyhole? You've experienced stress-induced loss of fine motor control.) During the research I conducted in preparing this book, I received a number of case reports of tops who had cut either themselves or their bottom while trying to use a knife to free the bottom during the stress of an actual emergency. (It also seemed that larger knives were clumsier to use than smaller knives.) That being the case, it is my recommendation that knives not be relied upon as a "first resort" means of cutting a bottom free from bondage in the event of an emergency.

That leaves scissors.

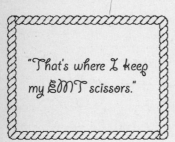

"That's where I keep my EMT scissors."

There is a very wide variety of scissors on the market, and in an emergency having any kind of scissors quickly available may be much more desirable than having no scissors available. Still, some types of scissors do seem to work better than other types.

Cutting a bottom free from bondage during the stress of an actual emergency may happen during extremely turbulent conditions. For example, in California a top may have to attempt to free a bottom during an earthquake. Furthermore, this cutting loose may have to be done under low-light conditions, or even in complete darkness. Given these "worst case" factors, scissors with relatively blunt tips are less likely to cause injury than scissors with sharp tips.

Also, emergency release scissors should be sharp enough to cut through material smoothly – this is not the time to have to take a "gnaw and saw" approach. As a standard, I recommend that emergency release scissors be able to cut through a quarter-inch-thick piece of cotton sash cord with a single, clean, smooth snip.

Keeping in mind that an emergency bondage release may have to be done in low-light conditions, it's only reasonable that these scissors be relatively easy to find in the dark. Finding your scissors can be much easier if the handles are of a relatively bright color such as white or neon yellow as opposed to black or dark blue.

So what we need, if we can find them, are scissors that have relatively blunt tips, cut smoothly, and have bright-colored handles to make it easier to find them under low light conditions. Do such scissors exist? They certainly do!

There is a type of scissors on the market that is widely used by emergency medical personnel. These scissors were originally developed for use by field medics during the war in Viet Nam. Field medics rapidly discovered that standard bandage scissors worked fairly well at cutting what they were designed to cut – bandages and other types of relatively light cloth – but they were never designed or intended to cut through heavy cloth, leather straps, combat boots, and so forth. Thus, they developed heavier scissors with thick, easy-to-grip handles; these are now sold as "EMT scissors."

EMT scissors are sold in many drugstores, medical supply stores, and in a fair number of erotic boutiques. Their handles are available in more than half a dozen colors. (I personally recommend handles that are either white or neon yellow in color.) Also, they are relatively cheap. As of this writing (late in 1999) you can buy EMT scissors of excellent quality for ten dollars or less.

Bonus Tip: EMT scissors come with a flattened lower edge that has a small flange of metal protruding from one side. This flange can often be used to very good effect when it's necessary to do something such as loosen a rope that is wrapped around a wrist or ankle. Simply slip the flange under the rope in question and you should find that it's fairly easy to loosen it a bit.

The top needs to keep EMT scissors in some location where they can be grabbed very quickly, even in the dark, in the event of an emergency. Pursuant to this, I've seen scissors kept in a particular location inside a toy bag, hanging on hooks on bedroom walls, tucked away into nightstand drawers, and even worn on belt holsters as part of an SM costume.

I recommend that tops get as much experience and practice in using their EMT scissors as they can. For example, when it's time to cut up a long new length of rope into the desired shorter lengths, make a point of using the EMT scissors to do the cutting. Take a similar approach regarding any opportunity to use the scissors to cut rope, fabric, or some similar material. Doing so will give you a feel for how well the scissors cut that will serve you very well in an emergency situation.

In summary, EMT scissors are probably your single most important item of bondage-related emergency equipment. A good top will have at least one pair handy in an easy-to-reach location (many tops keep more than one pair handy) and will have prior experience with using them.

Your "Get Loose" Kit

Every bondage practitioner should have a few tools handy for those inevitable times when an item of bondage equipment simply refuses to let go of the bottom.

"I don't think I can get out of this."

If you have an adequate "get loose kit" on hand when such a situation happens (and it *will* happen sooner or later), the situation can be nothing more than a somewhat amusing misadventure. On the other hand, if you lack the proper items, the situation can be unpleasant, stressful, and even dangerous.

A few items in a good "get loose" kit would include:

- At least one extra key for every different type of lock that is being used. (If quick-links, described later in the "Equipment" chapter, are being used, an extra wrench will serve as your extra "key" for them.)

- If you're using metal items, you will need bolt cutters, a hacksaw, numerous good-quality hacksaw blades (buy more than you think you'll need), a small amount of oil, and a small vise or other means of holding the metal item still while it's being sawed.

- If a leather cuff or a metal cuff locks into place and refuses to come off, but the cuff can almost be slipped off, the bottom's hand can often be slid out of a cuff if the hand is first coated with something like baby oil.

- Obviously, when dealing with item made of rope or leather, your trusty EMT scissors should be nearby.

- To help pry stubborn knots loose, a crochet hook can be handy. Also frequently very handy is a piece of strong metal that comes to a hard point. Depending on the thickness of the rope, your needs may be adequately served in this regard by an icepick, an awl, a knitting needle, or the marlinspike of a boating knife.

- A small-sized hemostat made of good-quality metal can be useful for gripping or prying to release a stubborn knot. Two such hemostats can help you both grip and pull in opposite directions.

- A pair of needle-nosed pliers be useful in gripping and pulling. As with the hemostats, two such pairs of pliers can aid in release.

- Finally, if all else fails, you may need to cut the rope. If it comes to this, I recommend a sharp knife with a relative short, narrow blade. Be sure to use the knife in a controlled manner and with adequate visualization.

Footnote: Release Rings. If you have reason ahead of time to believe that a knot such as a square knot may become very difficult to untie, you can pre-position one or two rings that I call "release rings" inside the knot. These small rings are often made of metal, but they can be made of small, firmly knotted loops of sturdy cord as well. To understand how to use them, tie the first half of a Square knot (see p. 135) in place, then drop one ring over each free tail and let it fall down to where the knot is. Finish the knot in the usual way. The presence of the release rings will not affect the security of the knot at all (unless the bottom can reach them) but can make even a tightly pulled knot substantially easier to untie. They can convert many knots that are otherwise difficult and time-consuming to release into what amount to quick-release knots. Try using either one or two release rings when tying various knots, particularly knots that you might need to release quickly, and you'll understand how they work. Release Rings are kinda neat.

"I'LL BET YOU CAN'T GET LOOSE"

One of the more fun and popular bondage games is the one often called, "I'll bet you can't get loose." This type of game is particularly popular with "escape artists" (aka "eels") who like to be tied up and then see if they can escape.

This game can be a great deal of fun. It can also be very educational for both the top and the bottom.

"I'll bet you can't get loose" can be fun for a certain type of bottom because, in part, it offers them a chance to struggle and see if they can escape from their bondage. Some of them love doing this, either because they enjoy the "triumph" of escaping or because it proves to them (and to the top) that the bondage they are in is essentially inescapable.

(Some bottoms would never even think of trying to get loose from their bondage, no matter how loosely or even sloppily it is applied. Others think that any bondage that can be escaped from *should* be escaped from. I confess that I personally tend to be of the second viewpoint, to the annoyance of some people who top me.)

Playing "I'll bet you can't get loose" can also be fun for the top because, in part, it offers them a chance to watch the bottom try to escape from their bondage. This can be educational as well as entertaining because, as the top watches the bottom try to escape, the top can learn from this and alter how they tie the bottom in the future. I know one dominant woman who became very good at bondage by using this "trial and error" technique. She would tie a bottom up, order them to try to escape, and then watch them carefully as they did so. The next time she tied them up, she would tie them in a way that made it very difficult or impossible for the bottom to escape in the same way. Using this approach allowed her to become very good at bondage in a relatively short time without her ever being "formally" instructed in how to do it.

Playing "I'll bet you can't get loose" can be a very fun bondage game to play, but, as with all games, establishing a few ground rules ahead of time can prevent problems and make it more fun for both parties.

Here are a few good ground rules for the game:

- Agree upon a time limit. It is actually very difficult, using ordinary rope-like materials, to tie someone up so that they absolutely cannot ever, in any amount of time, get free from the bondage (unless you tie them so tightly that the bondage damages them). Among other things, most rope-like materials are at least somewhat stretchy and thus usually loosen a bit over time. Also, skin that was initially non-sweaty when the bondage was applied can become very sweaty, and thus very slippery, as the bottom struggles to free themselves. Finally, most human tissue compresses at least somewhat. Thus bondage that was comfortably tight when first applied often becomes too loose as the underlying tissue compresses. Indeed, if the bottom is really trying with all their intelligence, strength, and flexibility to get free, holding them for even five minutes can be a real challenge.

> "I love looking at the various types of rope in the boating supplies catalog."

I have found that most bondage can be adequately tested in a maximum of about fifteen minutes. Bondage that cannot be escaped from within thirty minutes is unlikely to be escaped from at all. Plus, the game usually remains exciting and fun for both parties for only about fifteen to thirty minutes.

Tops, keep in mind that a bottom who has failed to escape may not be in the most positive state of mind. While they might be blissfully happy, there is also a decent chance that they may feel frustrated, feel like a failure, feel angry with themselves (or even with you), or otherwise be in something of a negative frame of mind. They frequently also feel physically tired, even nearly exhausted, from their exertions, and they may have some scrapes and strains.

- *Agree upon what happens if the bottom cannot escape within the agreed-upon time.* Does the session continue, with various sexual and/or sado-masochistic acts, or does everything end at that time? Is the bottom entitled to be freed if they have given up? In other words, before playing this game, clearly agree ahead of time regarding who will win what if the bottom either succeeds in escaping or fails to escape.

- *Is the top allowed to watch the bottom try to escape?* In general, I recommend that the top be allowed to watch. First, because it can be an important safety precaution. Second, because it can be educational for the top. Third, because it can be enjoyable for both parties. If the top is not allowed to watch, they should at least remain within "yelling distance" so that they can promptly come to the bottom's aid in the event of an emergency.

- *Is the bottom allowed to use any foreign objects in the escape attempt?* For example, if they can reach a knife, are they allowed to use it? If they can reach something "breakable," can they break it and try to use the resultant sharp objects to cut themselves free? Is the bottom allowed to rub against various items of furniture, outcroppings from the wall, and so forth in an attempt to get free? It can be dangerous for the bottom to use a knife or other sharp object to cut themselves free if they cannot see where they are cutting. "Blind" cutting can result in injuries, and it can be difficult to tell the difference between sweat and blood by feel alone.

- *Is the top allowed to intervene if they see that the bottom is succeeding in their escape attempt?* In general, I recommend against this. The top had their turn "at bat" when they were doing the tying. It is now the bottom's turn at bat, and they should be allowed full opportunity to take advantage of it. Indeed, an intervention by the top that was not agreed to ahead of time can cause the bottom to feel cheated and angry.

- *The bottom should not be allowed to do anything likely to seriously injure themselves during their escape attempt.* It's common for the bottom to lose a few layers of epidermis as they twist and squirm in an attempt to escape, and there may be a few aching muscles and a slight strain or two afterwards. However, anything more severe (for example, twisting within the bonds to the point that the skin starts to bleed), is usually not that great an idea. As one dominant woman I know put it, "I don't like to see a partner of mine limping afterwards."

- *Is the top allowed to tie the bottom to something such as a chair, bed, or post?* I generally like the bottom to be lying or sitting on a carpeted floor for this game. This allows them a fairly high degree of movement without exposing them to the danger of a fall. (I suggest that the bottom not be allowed to stand up if their feet or legs are tied in any way.)

Be advised that a bottom who is tied to a chair may be at greatly increased risk for injuring themselves if the chair topples over.

- *Is the top allowed to blindfold and/or gag the bottom?* Using a blindfold makes it much more difficult to escape because it limits how closely the bottom can study their bondage. A gagged bottom has a much more difficult time using their teeth to open a knot.

A final cautionary note: "I'll bet you can't get loose" is a game that you should only play with people that you know very well and trust a great deal. Remember that there are some serious predators out there that may trick you into playing this game with them by misrepresenting how good they really are at bondage. The decision to consent to allowing yourself to be bound is always one that you should take a moment to think carefully about. You should always assume that the person will succeed in tying you so that you cannot get loose, and make your decision accordingly. If you are not comfortable about being inescapably tied up in this person's presence, don't play this game with them.

Footnote: Some predators try a variant called "You tie me up, then I'll tie you up." They know that they are probably much better at bondage than you are, and so they'll probably be able to get out of what you put them in. Furthermore, once you've had your turn it can seem only fair that they now be allowed to have their turn. This can be taking advantage of your sense of fair play. Be careful here. Again, only play this game with someone that you know well and feel very comfortable with.

How They Get Loose

All ropes stretch somewhat, all tissues compress somewhat, and sweaty skin is slippery skin.

It can actually be very difficult to tie someone in such a way that they really cannot eventually free themselves by one means or another. This is particularly true if you care about not tying them so tightly that you damage them. Even handcuffs are rated as temporary restraints.

People vary a lot in their body type. Some have wider hands than others have. Some people are much more flexible than others. When studying how to tie someone up, and how to keep them tied up once you have them in that condition, it can be very useful to make a separate study of how people escape from their bondage. Most escapes from bondage involve a relatively small number of techniques. Let's look at each of the common ones.

- *Reaching the knot.* This is probably the easiest and most basic means of escaping from bondage. Any knot that can be reached with a finger, a toe, or a tooth is very likely to be worked loose sooner or later. (To keep things simple, henceforth I'll only refer to knots that can be reached by the bottom's fingers.)

  Keep in mind that bound bottoms may have lots of time to study their bondage and thus figure out ways to either move their fingers to the knot or move the knot to their fingers. They may devise very ingenious ways of accomplishing this. (Bondage is, in many ways, a mental game.)

  One of the ways that the top can help ensure that the bottom remains bound is to limit their ability to study their bondage. This can involve means such as blindfolding them, or means of keeping their mind busy on other things such as enduring pain, counting, or some other method of keeping those neurons busy.

  Tops should be wary of placing bondage knots "just out of reach" of the bottom's fingers. This leaves almost no margin for error, and thus any unexpected development may result in the bottom's being able to reach the knots and thus escape.

- *"Coneing out."* I bound a fairly large number of different people during the research phase of this book, especially their wrists. Over time, I learned to appreciate how very variable were the shapes of the numerous hands and wrists that I encountered. In particular, I learned to appreciate how much the size of a hand can vary in relation to the size of its wrist. At one end of the spectrum, some people (mostly men) have large, meaty hands out at the ends of relatively narrow wrists. At the other end of the spectrum, some people (mostly women) have hands that are little more than "slightly wider areas of the road" as you travel the "highway" that runs from their elbows to their fingertips.

Hands that are relatively broad in relation to their wrists can be fairly easy to bind. On the other hand (so to speak), hands that are only slightly wider than the wrists can be incredibly difficult to bind in any lasting way. The bottom can often escape relatively easily by making their hand as narrow as possible. This is often done by bringing the four fingers tightly together, placing the tip of the thumb at approximately the base of the ring finger, and curling the bones of the hand into a rounded arch. Given its shape, this can be called a "cone." If even a small amount of slack exists in the wrapping turns, the bottom may, with time, determination, and sweat, be able to "cone out" of their bondage by pulling their hand through a relatively narrow set of wrapping turns. (As one bottom put it, "This is like fisting in reverse.") This is especially true if they can move other parts of their arms with relative freedom and/or bring a large amount of muscular effort to the task. Thus, if the bottom has relatively narrow hands in relationship to the width of their wrist, immobilizing their upper arms can be even more important. (See the "Arm Harnesses" chapter for more information.)

Note: Some bottoms have noted that the "cone out" escape maneuver is sometimes enhanced if they can move the knotted portion of the rope over to the little-finger-side of their hand.

• *Slipping a wrapping turn.* This is a fairly sneaky technique that can take a bit of dexterity and patience, but has a very good chance of working. Bound-together wrists are particularly vulnerable to this technique.

To escape by this technique, using its simplest form, the bottom grasps the wrapping turn closest to their hand with the fingers of their other hand and pulls it away from the skin of the wrist. The idea here is to intentionally create some constriction in the other wrapping turns (for a relatively short time) in order to create some slack in this particular turn. Once adequate slack is created by this maneuver, the slackened wrapping turn is worked over the bound hand. This almost always allows enough slack to be created in the other wrapping turns that the rest of the bondage is defeated relatively quickly.

- *Thrusting a wrist "further up" the bondage.* This is something of a variant on the "slipping a wrapping turn" technique. When using this technique to escape from "hands tied behind the back" bondage, the bottom takes a moment to determine which bound wrist feels slightly looser than the other. (There is usually a small amount of difference.) After making this determination, the bottom pulls firmly on their bondage (and, if possible, twists their wrists) so that the wrapping turns are pulled as high as possible up (towards the elbow) of the looser wrist.

- *Simply waiting for the ropes to stretch and the tissue to compress.* It is a simple fact that all (non-metal) materials used for bondage have at least some degree of stretch. Also, almost all tissue except bone will compress at least a bit. (This is what allows some escapes from metal restraints.) Thus, over time, if the bondage material is under tension and the tissue is being pressed upon, almost all bondage eventually develops at least a little bit of looseness.

> *"I love the look that comes over your face when you're tied up."*

- *Offering the wrists in a T-cross.* This is a sneaky one. The bottom offers their wrists to be bound in such a way that the bones of the wrist on top are perpendicular to the bones of the wrist underneath. When the bondage is applied, the bottom can often create a substantial amount of slack by simply turning their wrists so that they are parallel to each other. The use of cinch loops (see p. 168) does a lot to defeat this technique.

- *Clenching the fists.* This is a simple technique in which the bottom clenches their fists and thus puts the tendons in their wrists under tension. The result is a slightly wider wrist. When the fists are unclenched, a small amount of slack can be created. (A small amount of slack may be all that an "eel" needs to escape.)

- *Flexing the feet as the ankles are tied.* This technique resembles the "clenching the fists" technique. The bottom "lifts their toes" as far up as they can while their ankles are being bound. This puts the tendons in their ankles, particularly their Achilles tendons, under tension. When they point their toes a certain amount of slack can be created.

- *Placing the ankles side by side.* A fairly subtle means of creating some slack in ankle bondage is to simply place the ankles side by side while they are being tied, and then crossing them to create some slack. This technique is usually easily defeated by the use of cinch loops (see p. 168).

- *"Working the rope" to create some slack.* Any rope that the bottom can move is at great risk of being loosened. In particular, a bottom whose wrists are tied behind their back but whose arms are not otherwise restrained may be able to work their wrists free within a relatively short time. Double-limb bondage is especially vulnerable to this, as spending some time watching a bottom twist, turn, pull, push, slide, and otherwise "work" their arms or legs within the bondage will usually make quite apparent.

- *Use of a foreign object.* Any foreign object that the bottom is able to reach may be of assistance to them as they attempt to escape. For example, the corner of a nightstand or of a chest of drawers can offer a hard, useful projection point to use to help move wrapping turns down (and off) the bound wrists. Another example would involve the bottom rubbing their face against a wall – or even against the bed that they are laying on – to remove a blindfold or gag. The bedframe or bedposts can also offer a hard point to rub against.

  If the bottom can reach something sharp, such as a knife or pair of scissors, they may be able to cut themselves free. *(Caution:* "blind cutting," such as is done when trying to cut bonds holding the wrists behind the back, can produce injury.) Bottoms who cannot reach a sharp object may be able to improvise one by breaking something made out of glass or similar material.

- *Using their own sweat to lubricate their skin.* The sweatier a bottom becomes, the more slippery they become. Ropes that would not move on dry skin will often slide with relative ease over skin made slippery by sweat.

- *"Stepping through" hands tied behind the back.* This technique depends a great deal upon the body type of the bottom and to a certain degree upon how their wrists are secured behind them. It involves the bottom bringing their hands down behind their back until they drop below their buttocks and to the backs of their knees, then "stepping through" and bringing their hands up in front of them. I could do this technique when I was a boy.

- *Using their own muscle strength.* This is typically done when the wrists are tied behind the bottom's back, but it can be done in other positions as well. It can be especially effective when the wrists are tied in the anti-parallel position (see p. 178). This technique is often a final technique used to assist in coneing out once the ropes have been worked as far down the bottom's wrists as possible. In the classic method, the bottom tenses the large muscles of their back and pulls as hard as possible in the anti-parallel direction. If things have been properly prepared, this maneuver often succeeds.

- *Sliding out of very smooth rope.* Basically, the smoother a rope is, the more a person can adjust it and struggle within it, and the less firmly it will hold a knot. (Some schools of bondage, particularly Japanese bondage, therefore intentionally use relatively rough rope such as hemp rope against the bottom's skin as a very persuasive means of discouraging struggling.) One escape artist's trick is to rub wax into a rope as a means of making it exceptionally slippery.

On Self-Bondage

Self-bondage (basically, tying yourself up – usually when nobody else is around) is one of the most controversial areas of bondage – and of BDSM in general.

Motivations for wanting to do self-bondage vary. Most people who want to be tied up would rather be tied up by a skillful, trustworthy top. However, this is not always possible. As one bondage expert I interviewed for this book mentioned: "Men tend to tie themselves up because they do not have a partner, while women tend to tie themselves up because they do not trust their partner."

The person who desires to engage in self-bondage (and, because it is frequently erotically based, this desire can be very strong) faces a serious problem.

On one hand, they want to end up bound to a satisfying degree, and this often means being tied up to the point where they can't get loose. On the other hand, they eventually *will* want to get loose, so they have to try to figure out a way to accomplish that.

To engage in self-bondage is to attempt to predict the future, and that can never be done with perfect accuracy. Self-bondage can be exciting, intense, erotic, and enjoyable, as long as *absolutely nothing* unexpected happens. Any unexpected occurrence can have severe consequences.

One of the more obvious problems is that being in bondage can reduce the bound person to an infant-like state of helplessness, and there is the rule of "always stay as close to a bound person as you would to an infant left in your care – and if you gag them, stay even closer."

Unfortunately, there have been many deaths among self-bondage practitioners. I have many such case reports in my files. (I even have a case report of a self-bondage double fatality.) Indeed, even if you set aside cases of suffocation and/or strangulation done either alone or with a partner for erotic reasons (and these practices are not necessarily related to BDSM at all), self-bondage mishaps appear to account for the overwhelming majority of BDSM-related deaths.

Unfortunately, there seems to be no simple way to significantly reduce the danger involved while still preserving the essence of what the self-bound person wants to experience.

Some self-bondage fans recommend "emergency escape plans." I have seen a number of these plans. None seem reliable enough for me to want to bet my life on one of them. (In fact, one self-bondage enthusiast pointed out that few self-bondage practitioners have actually practiced using their emergency escape plan ahead of time.) I should also note that in the forensic pathology literature, "failed self-rescue mechanism" is a common cause of deaths among self-bondage people. (This serves as an excellent example of the advice to take at least one more precaution than you feel that you need to.)

I confess that I went through a phase in which I did some significant experimenting with self-bondage. The thought of being naked and tied up, even if I had no partner, had distinct appeal. I even found a fairly good "how to do it" article in a bondage magazine and immediately went home to try it out. The technique worked reasonably well. Thoughtful person that I am, I even figured out how to improve the technique that the article mentioned. Unfortunately, the "improvement" worked even better than I anticipated (and, in one terrifying incident I won't describe here, almost cost me my life).

Self-bondage can be affected by other factors out of the control of the self-binder. Out here in California, one of the things we BDSM enthusiasts must always keep ever-so-slightly in the back of our minds is the fact that an earthquake might strike at any time, with no warning whatsoever. Thus, particularly if we are taking the dominant role, we must always give at least a bit of thought to the question of "how will I deal with this situation if an earthquake strikes?"

At the time I was doing my greatest experimentation with self-bondage, I was living in a building made of standard red bricks. (Such buildings can disintegrate in an earthquake.) A few weeks after I gave up experimenting with self-bondage, a fairly strong quake struck and the building started shaking like mad. Fortunately, I was able to get to a safe place, but I still remember running down the stairs while the building shook and the plaster fell. Afterwards, when I had time to reflect, the thought that I might have been in my room, in self-bondage, in that red brick building when that earthquake struck, occurred to me. It was, as I'm sure you can imagine, an utterly chilling thought.

I've had some other self-bondage incidents. Once, a few years ago, on something of a whim, I decided to show Janet one of my self-bondage techniques. I managed to apply the tie without too much difficulty (it puts you into a hog-tied position) but when I came to the final "pull it tight" part that makes escaping from the tie very difficult, I accidentally bumped the room's electric space heater as I did the "pull it tight" maneuver. Thus both Janet and I watched as the space heater fell over, face down, onto the carpet and began to heat up the rug. I knelt on the carpet, naked and hog-tied, and she sat on the bed, dressed and fully able to move, and we both watched for a moment in shocked horror as the heater began to direct its full force onto the carpet. Fortunately, she was able to quickly and easily correct the situation (thanks, Honey!), but we were both left contemplating the possible consequences of what might have happened if I had been there by myself.

On another occasion, we were visiting a resort. Janet had gone off to soak in the hot tub and I had stayed in our room, reading. We had brought along some rope with the intention of playing later. I finished the book, did not feel like joining Janet in the hot tub, and was generally feeling bored. So I decided to try a small amount of self-bondage.

I had been, from time to time, mulling an idea around in my head on how to improve a certain self-bondage technique that was designed to tie the wrists together (frequently the trickiest part of the process). I also had an idea as to how I would loosen the bondage when I wanted to get loose. Figuring like there was no time like the present, I decided to give it a quick try. Still, I had to be a bit careful. (I still very clearly remembered my earlier scare.)

I decided to tie my wrists in front of me, and to remain fully dressed. That way, if there were an earthquake or something similar, I could simply just walk out the door of our room. Yeah, that would be embarrassing, but I'd still be alive. I also, as a backup, took out my Swiss Army knife, opened out the main blade, and put it on the desktop.

Those precautions taken, I then got the ropes and proceeded to apply the wrist tie. I did the "pull tight" maneuver, and the ropes cinched down very nicely indeed. I had a bit of fun wiggling around in the bondage for a while, but after a time I decided that it was time to free myself. I tried my "escape" technique, and it didn't even begin to work. Uh oh! I tried again, a bit harder; no luck.

I sat there on the bed, looking at my very securely bound wrists (thank God that they weren't bound so tightly that the nerves and blood vessels were dangerously compressed), and tried to figure out what to do next. I could, of course, use my Swiss Army knife if I really needed to. (Thank goodness the blade was already out. Whether or not I could have gotten out with my hands in their present state, I wasn't at all sure.) I could also, of course, if things really got bad, simply walk out of the room and ask for assistance. I decided that things weren't yet that bad, so I decided to try another approach to loosening the ropes around my wrists. No luck. Well, Janet should be back eventually, right? Right?

And so I sat there for what seemed like a very long time. When Janet finally returned to the room, after what turned out to be about an hour and fifteen minutes (but which seemed much longer) there I waited, still bound. When I looked at her, I'm not sure which was redder – the skin on my wrists or the skin on my face. Long-suffering woman that she is, she released me (it was rather easy for her to do) and after the redness faded slightly from the various parts of my body we went out to dinner.

There is a postscript to this incident. The next day, while we were still at the resort, Janet agreed to stay in the room with me while I tried out some variations on the self-bondage techniques that I had been mulling over. I tried out four different techniques. In all four cases, after I had done the final tightenings, I found that the effect was not quite what I had predicted. In three of the four cases, the bondage ended up being looser than I had wanted, but in the fourth case the bondage was much tighter than I had wanted – so much so that it was cutting off circulation. In all cases, the presence of a second person made these unexpected results easy to correct, but we were certainly left wondering what would have happened if I had tried this while alone – especially in that fourth, dangerously tight, case.

So where does this leave us? What should I, as a responsible SM author and educator (which I certainly hope that I am) advocate regarding self-bondage? What recommendations on this subject am I willing to back with my good name and reputation?

One of the things that makes this hard is that we have no overall statistics regarding who is engaging in self-bondage (interestingly enough, while the common belief seems to be that this is a practice engaged in almost exclusively by men, I have heard from a significant number of women who say that they engage in it). We don't know how many people are doing it, or how often they are doing it, so we cannot evaluate the degree of risk from a statistical viewpoint. All we can go by are case reports in the medical and police literature, and by reports from practitioners.

I cannot make myself comfortable with saying something like "Self-bondage is great. Go ahead and do it. Have a ball!" I have simply heard too many stories of accidents, mishaps, and injuries, and even a few reports of fatalities, for me to feel comfortable saying something like that.

I can say the following things:

- The risk level involved in self-bondage seems to dramatically increase if any sort of gag is involved.

- The risk level involved in self-bondage seems to dramatically increase if any sort of ropes are around the bound person's neck.

- The risk level involved in self-bondage seems to dramatically increase if the bound person is tied to some sort of fixed object such as a bed.

- The risk level seems to dramatically increase if the self-bound person unexpectedly falls.

- Many self-bondage fans have an "emergency escape" plan in place, but they've never actually tested it to see if it works. (For example, it may be impossible to open a lock if you have to use oil-covered keys on a keyhole that is located someplace where you cannot see it.)

- Bondage that might not be tight enough to cause the self-bound person's hands to become numb immediately might still be tight enough to cause the bound person's hands to become numb after the passage of many minutes or a few hours. This could make escape impossible. (A friend of mine who is a surgeon suffered numbness on one of their thumbs that lasted for several weeks after some self-bondage of their wrists unexpectedly became too tight.)

> "This new chair I got works great for bondage."

- Almost all BDSM-related fatalities that I have heard about have involved self-bondage mishaps. The presence or absence of a sympathetic monitor emerges as a major landmark in this regard.

- A self-bondage position that makes it slightly difficult to breathe may be tolerable for up to several hours, but if the bound person is unable to escape, their breathing muscles may eventually tire to the point where they cannot function and the bound person will die of what's called positional asphyxia (see p. 273). If the bound person is overweight or has impaired breathing, they are at greater risk for this problem.

- Any unexpected event that affects a self-bound person can have major consequences. For example, I was consulted a while back on an incident in which a person who was bound, gagged, and alone (whether he did this to himself or had help was not clear) developed a nosebleed, and died when the clotted blood blocked his nose.

- People who are in bondage sometimes suffer what can be called a "panic reaction." This reaction can come on very suddenly and with no warning whatsoever, sometimes for reasons entirely unrelated to the SM play. A panicked bottom in bondage can be very difficult for even the most experienced top to deal with. A panicked bottom who is in self-bondage may not survive.

- Knives may not work well as self-rescue devices. It is very easy to drop a knife, or to have it fall some place where you cannot reach it, or to injure yourself with it. (For example, it can be fairly easy to cut yourself if you are trying to use a knife to cut ropes that are holding your wrists tied behind your back.)

As I've mentioned in other places in this book, to engage in bondage or some other aspect of BDSM (or any other aspect of life) is never a simple, binary decision of choosing the safe versus the unsafe. It's always a matter of "choose your risk level." Each of us must decide what level of risk we feel comfortable facing. I play at a higher risk level than some bondage fans (and have had the scares and mishaps to show for it), and there are people who play at higher risk levels than I do. Given that these people are informed, consenting adults, I'm not going to say that they are reckless or irresponsible for doing so. Still, they know perfectly well that they may someday face a major mishap.

The core of the problem may well be that the actual risk level of self-bondage is unappreciated. I interviewed some self-bondage fans while working on this book, and the ones who have made a real study of it fully understand that there are serious risks involved. One person proudly showed me their "triply redundant" escape mechanisms. As they put it, "If the first one fails, the fact that you still have two more options helps a lot to steady your nerves so that you can make the second one work."

There is an excellent saying, particularly popular in the Southern California BDSM community, that goes "think with your head." Self-bondage fans would do well to heed this advice. It seems that many people rush into self-bondage situations without adequately asking some of the hard "what if?" questions. While all bondage involves risk, self-bondage emerges as the bondage practice associated with what is by far the highest number of known fatalities.

RISK FACTORS AND WARNING SIGNS

*L*EVELS OF RISK. One of the most frequent questions to come up regarding erotic bondage is the question of "Is it safe to do this?" This can be a very difficult question to answer meaningfully.

What does the word "safe" mean? One of the definitions in my dictionary is "freedom from risk." In that context, it is never entirely safe to do erotic bondage, because the risk level can never be reduced to zero. Thus, the only entirely safe way to engage in erotic bondage is to not engage in it at all. On the other hand, I've certainly heard many people try to rationalize various extremely dangerous behaviors on the grounds that, "Hey, everything is risky." This seems like a very dangerous line of reasoning to me.

While it is, of course, true that "everything is risky," trying to summarize the risk levels in this very crude way seems to lump all forms of risk in together. Yes, "everything is risky" – but not to the same degree!

Actually, the concept of "degree of risk" may be a very productive concept in determining how to consider various aspects of erotic bondage. After a great deal of research and contemplation, I have come up with what seems to be a workable plan to categorize the degree of risk associated with various aspects of erotic bondage.

They are:

1. Average level of risk.

2. Above average level of risk.

3. Extremely high level of risk.

I should note that, among bondage fans, not everybody agrees about which bondage practices fall into which category.

"Average level of risk" erotic bondage is bondage that is, in general, done in compliance with widely recommended safety principles. When people engage in erotic bondage in this way, there are almost no case reports of bad outcomes or significant injuries. Problems that are reported seem to involve emotional issues (such as the inadvertent triggering of a phobia or a panic attack) with a lack of adequate BDSM education, or with relationship difficulties.

"Above average level of risk" erotic bondage is bondage that is done in a way that places the bottom, and perhaps also the top, at a significantly increased, but not extremely severe, risk of physical or emotional injury. While there seem to be an increased number of reports of bad outcomes, most injuries that occur can be treated on an outpatient basis.

In my experience, the most frequently reported cause of lasting injuries is bondage applied so tightly that the bondage feels painfully tight. The single most common cause of bondage-related injuries severe enough to require an actual visit to a hospital emergency room involve having a bottom *fall* while in bondage. These falls are frequently due to some kind of equipment failure, such as having an overhead screw eye pull loose, or having a larger item of bondage-related equipment such as a whipping post suffer some sort of structural failure. They are also often due to placing a bottom in an unstable position while in bondage such as standing upright with their hands tied behind their back and their feet tied together.

"Extremely high level of risk" erotic bondage places the bottom, and perhaps also the top, at direct, immediate risk of very severe injury. When bondage is done in this way, there are a very significant number of case reports of bad outcomes in which someone is hospitalized or even killed.

As far as I've been able to discover, by far the single most common cause of bondage-related fatalities involves engaging in bondage while alone. This can be either a form of autoerotic asphyxiation (which the participant might not regard as bondage at all), or some form of self-bondage that does not involve any strangulation. If a gag is involved in bondage of this sort, the risk level is increased even further.

A comment about the right to choose one's own risk level. In various writings about bondage, and about other aspects of SM, there are frequent messages along the lines of "never do this" or "that is unsafe." These comments, while usually well-intentioned and often useful, can send something of a mixed message.

It is not necessarily wrong, unethical, reckless, or irresponsible to take risks of an above-average level. However, we as a society tend to look a bit askance at risks taken for the purpose of achieving pleasure, such as the risks associated with activities like auto racing, white water rafting, skydiving, and so forth. Furthermore, we especially tend to look a bit askance at risks taken for the purpose of achieving sexual pleasure. (Indeed, a large percentage of the population regards taking the risks associated with doing any sort of bondage for the purpose of heightening sexual pleasure, no matter how mild and relatively risk-free such bondage seems to its participants, as being well above the acceptable level of risk.)

RISK FACTORS AND WHAT TO DO ABOUT THEM

Here's a list of the top thirteen – a baker's dozen – of the most common bondage-related problems and what to do about them.

While I have mentioned various risk factors associated with bondage throughout this book, I thought it would be useful to compile the major ones in one location and discuss each of them. In many cases, of course, simply describing the risk factor suggests obvious means of mitigating it.

Keep in mind the "Take one more precaution than you think you need to" rule.

Risk Factor Number One: Playing bondage games while alone. From what I have been able to determine, after talking with large numbers of people and doing other research, the number one cause of bondage-related fatalities is playing bondage games while alone – i.e., self-bondage games or activities in which the top bound the bottom and then went beyond "yelling distance."

There were case reports in which the person died of some unrelated cause such as a heart attack while engaged in bondage or some other SM-related activity. (Deaths during sex are actually not all that rare.) However, doing bondage while alone was, by a huge margin, the most common activity in which a fatal outcome was directly caused by what was going on. If a gag was used, the risk level increases even further.

Please note that I am not referring to autoerotic asphyxiation games (activity in which a person suffocates or strangles themselves in order to heighten erotic sensation) here. While it is possible to play such games in conjunction with bondage, they are not necessarily the same thing. Many people who play such autoerotic asphyxiation games would deny that what they do is intrinsically a form of bondage.

"Master, I can't feel my hands."

Most self-bondage fans who are not killed by autoerotic asphyxiation seem to die from some form of what called positional asphyxia (see p. 273).

There is just no question that if another person is not within yelling distance, then the bound person is very much "working without a net."

Risk Factor Number Two: Falling. My interviews, experience, and research led me to the conclusion that the number-one cause of bondage fans ending up in a hospital emergency room was for treatment of injuries – including many fractures – that were sustained in a fall. A bound person, particularly a person whose feet are bound, is at increased risk for falling. This risk level can be increased by activities such as wearing high-heeled shoes. Furthermore, if a person has their arms bound in any way, they are limited in both their ability to steady themselves to prevent a fall or to catch themselves and reduce their chances of being injured if they fall. If their hands are bound behind their back when they fall, they may be at very great risk of injury.

In my experience, the single most common cause of an injury-producing, bondage-related fall is the pulling loose or other failure of an overhead eyebolt or similar item while the bottom is in a standing position with their hands tied over their heads to this item.

When moving a person who has been bound in any way, keep close to them so that you can steady them as soon as they start to lose their balance.

A warning about panic snaps: One of the items of conventional wisdom in the SM community is that panic snaps – special snaps designed to be opened readily even when under stress – should be used when the bondage involves a vertical rope under tension. I am growing more and more disenchanted with this recommendation. (For my reasons why, see p. 297.)

I feel far more comfortable with block-and-tackle devices that allow a more controlled, gradual lowering of the bottom if necessary. Even winding the rope once or twice entirely around the loop in the eyebolt can make such a lowering much more simple. (If you want to learn more about this, look at what the climbing and boating books have to say about "belaying turns.")

Risk Factor Number Three: Painfully tight bondage. While it is probably always risky to tie someone so that numbness and/or tingling results, most reports of tingling that persists after the bondage is removed seem to be strongly associated with painfully tight bondage. It seems to be true that most bondage which causes some tingling or numbness but is not painful goes away almost immediately after the bondage is removed. On the other hand (so to speak), most bondage that causes persistent tingling, numbness, or even weakness in the limb causes not only numbness and tingling, but is itself painful.

Risk Factor Number Four: Playing while intoxicated. I'm something of a student of "SM horror stories." Whenever I heard of an SM scene that ended badly, I always try to learn as many details as I can. Whenever possible, I try to talk personally with the people involved. One of the items that is mentioned with astonishing frequency is the use of intoxicants by one or both parties. It has become very obvious to me that intoxicant use was an "essential co-factor" in many SM-related disasters, and that had intoxicants not been used it is quite plausible that the incident would never have happened. Based on my research, I have concluded that intoxicant use by any person in the scene automatically increases the degree of risk by one level, and that intoxicant use by both people automatically takes the scene up to the "extreme" degree of risk.

Risk Factor Number Five: Playing with an abusive top. While many people perceive this to be the major risk factor associated with bondage, I have found that case reports of this type of incident are actually somewhat rare. Still, they most definitely do happen. Happily, this is one case in which the conventional wisdom does seem effective: Take your time and get to know someone before you let them tie you up. If possible, get references from previous play partners. Make sure that a third person knows where you are, who you're with, what you're doing, and when you're expected back – and that your bondage partner credibly believes that this is true before the play starts. Don't do too much bondage on the first few play dates.

Risk Factor Number Six: Playing in isolated areas. An isolated area can be defined as an area in which a bound bottom cannot readily get the attention of a third person if the top were to become unconscious. Incidents of this type are rare, but they do sometimes happen. (One fictional account of such an incident, in which a top dies while a bottom is in bondage in a cabin in the woods, appears in the book "Gerald's Game" by Stephen King.)

It should be pointed out that if a top were to have a severe medical emergency under these circumstances, such as a sudden cardiac arrest, any reasonable life-saving attempt may well be impossible.

The risk level associated with this practice can be greatly mitigated by a little foresight – for example, telling someone where you'll be and when you're expected back. Other steps include making sure that a bound bottom can reach something like a telephone or an alarm panic button if they really need to.

Limiting the bondage can also be useful. For example, I know one bottom who will let herself be put in fairly stringent bondage under such circumstances, but she will not let herself be tied to any fixed object such as a bed, chair, or overhead eyebolt.

I would suggest that there be at least two different methods available to the bottom to either free themselves or summon help under such circumstances. Because two lives may be at stake here, this is an excellent example of a "take one more precaution than you think you need to" type of situation.

Risk Factor Number Seven: Withholding information from your partner or giving them false information. Unfortunately, this mistake is fairly common, and can cover a wide variety of topics. I know of cases in which people have not told their prospective partner of important medical conditions (such as a heart condition or seizure disorder). I also know of cases in which people have claimed to not have a sexually transmitted disease when they knew that they did.

There are people who overstate how much experience they have, either as a top or a bottom. There are people in committed relationships who claim that it's fine with their spouse or life partner if you play with them, when in fact it's not.

The list goes on and on.

Risk Factor Number Eight: A medical emergency occurring during the play. Medical emergencies do occasionally occur during SM play, and they may not even have any direct relationship to what is happening. Probably the most common medical emergency is a bottom who faints while in a standing position. Other emergencies can include injuries caused by falls or burns, or heart attacks and seizures.

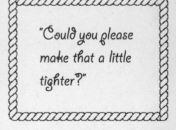

"Could you please make that a little tighter?"

Thus, many sadomasochists make a point of taking classes in First Aid and CPR. Some SM clubs go as a group; some even have their own "in-house" instructors. (I have been regularly teaching classes in First Aid and CPR within the SM community for many years.) If you're not sure where you can go to take a class, look under "first aid instruction" in your local yellow pages.

Risk Factor Number Nine: Failure to deal promptly with "bad pain." Experienced SM practitioners come to know the difference between "good pain" and "bad pain." "Good pain," such as might be produced by pinching the bottom's nipples, typically has an erotic component to it, is not significantly damaging, and adds to the energy of the play. "Bad pain" such as painfully tight bondage typically does not have an erotic component, may be significantly damaging, and detracts from the energy of the play. "Bad pain" also has a way of involving a joint, especially the neck, lower back, shoulders, or wrists. Failure to promptly alleviate "bad pain" can lead to long-term problems.

Risk Factor Number Ten: Loss of emotional balance. This is a relatively rare condition that, when it occurs, usually happens to the bottom. It is commonly associated with the top increasing the intensity of the activity too quickly (the classic mistake of the inexperienced or careless player.) It is also commonly associated with a bottom's having waited much longer than they should have waited to use their safeword or to express a concern in some other way.

The most dangerous aspect of this problem is that the bottom may have become so emotionally overwhelmed by what's going on that they have lost their ability to use their safeword, even though they desperately want to.

For this reason, tops are well advised to do occasional "affirmative check-ins" with their bottoms. They should not assume that all is well simply because their bottom has not called a safeword or expressed concern in some other way.

If the top determines that the bottom has lost their emotional balance, it's almost always best to stop the SM play and become a sympathetic supporter. Reassure them, remove the bondage, make sure that they're adequately warm (a blanket can help), and offer them something to drink. This is not the time to argue with them or to become personally defensive. This is also not a good time to discuss in detail what happened during the scene.

While loss of emotional balance occasionally happens suddenly and without warning, as might happen when the play unexpectedly triggers a phobia, most of the time there is significant warning before this occurs, so stay alert.

Risk Factor Number Eleven: Playing with unfamiliar equipment. This is a common error, and it tends to happen to overly egotistical tops who should have known better. You wouldn't think that I would have to advise people not to do things like try to use a piece of SM equipment until they clearly understand how to apply and remove it, or how to raise and lower it, or how to make sure that it's securely locked into place. But the human condition being what it is…

Risk Factor Number Twelve: Environmental emergency. Just as medical emergencies may occur during an SM scene for reasons entirely unrelated to the play, so may other emergencies occur. For example, every now and then an earthquake strikes while an SM scene is in progress, or someone glances out the window and sees that the house next door is on fire. Therefore, the top needs to have a clear, workable plan for freeing the bottom with a high degree of speed and safety.

Power failures may occur at any moment, and may even be associated with something such as an earthquake. Thus, many bedrooms and playrooms have power-failure lights in them. These lights go on automatically if the power goes off.

Risk Factor Number Thirteen: Equipment failure. Every now and then, an item of SM equipment just simply fails. Probably the most common equipment failure that I have seen or heard about is an overhead eyebolt (or, especially, a screw-eye) pulling loose. This typically happens when the force of the pull is along the same axis as the axis in which the eyebolt or screw-eye is attached. For example, a screw-eye is placed straight up into some wood and the direction of the pull is straight down.

Locks sometimes fail, and the reason is often unclear. For this reason, people who like metal bondage equipment should make sure their "get loose kit" includes extra keys, a good pair of bolt-cutters, a hacksaw and several high-quality blades, and related items.

Knots sometimes get pulled much more tightly into rope and rope-like materials than was expected. Items useful in helping to work such

" My right foot is starting to go numb."

knots free are listed on p. 50. Of course, as a final option, you can use a knife blade or your EMT scissors. (Note that knots put into nylon stockings can easily be pulled so tightly that it will be impossible to untie them by any means.)

WARNING SIGNS AND WHAT THEY MEAN

When a limb is bound, it may develop an unusual color, an unusual temperature, an unusual size, and other abnormalities. How should we evaluate these abnormal findings, and when should we become concerned about them?

When emergency medical personnel evaluate a limb that may be injured, they usually evaluate the blood supply and nerve function of the limb in addition to checking for any injuries. This is sometimes referred to as checking the circulation, sensation, and movement, or the "CSM," of the limb. We bondage fans should know something about how to do this, so let's take a look at each component.

To evaluate the circulation in the bottom's limbs, the top should first ask about the presence of any underlying medical condition that might impair the bottom's circulation. These matters are usually covered in pre-session negotiations. Diabetes is one common example of such a condition.

Then the top should briefly inspect the bottom's limbs. This inspection is especially important when playing with a new partner. Normally, this will only take a very short time. Briefly look at and touch each hand and/or foot to get a general impression of its color, temperature, and size. This is important because, among other things, some people's limbs are naturally cooler and/or paler than other people's are.

Key Point: It's difficult to know if a limb has become unusually cold or pale after you have applied bondage to it unless you first noted its color and temperature before you applied the bondage.

It is especially important to note any differences between the two limbs upon this initial examination. For example, if one of the bottom's hands is noticeably cooler, paler, or bigger than the other, the top should ask about this. (This bottom might need to see a doctor.)

By the way, both as a convenience and as a safety measure, it is usually a good idea to remove rings, watches, bracelets, and other such items from the bottom's limbs before applying the bondage. In particular, large bracelets, or rings with precious stones prominently attached, might cause problems.

If the bottom has adequate circulation to their limbs, this brief "look and touch" exam will likely be adequate. However, if the bottom has problems with their circulation, the top may want to examine them a bit further.

To check further for adequate circulation, the top can perform what's called a "capillary refill" test. To perform this test, simply press down on a fingernail so that the nailbed blanches white and then release the pressure. The normal reddish color should return within about two seconds. This test is more accurate if the limb is raised above the level of the bottom's heart.

A "squeeze test" can also be done to check capillary refill. To perform this test, simply have the bottom squeeze a tight fist for a few seconds, then have them open – but not fully extend – their fingers. Their palm should be a whitish color when their fist is first opened but due to capillary refill should return to its normal color within a few seconds.

The top can, if they wish, learn how to feel for the pulses in the bottom's wrists. Various medical books and first aid courses will teach how to feel for the radial and ulnar pulses in the hand and wrist, and the posterior tibial and dorsalis pedis pulses in the foot and ankle. However, if the bondage is tight enough to cause problems, this will usually become much more apparent by other signs. Thus, absent or diminished pulses in a bound limb is usually more of a secondary warning sign than a primary warning sign.

To evaluate the status of the nerves in a bottom's limb, check for sensation and movement by asking the bottom to move the limb and its digits, and to report back on the sensations they feel. Normal sensation has no associated tingling, numbness, or pain. Normal movement involves full range of motion with no loss of strength or dexterity.

With these signs understood, bondage can be thought of as having three basic levels of tightness: average tightness, above-average tightness, and extreme tightness.

Average tightness. With average tightness, the bound limb remains essentially normal in its appearance and function. There is no obvious increase in redness, paleness, or size of the limb. (An increase in redness or size would be due to some restriction of venous and lymphatic return; this is usually not harmful for brief periods.) The limb does not become cooler to the touch and there is no increase in capillary refill time. Pulses can be felt, and the bottom reports no numbness, tingling, or pain. In essence, the status of the limb is identical to its pre-bondage state. When bondage is done to this degree of tightness, I have heard almost no reports of post-bondage problems such as persistent tingling, weakness, loss of strength or dexterity, and so forth, as long as the bound limb is kept this way no longer than the two-hour maximum bondage time recommended by this book.

(Every now and then a bottom will report some post-bondage problems even when tied in this most conservative manner, but these reports are very rare and the problems reported tend to be minor.)

Above-average tightness. With above-average tightness, there is frequently some change in the appearance of the limb. The limb may become redder or paler in color, or increase a bit in size due to inhibition of venous and lymphatic return. It may also become cooler. (These changes can also be caused by raising the limb above the bottom's heart, regardless of the tightness of the bondage.) However, these changes do not seem to be associated with post-bondage problems if the bondage is kept on for no longer than two hours. Pulses can still be felt and capillary refill time remains normal or is only slightly prolonged.

While this level of bondage is not painfully tight, tingling in the bound limb may appear. This type of tingling typically develops gradually and is often quickly relieved if the bottom can shift position or have one or more of the coils of rope slightly moved or eased. (The top can use the curved portion of the blunt, bottom edge of their EMT scissors for this.)

Note: The bottom will often still be able to move fingers that have become numb. This is because the muscles that move the fingers are themselves located on the bottom's forearms and not on the hands themselves. Thus they are "above" the bondage and not subject to its risks. This being the case, the top should *not* rely overly much on whether or not the bottom can move their hands to evaluate the degree of tightness.

One possible exception to this phenomenon are the muscles that spread the fingers apart in a lateral direction. Thus a command to the bottom to "spread your fingers apart" can be revealing. (Note that many of the muscles that move the thumb are above the bondage. Therefore, the ability of the bottom to move their thumb may not provide much valuable information.)

The question of how to evaluate tingling (which often progresses to numbness) in bound limbs is not a simple question to answer. This tingling is generally due to moderate but non-damaging pressure by the ropes on the nerves themselves rather than bondage that impairs circulation.

While as a general rule, it's safer to not tie someone so tightly that tingling develops, and to loosen the bondage if such tingling does appear, for the sake of intellectual honesty I should note that many people have shared with me that they have routinely been doing bondage that causes tingling or even numbness in their hands on many occasions for a number of years with no reports of significant post-bondage problems.

There are many case reports of persistent tingling that persists for a period of days or even weeks, but this tingling does not seem to be associated with significant weakness, loss of dexterity, or compromised circulation.

So this is, admittedly, something of a gray area. While the risk level is somewhat increased, and there are a significant number of reports of post-bondage problems, these problems are often more annoying than serious.

Extreme tightness. When bondage is applied that is extremely tight, virtually all the warning signs appear either as soon as the bondage is applied or very shortly thereafter, and there are many reports of serious post-bondage problems. These problems include persistent severe tingling, persistent numbness, and loss or strength and/or dexterity in the limb.

With extreme tightness, the limb quickly becomes redder or paler in color and may even become somewhat bluish in color (or even greenish... yuck!) after a few minutes. It is almost always cooler to the touch. Pulses are often absent. Due to no inflow of blood, the limb may not swell in size. Capillary refill is greatly delayed or entirely absent. Tingling develops almost immediately and rapidly progresses to numbness.

In particular, this degree of bondage is often *painful* when it is first applied. Thus, we have something of an especially useful warning sign. If the bondage is not immediately painful, there may be some post-bondage problems but they are usually minor. However, if the bondage is immediately painful, we have entered a definite danger zone. If the painful bondage is also associated with immediate signs of compromise to the blood supply and nerve supply to the limb, then there is no doubt that the risk of substantial post-bondage problems has become very high indeed.

In BDSM circles, there is talk of "good pain" which is experienced as being, in some way or another, rewarding for the bottom to receive and is not associated with significant damage. A well-placed paddle stroke upon the bottom's rump often produces "good pain." There is also talk of "bad pain," which is experienced as being unrewarding to receive and is often associated with significant damage. A whip stroke which "wraps" around the bottom's ribs instead of landing squarely on the back often produces "bad pain." Many experienced bottoms can tell instantly if a given sensation produces "good pain" or "bad pain."

This concept can frequently be extended to bondage. I've had several experienced bottoms tell me that they can quickly tell the difference between bondage that is "good tight" as opposed to bondage that is "bad tight." Thus, feedback from the bottom, especially if the bottom is experienced in being tied, is especially important. In particular, if the bottom reports that the bondage is "bad tight" the top should promptly adjust the bondage – or remove it entirely if necessary.

A final caution about cumulative effect. We live in an age when repetitive stress wrist injuries such as carpal tunnel syndrome have become epidemic. Obviously, bondage could be looked at as one form of repetitive stress.

The obvious question emerges: Is there a significant potential for cumulative damage from activities like the repeated compression of bound tissues?

At this point, based on the best information I have available to me, I have seen no evidence that such cumulative damage is highly likely. The SM community is large, contains many practitioners of more than 20 years' experience and, due to the Internet, is increasingly well interconnected. While there have been some occasional case reports of problems, there has certainly been no groundswell of warnings associated with the cumulative effects of doing bondage. If it were true that there was a significant risk of cumulative damage, I would think that such reports would have emerged.

Certainly there are many case reports of injuries associated with something like an overhead screw eye pulling loose, so I don't think that this relative lack of reported problems is due to inadequate reporting.

I have heard some case reports that indicate that once a nerve has been damaged, it might be easier to damage it in the future. But exactly how to interpret such reports, or what conclusions to make from them, is not immediately clear.

From what I can gather, if you follow the advice in this book, particularly about not leaving the bondage on for longer than two hours without at least a ten-minute break before reapplying the bondage, and steer clear of painful, numbing tightness, your risk of cumulative damage, while not nonexistent, seems to be very low.

Rope

o ya wanna engage in some rope bondage, eh? OK, then it would make sense for you to learn a little bit about rope. Let's take a closer look at it.

An Introduction to Rope

When many people (including, by the way, me) think of bondage, they think of someone tied up with rope.

Certainly, from our earliest days of "cowboys and Indians" games, the idea of using rope to tie someone up is well established. (I remember when I was four years old, although I wasn't specifically into bondage at the time, begging my mother for a comic book specifically because it had a picture of Dale Evans tied up in it. For some strange reason, that picture fascinated me.)

So, if rope bondage involves, well, rope, what should we know about it?

Rope: A closer look. Various types of rope are sold all over the place. In fact, if I suddenly need some rope and have none (as has occasionally happened to me), I can run down to my local convenience store and probably buy some rope that will usually be at least minimally adequate for my nefarious purposes. Indeed, I can get all the material I need for a pretty good SM scene at my local convenience store. Let's see, in addition to rope, they sell clothespins, duct tape, candles, ice cubes, matches, Ben Gay, elastic bandages, first aid tape, knives, fly swatters, wooden spoons, and… Hey, when did this place turn into an adult toy store?

Anyway, there are various types of rope readily available for purchase. As a bondage fan, you should know at least something about the various types of rope on the market. Let's take a look at the major aspects of ropes.

There are two basic designs of ropes: twisted rope and braided rope. What's the difference? Well….

Twisted rope. The type of rope often sold as "twisted rope" is more properly called laid rope (it's also sometimes called hawser laid rope or three-strand rope). Laid rope is constructed of strands of rope (usually, as I mentioned, three) twisted together to give it a sort of "barber pole" appearance. A real rope purist is capable of saying about laid rope: "Fibers are combined to make a yarn. Yarns are combined to make a strand. Strands are combined to make a laid rope."

This type of rope is called a laid rope because the direction of its twist is called its "lay." There are two types of lays: "S" laid (also called left-laid) and "Z" laid (also called right-laid). To determine the lay of a rope, hold it upright and note the direction of the twists. An S-laid rope will twist from left to right as you look from top to bottom (thus looking like the center part of the letter "S"). A Z-laid rope will twist from right to left as you look from top to bottom (thus looking like the center part of the letter "Z). Most laid rope is Z-laid rope.

I will bow before the pressures of popular usage and henceforth refer to laid rope as twisted rope.

Twisted rope is very popular for decorative use and, in addition to being sold in places such as hardware stores and boating stores, is often sold in fabric stores as trim for pillows, curtains, and so forth. It comes in a wide variety of colors, materials, and thicknesses.

From a bondage point of view, twisted rope can leave a distinctly telltale pattern on the skin of a person who has been

z-laid rope

bound with it. This pattern usually disappears within a few hours unless the bondage was especially tight. How bottoms feel about having this telltale pattern on their skin varies. (How bottoms feel about everything varies.)

Braided rope. Braided rope is usually made of a braided outer sheath consisting of 16 or more strands. This outer sheath usually encloses an inner core strand of yarns (that is sometimes called a "heart strand"). This inner core is sometimes itself made of braided rope (often not as tightly braided as the outer sheath), but can also be made of twisted rope or of another material entirely.

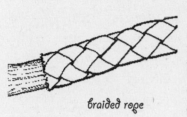

braided rope

Occasionally braided rope is made of four stands of twisted rope (two S-laid and two Z-laid) braided together.

Some braided ropes, particularly the smaller-diameter ones, have no inner core. This type of rope is often sold as "solid braid" rope.

ROPE MATERIALS

What is rope made of? There are two general categories of rope materials: natural and synthetic.

Natural Materials. Natural materials include cotton, hemp, sisal, and manila, with cotton and sisal being somewhat more commonly available in the United States.

Sisal rope is very inexpensive (it's often the cheapest type of rope readily available) but usually feels very scratchy to the skin. With the exception of people who like their bondage to be painfully chafing, it is not a popular rope for bondage and is thus only rarely used. Hemp and manila rope are also rarely used for bondage.

Cotton rope is fairly soft, particularly after it's been washed a few times, and tends to work well for bondage. However, a lot of cotton rope, particularly that made for use as clothesline, is in fact a braided cotton sheath over a core of some other material – frequently some type of plastic. This type of material may do in a "bondage emergency" (remember my need for a quick trip to the local convenience store?), but in general it is not all that good for bondage.

Rope made entirely out of cotton can work very well for bondage. Unfortunately, it can be somewhat difficult to find. One place that can be a source for pure cotton rope is a magician's supply house. The soft, supple "magician's rope" that they use for their performances can work very well for general bondage. (An important safety warning here: While magician's rope can work well for "plain ordinary people tying," it is somewhat more stretchable than some other types of rope, and is usually not rated in terms of its breaking strength, so I definitely do not recommend using this type of rope for doing any sort of suspension bondage.)

> "How close together can you get your elbows?"

One type of rope that can work well for bondage and is fairly widely available at places like hardware stores and variety stores is called sash cord. However, you need to read the label closely. Some brands of sash cord contain no cotton at all. Other brands of "cotton" sash cord do indeed have a cotton outer sheath but their core is made of synthetic (or even "unknown") materials.

Synthetic materials. Some synthetic materials commonly used to make rope include nylon, polyester, and polypropylene.

There are many types of nylon rope on the market, and it is a very popular rope for bondage. It is generally soft on the skin (although that can vary) and comes in a variety of colors and thicknesses. One major disadvantage of nylon rope is that, because its outer sheath can be very smooth, it is sometimes difficult to get to hold a knot properly.

Polyester and polypropylene ropes are often sold in hardware stores and boating stores. They are popular rope materials and can work well, but unless a rope made of such materials was manufactured with the expectation that it would be repeatedly exposed to wet environments, it may not stand up well to repeated washings. (More on this later.)

Two special categories of ropes. There are two special categories of ropes that can be truly excellent for bondage. These can be thought of generally as climbing ropes and boating ropes. (Nautical types, of course, refer to ropes as lines.) As you may have guessed, you will probably have to contact either a climbing supply store, a boating supply store, or an outdoor adventure store if you want to buy some of these types of ropes. They are often noticeably more expensive than ordinary ropes, but they give excellent value for the money.

The two types of climbing ropes that we bondage fans should know about are called tubular webbing and accessory cord (also sometimes called Prussick cord). Let's take a closer look at each.

Tubular webbing. There is a special type of nylon "rope" that every bondage enthusiast should at least know about. It's called tubular webbing and has so many fans that it has something of a cult following.

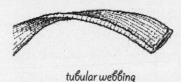

tubular webbing

There are basically two types of webbing: flat webbing (sometimes called seat-belt webbing) and tubular webbing. Both are a type of "flat rope" and are often used as accessory ropes, but not the main ropes, for mountain climbing and rescue work. Flat webbing and tubular webbing look similar at a distance, but upon close examination of an unsealed end you can see that tubular webbing can be "pinched open" to reveal a channel while flat webbing has no such channel and is more similar to the webbing found in seat belts.

Flat webbing tends to be somewhat stiffer than tubular webbing, and generally does not hold knots as well as tubular webbing, so it is not used very often for bondage.

Tubular webbing is available in widths of (approximately) half-inch, one-inch, and two-inch. Both the half-inch and the one-inch thicknesses are popular for bondage, with the half-inch thickness possibly being the more popular.

Tubular webbing can work very well for bondage purposes. There are a number of reasons for this:

- Tubular webbing is more "tape-shaped" than "rope-shaped" so it tends to lie flatter on the skin and thus distribute its force over a wider area. This quality can reduce the amount of marking left on the skin.

- Tubular webbing can be bought in a wide variety of colors. One vendor lists it for sale in orange, blue, red, purple, black, green, and yellow.

- Tubular webbing usually comes off the spool in an acceptably soft state. It can become even softer with a few washings.

- Tubular webbing withstands washing very well. Remember, though, that it's nylon and therefore it will melt if exposed to high levels of heat. Avoid putting tubular webbing in your dryer until you've first made certain that you've set your dryer to either "low heat" or "no heat," unless you want a bunch of melted nylon messing up your dryer. In general, it's probably best to let tubular webbing (and all other ropes made of synthetic materials) simply air dry.

- Tubular webbing is very strong. Some brands of one-inch "mil-spec" (built to military specifications) webbing is rated at a strength of about 4,000 pounds. Some brands of half-inch webbing are rated to a strength of about 1500 pounds, and some are rated even higher. Even the lowest strength rating of tubular webbing should be much more than adequate for the bondage purposes set forth in this book.

> *"Have you seen the red tubular webbing anywhere?"*

Tubular webbing can be noticeably more expensive than ordinary rope, but given that it can easily last for more than a decade, many bondage people consider tubular webbing to be much more than worth the extra cost.

Climbing rope – another special type of nylon rope. Climbing rope – or, to put it more correctly, the rope sold in stores that sell mountain climbing supplies – is another type of nylon rope that can work very well for bondage purposes. However, I should note that the types of ropes most often used for the actual "hold a person in mid-air" type of climbing applications are usually around one-half an inch in thickness, and that is a little too thick for most bondage fans. Instead of using actual climbing rope (which, among other things, can be very expensive) we bondage fans tend to use the smaller-diameter "accessory cord" that such stores sell.

Note: The diameter of accessory cord is usually expressed in millimeters, not fractions of an inch. Keeping in mind that one inch equals 2.54 centimeters or 25.4 millimeters, remember that six-millimeter or seven-millimeter rope is about one-quarter of an inch in thickness and that eight-millimeter rope is about five-sixteenths of an inch in thickness, and that nine-millimeter to ten-millimeter rope is about three-eighths of an inch in thickness.

Like tubular webbing, the type of rope known as climbing accessory cord can work very well for bondage, and shares many of the excellent qualities of tubular webbing. While accessory cord does not lie as flat on the skin as tubular webbing does, it comes in an even wider variety of colors, including mixed colors as well as single colors. (For my money, it's by far the prettiest type of rope used for bondage.) It also frequently is acceptably soft when bought "off the spool" and usually becomes even softer with a few washings. It withstands washing well, is very strong, and the ends are relatively easy to seal. Like tubular webbing, and all other forms of rope made from synthetic materials, it was not designed to stand up to high heat, so you should avoid tossing it into a clothes dryer.

Boating rope. Other types of rope that can be truly excellent for bondage purposes are the ropes (more properly called lines) sold in boating supply stores. These are available as either twisted ropes or braided ropes, and are commonly made of either nylon or polyester. They come in several different colors and many different widths, especially the braided ropes. Boating ropes also stand up very well to repeated washings. (Please note that I did not find this to be especially true of the nylon, polyester, or polypropylene ropes that I bought in hardware stores, particularly the braided ropes that had a core.)

Also, boating lines are rated in terms of their stretchiness in a way that climbing ropes are not. Most rope used for bondage is somewhat stretchy, and tends to "give" a bit once it's been on the bottom's body for a while. Being bound with low-stretch boating line can be an entirely different matter. As I can tell you from experience, being tied up with this stuff can feel like you have been positively encased.

Boating line can be somewhat stiff when you first get it home from the store, but with a few washings it can become amazingly soft and supple. I've found this to be particularly true of braided boating rope.

Boating rope: It's definitely worth checking this stuff out.

Big Savings Hint: Both climbing stores and boating stores often have something along the lines of what's called a "rope remnant bin." This bin will contain lengths of rope that have been left over from other cuttings, have been returned for one reason or another by customers, and so forth. Such ropes will typically be too short for their "legitimate" uses, but will do very nicely for our nefarious plans. Additionally, such remnants are usually for sale at a far cheaper price than the off-the-spool ropes cost. I have picked up some tasty bargains on very high-quality ropes this way. (This one tip may save you more than you paid for this book.)

Stretchiness. All ropes and all rope-like materials have at least some degree of stretchiness (more properly called degree of elongation). This is true even for chains. However, this degree of stretchiness can vary widely; nylon rope and pure cotton rope often have the most stretchiness.

Warning: Stretchiness can build up significant tension. The package that comes with the rope may contain a safety advisory to never stand in line with a rope under tension. In particular, nylon rope may store up a very large amount of energy while under tension, and if it breaks it may have a "snap back" potential that can be outright deadly.

In general, I recommend materials of relatively low stretch for bondage. I've tried using very stretchable materials, such as bungee cords, for bondage, and have usually found the results very disappointing. In particular, in order to apply the material tightly enough to prevent the bottom from easily escaping, it is usually necessary to apply it so tightly that it creates a dangerous and damaging amount of pressure on the bound tissues.

Also, because all rope used for bondage will stretch out at least somewhat over time, a cunning bottom may know that all they have to do is wait patiently. A rope whose tightness was definitely inescapable when it was first applied may loosen over time to the point where it can be easily escaped. Using low-stretch ropes can definitely help prevent this eventuality.

Stretchiness is often described in terms of a rope's percent of stretch at what is called "safe working load." What is considered "safe working load" varies, but is usually considered to be somewhere around 15% of the load at which the rope is expected to break. Most bondage-related uses of rope, other than special applications such as suspension bondage, are not likely to stress a rope to anything close to its breaking strength. This is true even if the rope's core has been removed. (See p. 98.)

One of the nice things about buying rope at climbing stores or boating stores is that a rope's degree of elongation is often numerically quantified as one of its various specifications. In particular, many types of boating rope stretch less than two percent at their safe working load.

At the climbing store, actual climbing "hold a person in the air" rope may be sold as "dynamic" and "static" rope, with the static rope having much less stretch to it. However, both such ropes are often too wide for routine bondage use. The accessory cord and the tubular webbing sold in such stores seems to be fairly low-stretch ropes.

Width. One of the more important questions regarding rope that will be used for erotic bondage is the question of how wide it should be. This is, as always, something of a matter of taste. I've seen everything from very thick mountain climbing ropes down to the thinnest dental floss used for bondage.

"Can I be tied up while we watch that video?"

In thinking about how wide bondage rope should be, it helps to keep the principle of "acceptable pressure" in mind. People usually want their bondage to be tight enough to prevent escape but loose enough to not damage the bottom. Tightness is a matter of pressure.

Basic physics: Pressure is defined as the amount of force divided by the amount of area. Thus, lots of force applied to a small area equals high pressure. Alternatively, very little force applied to a large area equals low pressure.

What does this mean to us bondage fans? Basically, the thinner the rope we use, the more "wraps" of rope we need to distribute the pressure on the bound body part enough to keep it within tolerable limits.

While tastes vary, most bondage folks seem to end up preferring to use ropes that are about one-quarter-inch – aka 4/16 of an inch (4/16") – in thickness. Some people prefer a 5/16" thickness in their ropes, and some go up to 3/8" (6/16") in thickness.

Rope that is thicker than 3/8" is usually not used for bondage, except for special applications such as suspension bondage. (The one significant exception that I've found to this is one-inch-wide tubular webbing.) Some people like rope that is somewhat thinner than 1/4" (4/16") so they may use 3/16" thick rope or even the one-eighth-inch (2/16") thick "parachute cord" rope, but if they do then they usually need to use more wraps around the bound body part than people who use thicker ropes need to use.

One place where thinner ropes can work especially well is for breast and genital bondage. (More on those very interesting topics later.)

For your "bondage starter kit" I recommend that you buy rope that is either 1/4" (4/16") or 5/16" thick.

PREPARING THE ROPE

Length. The question always comes up: how long should the ropes I use for bondage be? As always, this is a matter of taste, but I have found that rope lengths which are either about six feet long or multiples of six feet long – such as 12-foot, 18-foot, 24-foot lengths – tend to be the most generally useful.

Big hint: As a general rule, it's both easier and more effective to work with several shorter lengths of rope than it is with one very long length. Using shorter lengths makes the bondage easier to adjust to a particular bottom. Plus, if you have to rearrange one part of it, you don't have to undo everything that you applied after that part.

For example, let's say that I buy a 50-foot length of rope at my local hardware store and want to prepare it for bondage use. A 50-foot length is itself pretty long for all but the most exceptional usages, such as an elaborate body harness, so I probably want to cut it. It's logical to cut it in half, so that gives me two lengths, each 25 feet in length. This is pretty good for a comprehensive all-body tie, but it's still long enough that using it, and especially readjusting it, can be awkward.

By the way, when making the cuts in your new ropes, I suggest that you use your EMT scissors. It can be a good idea to get as much familiarity as possible regarding how well your scissors cut ropes before trying to use them in an actual emergency.

So you cut the 25-foot length in half and this gives you two (approximately) 12-foot lengths. Now you're getting somewhere. The 12-foot length frequently works very well for a wide variety of purposes. It fact, I would say that the 12-foot length of rope is the most useful overall length for bondage purposes.

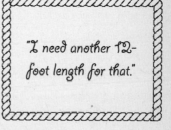

"I need another 12-foot length for that."

If you cut the 12-foot length in half, this will, of course, give you two lengths of rope, each six feet long. This is about as short a length as you want for most bondage purposes. I've found that the six-foot rope often works especially well for tying the bottom's ankles or knees together, or for tying their legs out in a spread-eagle fashion. However, it's often too short for tying wrists either together or separately outstretched in a "spread-eagle" position. I'll explain why this is so later on.

Given all of the above, you could make a pretty good "bondage starter kit" out of your 50-foot rope by cutting it until you have two 12-foot lengths and four 6-foot lengths.

An 18-foot length can be especially useful for tying the bottom's hands behind their back (I'll explain the technique later). So if you had a 100-foot length, you might create a "bondage starter kit" as follows:

First cut the 100-foot length of rope in half, then cut one of those halves into four lengths of rope, each just slightly longer than twelve feet long.

Next, take the second 50-foot length of rope, and cut it in half to make two 25-foot lengths. Keep cutting one of those 25-foot lengths in half until you have four six-foot lengths. Then (please pay especially close attention here) use one of those six-foot lengths to measure out a six-foot length on the remaining uncut 25-foot rope and make a single cut in it. This will give you one (approximately) 18-foot length of rope and an additional six-foot length.

Your overall total will be: One 18-foot length, four 12-foot lengths, and five six-foot lengths. A very nice "starter kit" indeed.

Removing the core. Braided rope, unless it's "solid braid" rope, will consist of an outer sheath and an inner core. One interesting approach to preparing this rope for use in bondage is to remove its core. (Obviously, this will have to be done before you seal the rope's ends shut.) Removing the rope's inner core will do a number of things to the rope.

First, obviously removing the core of a rope will weaken it considerably — by as much as 70%, according to some estimates. For applications such as suspension bondage, this could create a very dangerous situation. However, for "plain, ordinary people-tying," removing the core seems to create no significant problems. Most of the ropes I recommend for bondage still remain more than strong enough for our purposes.

Second, and more to the point, removing the core converts the rope into a sort of especially narrow tubular webbing. This means that the rope will now tend to become *much* more flexible and easy to work with, and to lie flatter on the skin. The increase in flexibility frequently makes it possible to use the rope much more effectively for bondage as it can be molded more closely to the bottom's body.

Third, removing the rope's core will tend to allow the rope to stretch out in length a bit more, making the remaining sheath slightly longer than it was.

Braided ropes are made of either natural or synthetic materials. In general, I've found that removing the core from a rope made of synthetic materials to be relatively easy, but removing the core from a rope made of a natural material, such as cotton, can be a challenge.

braided rope with
core exposed

To remove the core from a "challenging" rope, consider the following tips:

First, it may be a good idea to first cut your rope into the desired lengths. You will likely find that it is much easier to remove the core from several short lengths of rope than it is to remove the core from a single long length of rope.

Second, it may be a very good idea to wear some sort of sturdy gloves, such as a leather gardening gloves, while trying to work out the core. Otherwise, you increase your chances of getting what you might think of as "rope splinters" in your hands.

Third, the process may go significantly easier, particularly when working with a longer length of rope, if you pull out a few inches of the core and tie this core around a fairly sturdy, immovable object such as a strong part of a stairway banister.

To remove the core, the basic process is: pull out several inches of core (perhaps winding the core around your gloved hand as you go) until it resists further such pulling. Then straighten out the bunched-up outer sheath – this usually works better if you work from the far end to the near end – and repeat as necessary.

I suggest that if you have four lengths of rope, each twelve feet long, you remove the core from two lengths and leave the core in the other two, then compare how they perform.

Sealing the ends. OK, you're just back from the store and with you is your newly bought 50-foot length of braided rope that you plan to use for bondage. Excellent.

However, before you haul out your EMT scissors and start cutting away, it is only wise to give a moment of thought to contemplate what will happen to the ends of rope that will be created by this cutting.

What will happen, unless you prevent it from happening, is that the ends will immediately start to fray. This will result in an untidy-looking mess of loose strands at the ends of your ropes. (If you use twisted rope, this effect can be even more pronounced as the strands can actually spin, unwinding the rope for quite some distance and looking really messy.) Remember that messiness and sloppiness are often considered to be ominous signs, particularly in a top.

So, how does one go about keeping the ends from fraying? Let me count the ways. (More than a dozen are listed below. This was one aspect of researching this book that turned into something of an odyssey.)

There are several different categories of end-sealing techniques. These can be roughly categorized as chemically sealing the ends, taping the ends, sewing the ends, and melting the ends. Let me describe each in turn.

1.   **Chemically sealing the ends.** In this approach, various types of liquid chemicals that harden upon drying are applied to the ends, thus sealing them.

     •   *A liquid rope sealer.* There are compounds specifically intended for this usage that is sold in boating supply stores and in climbing stores. While this compound is usually sold in a clear version, it is also possible to buy it in red, white, and green. (The climbing vendors seem to stock a wider variety of colors than the boating vendors.)

         Because you will probably be trying to seal an end created by a fresh cut, I suggest the following approach: Find the point in the rope where you wish to make your cut, then "paint" that section of the rope with about a one-inch wide band of sealant. (Some brands of sealant come with a convenient brush that facilitates this process.) Allow the sealant to dry, then cut through this coat with your scissors. If you did an adequate job, the ends will not fray. As a finishing touch, you can then dip the ends in the sealant one last time to entirely cover the ends. Use the brush to remove any obvious excess dip solution, and you're done.

         This kind of sealant can work particularly well when dealing with relatively large ropes such as the 3/8" diameter.

     •   *Tool dip.* My local hardware stores sell a special sealant known as "tool dip" that can work well for sealing the ends of ropes. This material does not come with a brush so it doesn't work as well for painting a section prior to cutting. Of course, one can simply fold the rope into what's called, in ropespeak, a "bight" and put the bight into the dip. As with the rope sealant, you may need to do a second dip of the freshly cut ends after the first coat dries. My local stores have this material available in the colors of red and black.

Note: This material uses some serious chemicals to keep the sealant dissolved. The instructions say to use this material only in a very-well-ventilated area. After using it a few times, I can certainly understand why.

- *Fingernail polish.* In the tests we did here at the "San Francisco Bondage Research Institute" we found that fingernail polish worked almost as well as did the more formal liquid sealant. Like many brands of the sealant, it comes with its own brush. Again, paint a one-inch band of nail polish, allow to dry, and cut through the midpoint of the dried portion. Then apply another coat to the freshly cut ends. We found that fingernail polish stands up well to repeated washings.

  One of the significant benefits of using fingernail polish, aside from its ready availability and low cost, is that it is available in a truly amazing variety of colors. This can make it easier to color-code your ropes in terms of length, width, etc. Of course, clear nail polish is also available and works well for sealing rope ends while allowing the original color of the rope to show through.

  Sealing ends with fingernail polish seemed, overall, noticeably less work and generally easier than using the "heavier" substances such as liquid rope whipping and tool dip. It was also easier to work with narrower-diameter ropes when using fingernail polish.

- *Anti-fray liquids.* Fabric stores sell various brands of "anti-fray" liquids that you can apply to different types of cloth to prevent them from unraveling. One is known as "Fray Block." I found the sample that I bought to be even easier to work with than fingernail polish was. While "anti-fray liquid" did not seem to stand up to repeated washing as well as fingernail polish did, it did seem to stand up to such washings adequately. (Some anti-fray liquids are actually designed to wash out. Check the label.) As with the other compounds, apply about a one-inch band of solution to the place where the cut is to be made, allow to dry, make your cut, and maybe apply a bit more anti-fray to the freshly cut end.

2. **Taping the ends.** With this approach, you simply apply some tape to the rope in a way that keeps the ends from fraying. While you can apply tape to the ends after the cut has been made, it's generally easier to wrap a few turns of tape (two or three wraps are usually sufficient) around the location in the rope where you want the cut to be, and then cut through the tape.

    Note: Newly purchased rope often "comes home from the store" with some tape sealing its two ends. However, this tape is often masking tape or some other type of not very durable tape. I suggest that you replace it with more durable tape.

    You probably won't need to apply much more than about half an inch of tape to a rope end to seal it adequately (larger-diameter ropes may need up to one inch of tape), and longer "tape tails" can be both awkward and unsightly. This is not a problem if you're using tape that is one inch wide. However, if you're using wider tape, you might want to either cut the tape in half lengthwise before you apply it, or apply it and then cut off the taped end of the rope until only about half an inch is left.

    Note: No brand of tape that I tested stood up really well to repeated washings. Understand therefore that you may periodically either replace the tape entirely or apply additional tape over it.

    • *Cloth athletic tape.* This type of tape is readily available, comes in a variety of widths, and because almost all brands of it are white, this type of tape blends in well when used on standard, white ropes. Cloth athletic tape also absorbs laundry markings that may be used to indicate length in a way that duct tape may not.

However, cloth athletic tape typically did not stand up to repeated washings as well as the various brands of duct tape did.

- *Silver/gray duct tape.* This is the classic duct tape, sometimes also known as cloth tape, that is widely sold in supermarkets, variety stores, hardware stores, etc., and frequently used in movies and television shows for bondage. (I'll have more to say about using various types of tape for doing actual bondage later in this book.) This type of tape frequently works quite well for sealing the ends of rope. It is normally sold in two-inch widths, so you may have to make some accommodations for that (as described above). Silver/Gray duct tape tends to withstand washing fairly well, perhaps the best of any type of tape that I tested. One potential drawback is that its color doesn't allow it to blend in well with the color of the rope it is being used on. Another potential drawback is that its slick surface often prevents permanent markings.

- *Colored duct tape.* This is another type of duct tape. Sometimes called "cloth tape," it is also frequently found in hardware stores, and is sometimes also found in supermarkets, variety stores, etc. This type of tape is typically sold in two-inch widths, although I have seen it for sale in inch-and-a-half widths. The brands of colored duct tape that I tested, by and large, were not quite as sticky as the traditional silver/gray duct tape, but usually still quite sticky enough for our purposes. One advantage of this tape is, of course, that it comes in a variety of different colors, thus allowing it to be used to color-code the ropes for various purposes. (For example, different lengths of rope could have different colors of tape on their ends.)

3. **Sewing the ends (and related approaches).** In this approach, the ends of the rope are sealed shut with thread or some similar material. This is something of a traditional means of sealing rope ends shut and some of the knot books present numerous methods for accomplishing it.

- *Tying a knot in the rope's end.* This is probably the easiest method of preventing the end of a rope from fraying. It also has the advantages of being both quick and simple to do, and needing no additional equipment whatsoever. To do this, you simply tie a basic knot such as an overhand knot (or maybe something like a figure-eight knot if you feel like getting fancy) near the end of the rope. While this will prevent fraying, it will also leave a knot of noticeable size and frequently of unesthetic appearance at the rope's end. Such a knot can also make using the rope somewhat awkward. While the "simply tie a knot in the end" approach may work satisfactorily for very narrow-diameter ropes, such as one-eighth inch thick ropes, or may be suitable for short-term use, I have not found it to be a good, long-term solution to preventing the ends from fraying.

"Cross your ankles!"

- *Using small rubber bands.* This is such a simple method that I hesitate to mention it, but I will for the sake of completeness. Among other things, you might find yourself in a situation where rubber bands are all you have available, at least temporarily.

The technique is simple enough: Simply place a rubber band over the end of a freshly cut rope, twist the rubber band, and repeat the procedure. If you're using a relatively small rubber band, it should take only a moment to seal the end.

Obviously, this approach is, at best, a short-term solution and it would probably be wise for you to seal the ends of your ropes in a more permanent way at an early opportunity.

- *Sealing with simple sewing.*

I'm not an expert with needle and thread, but I had quite satisfactory results by taking a fairly long length of white thread, putting it through the needle so that its midpoint was at the needle's eye, and simply passing the needle through the end of the rope a few times. (Note: I'm talking about braided rope here.)

One can use a rough figure-eight pattern here, perhaps followed by an additional figure-eight pattern perpendicular to the first one, to make sure that the entire outer surface of the rope is covered. Leave a small tail when you start and when you're done simply tie the finishing tail tightly to the starting tail with a Square knot or Surgeon's knot. (Do this once or twice and you should easily get the hang of it.) I have some magician's rope whose ends I sealed this way nearly twenty years ago and now, numerous usages and washings later, they are still sealed just fine.

sewn end

- *Formal whip-stitching.* "Whip stitching" is a time-honored, even ancient, method of keeping the ends of a rope from fraying. In this approach, several turns of a very-narrow-diameter rope are wrapped around the tip of a rope and then fastened in place. Sturdy thread is often used for this purpose, and dental floss is occasionally used. Boating stores frequently sell various types of whipping twine intended especially for this purpose. One common recommendation to wrap enough turns so that the width of the turns at least equals the diameter of the rope.

   One very simple, very quick to teach method would be to take about a six-inch length of thread, tie the midpoint around the end of the rope about an inch from its end in an Overhand knot and pull tight, then wrap the thread around to the other side of the rope and tie the thread in another Overhand knot. Repeat this a few times, working toward the end of the rope, and finish the whip-stitching with a Square knot or Surgeon's knot.

   For instruction on how to do other (and better) whip-stitchings, consult this book's Bibliography.

- *Back-splicing.* Back-splicing a rope is basically taking the frayed ends of the rope and looping them back onto the still-unfrayed portion of the rope and interweaving the two sections. Done adequately, this creates a very secure, tidy-looking rope end that is very resistant to further fraying and stands up well to repeated washings.

There are several methods to perform a back-splice, some of which date back into antiquity, but they can be classified into "formal" and "informal" methods.

"Formal" back-splicing can be done on twisted rope. However, this is a complicated technique and beyond the scope of this book. For more information, consult one of the knotcraft books in the Bibliography.

Formal back-splicing can also be done on braided rope, but is also somewhat complicated and usually requires the use of one or another special and somewhat expensive tools. These tools are usually sold in boating stores.

There is an informal "back-splicing" technique which can be done on braided rope that has a core. This technique requires no special tools and can work very well. (Actually, technically, it's not really a true back-splicing technique, but it seems to work just as well.)

To make an "informal back-splice" you will need, as I mentioned, a length of rope that has a braided outer sheath and a core. You will also likely need two tools. One will be a very narrow, fork-like device. (I found that the fishhook-remover on my Swiss Army knife worked well.) You will also need a very narrow, ramrod-like device. (I found that a 1/8" phillipshead screwdriver worked well.)

Assuming that the rope in question is about 1/4" thick, cut it where you wish, then pull out about three to four inches of the core from the braided outer sheath and cut off this part of the core. Work the braided outer sheath back out over the core as much as you can. Then take the fishhook remover and poke the outer strands of the sheath down into the hole in the interior of the rope that was created by the removal of the core. Use the screwdriver as needed to ram and pack the outer threads firmly down into place. (This may sound complicated, but it's actually rather easy. If you have the proper tools, you should pick it up very quickly with just an attempt or two.)

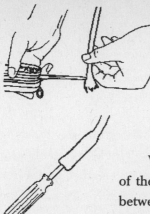

informal "back-splicing"

When finished, there will be a slight thickening of the tip, and maybe a short section of the rope between the end-packing and the rest of the core. This is a nice technique.

4. **Melting the ends.** The ends of ropes made of synthetic materials, such as nylon, polyester, or polypropylene, can be very nicely sealed by applying enough heat to melt them. There are a number of ways to do this.

- *Cutting with a commercially made "hot knife."* Stores that sell boating and climbing ropes frequently stock large spools of these ropes. The customer tells the clerk how much rope they want to buy, and the clerk then pulls the requested length of the rope in question off the spool and cuts it with a special device (sometimes called a "hot knife") used specifically for this purpose. This tool usually both cuts the rope and seals the ends in the same action. If you know ahead of time what lengths of rope you wish, and you don't want to remove the core of the rope, you can simply have the clerk do your cutting for you. For example, you might say to them "I want four twelve-foot lengths of that purple, six-millimeter accessory cord." The clerk will usually be happy to cut the rope to your specifications.

- *Heat shrinks.* Heat shrinks are interesting items. They are long, hollow cylinders of rubber-like or plastic-like material whose diameter shrinks when heat is applied to them. Heat shrinks are sold in boating stores, hardware stores, and electrical supply stores. The heat shrinks that are sold in boating stores are "marine grade" and sold with the intention that they will be used to seal the ends of ropes. The heat shrinks sold in hardware and electrical supply houses are sold with the intention that they will be used to seal bundles of electrical wires together. Predictably, I had by far the better results when I used the heat shrinks that were sold by boating supply stores.

Heat shrinks are easy to use and, as with most end-sealing techniques, your ability to use them will improve rapidly with experience. To seal an end, you will need a length of heat shrink that has an interior diameter which is slightly larger than the diameter of the rope that you want to seal (1/16"-1/8" wider). To apply, cut off a length of heat shrink tubing – I suggest you cut off a length of tubing that is half again as long as the diameter of the rope that you want to seal – and slide it over the rope in question. Make your cut (through the rope only, not through the heat shrink), then slide the heat shrink out to the freshly made end. You may slide it out so that a portion of the heat shrink entirely covers the freshly cut end or you may leave the last quarter-inch or so of the rope free. (The latter approach may produce a heat shrink with a better hold on the rope.)

You will need to apply heat to the heat shrink in order to get it to shrink. (Well, duh.) I have found that using a small candle flame works excellently for this. Hold the heat shrink slightly over the candle flame and slowly rotate it. (Be careful that the flame does not affect the rope itself.) Continue carefully rotating the rope until the shrinking stops, then set the rope aside to cool. The heat shrink will be very hot at this point, so be careful where you set it. Perhaps allowing the rope tip to dangle freely in the air might be best.

In summary, I found that heat shrinks did work quite well, although some types did tend to pop off during use. This tendency seemed especially true regarding non-marine-grade heat shrinks and heat shrinks that entirely covered the free end rather than leaving a small amount of it free.

- *Melting the ends.* Melting the ends of a rope is a well known and widely used sealing technique, and it can work very well, provided you keep a couple of points in mind.

    First, this only applies to ropes made of synthetic materials! If you try to melt the ends of your cotton sash cord you will end up looking very silly indeed.

    You will need a source of significant heat for this process. As with heat shrinks, a simple candle flame usually works well. There are two basic approaches: The widely known cut-then-flame approach, and the lesser known flame-then-cut approach.

    In the cut-then-flame approach, you simply cut the rope then cautiously apply the freshly cut ends to the flame. This can work just fine. In particular, tubular webbing is often excellently sealed with this approach with only a very brief exposure to the flame. (Regarding tubular webbing, please note that it's not necessary to seal the channel shut. Simply melt the ends just a bit so they won't fray.)

    However, some types of ropes unravel quite a bit almost immediately upon being cut and melting these ends shut may be difficult. This problem may be mitigated somewhat by wrapping a small amount of tape around the rope, making your cut through the midpoint of this tape, flaming the freshly cut ends, and then removing the tape. (You may have to re-flame the ends just a bit after the tape removal.)

    Sometimes the result of a cut-then-flame technique is a large, hard, ugly knob of melted rope at its end. This is particularly true if someone was a bit overenthusiastic in how long they applied the flame to the cut end. This knob can sometimes be reduced to an acceptable size by use of a nail file or something similar, but it may be easier to simply cut it off and try again.

    The flame-then-cut approach can work much better. This is especially true when dealing with synthetic ropes other than tubular webbing. In this approach, first hold the section of the rope through which you want to make your cut over the candle flame, rotating it slowly until you have slightly melted and fused together some of the outer strands. Allow this section of the rope to cool before cutting it (thus keeping you from getting melted rope on your EMT scissors), then make your cut. Finally, expose the freshly cut ends as needed to the candle flame to "touch up" the sealing job. In particular, the interior portions may need some sealing. The whole process is similar to how liquid rope whipping is used.

Marking the Rope

Very early in your bondage play, you will likely start to think along the lines of "well, let's see, I'll need two twelve-foot lengths of rope to tie their wrists apart at the head of the bed, and I'll also need two lengths of six-foot rope to tie their ankles apart," and so forth. In other words, you'll view the bondage tasks that you want to accomplish in terms of how long a length of rope you'll need.

"I like this type of rope for use on larger men."

While you may be able to tell the difference between a six-foot length of rope and a fifty-foot length of rope of the same type and color by merely glancing at their difference in bulk, it can be much harder to tell the difference between a six-foot length and a twelve-foot length, and so forth. Thus, your bondage play can proceed much more smoothly and efficiently if you can more readily tell the different lengths apart. There are a number of solutions for this problem.

1. *Color-code the ropes.* One very simple, elegant, and colorful solution to this is to simply have the different lengths be of different colors. This is especially easy with ropes that are sold in different colors, such as tubular webbing. For example, you might decide to have your six-foot lengths be blue in color, your twelve-foot lengths be red, and so forth. You can buy the rope in bulk and make the cuts yourself, or if the place where you buy the rope has a "hot knife" — boating shops and climbing shops usually have such a knife — you can have the

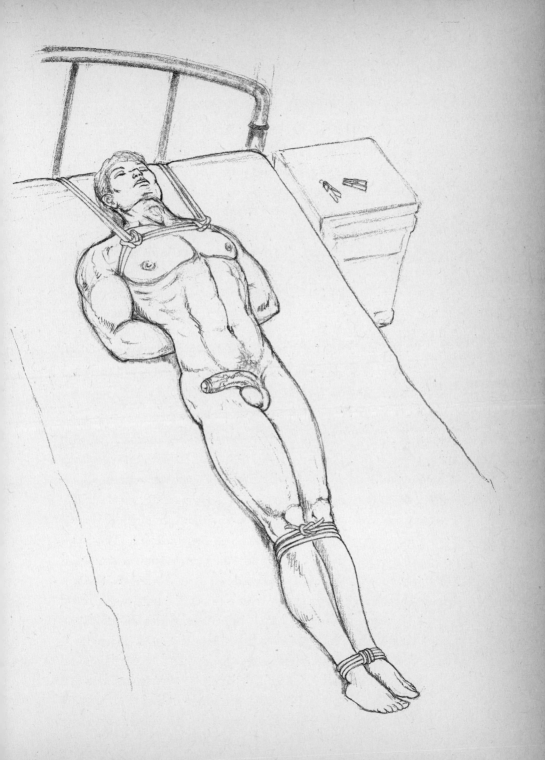

clerk make the cuts for you and to seal the ends as described above. An additional benefit of this approach is that you can tie your bottom into a very pretty package.

2. *Color-code the ends of the ropes.* If your ropes are all of the same color, you can often both seal and color-code the ends in various ways.

    Colored duct tape (sometimes sold as cloth tape) can work very well here. Thus, six-foot lengths of rope could have their ends both sealed with green tape, twelve-foot lengths could have their ends sealed in red tape, and so forth.

    You can also color-code as well as seal the ends of your ropes with nail polish of various colors. (Remember that you may have to apply more than one coat.) This technique will work better on some types of rope than on others. In particular, softer ropes may absorb the nail polish to the point where it becomes essentially invisible. Some types of tubular webbing can be particularly difficult in this regard. However, on many types of ropes, nail polish will work just fine. Note that while nail polish usually stands up well to repeated washings, an occasional touch-up may be needed.

3. *Mark the rope ends with bands of permanent ink.* This approach can also work well with ropes that are all of the same color and type. Let's assume that all of your ropes are either six feet long or are multiples of six feet long. Simply take a permanent-ink marking pen (a laundry marker can work well) and make a narrow band around both ends of the rope, with each band signifying six feet of length. Thus, you would know at a glance that a rope with a single band around each end is about six feet long, a rope with two bands is about twelve feet long, a rope with three bands is about eighteen feet long, and so forth.

    To fine-tune this approach a bit, you might mark a line about one inch long along a rope for each additional three feet of length. (I suggest you make two such lines on each end of the rope, each opposite the other on the rope's diameter.) For example, if you have a rope that is nine feet and a few inches long, you might mark it with a single band and a single line. Thus, you would be able to tell at a glance at a rope's end if it is about three feet, nine feet, etc.

You can also use permanent marking pens. These can usually be found without too much trouble in the colors of black, red, green, and blue, and those four colors should be sufficient for the four most common lengths.

Note: I tried using various types and colors of tape for this banding approach, but my results weren't very satisfactory.

4. *Marking the rope ends with thread of different colors.* The ends of some ropes may be quite nicely marked simply by sewing a noticeable amount of colored thread onto them. As with using colored tape or nail polish, this approach can also be combined with sealing the ends.

Finding the rope's midpoint. A lot of bondage techniques, especially the ones in this book, do not start at a rope's end. Rather, they start at the rope's midpoint. Thus, things can go a lot more smoothly if the approximate midpoint is marked on the rope in some fashion.

Marking the rope's approximate midpoint can often be done very easily with your marking pen if the color of the pen's ink contrasts noticeably with the rope's color. Simply fold the rope in half, make a small mark on the rope to note the midpoint, unfold the rope, and finally mark in a band around the entire rope's diameter.

Colored nail polish, colored thread, and a long, narrow piece of colored tape can also be used to mark the rope's midpoint.

Please note that most types of rope have some stretch to them, and thus the rope, or various sections of it, may shrink or stretch a bit with use. Thus, no matter how carefully you initially measure your rope's midpoint, you may find that the midpoint you so carefully marked has shifted a bit over time. Thus, midpoint markings should be taken as approximations.

Marking the quarter-point. Longer ropes, such as 24-foot ropes, are often folded in half and then used for bondage, so when using such ropes you may find it useful to mark "the midpoint of the midpoint" by making a mark at the approximate quarter-points of the rope. This can be done as described for marking the midpoint, but obviously the quarter-point marks should have a different appearance than the midpoint marks.

WASHABILITY

Interestingly enough, when considering a good rope to use for bondage purposes, the question of "washability" comes up fairly early. After all, ropes commonly go onto skin, where they will pick up dirt, sweat, and so forth. They therefore benefit from the occasional washing. Furthermore, our ropes may get certain body substances on them, including semen, saliva, vaginal fluids, blood, and traces of fecal matter. If they do, we'll want to wash them before we use them again.

While I know that some of you are diligent enough to wash your ropes by hand, frankly, that means you're more diligent than I am. Most of the time, unless I have some reason to suspect that my ropes might have become especially contaminated with something infectious, I'll settle for tossing my ropes into the washing machine along with the rest of my laundry.

Really Big Hint: I strongly suggest that you buy something commonly called a "lingerie bag." Dumping a bunch of loose ropes into your washing machine can be asking for disaster. The loose ropes can coil around the agitator and jam it fast. Drop your ropes into a lingerie bag and then drop the bag into the washing machine for a much more hassle-free experience. (If you really can't get a lingerie bag, you can use a knotted-shut pillowcase as an at least minimally adequate substitute – but I recommend that you go ahead and purchase a lingerie bag. Many drugstores and variety stores sell them, and they're fairly cheap.)

Note: I've tried lingerie bags that zip shut and lingerie bags that snap shut, and I've found that the ones which snap such seem more likely come undone in the machine, thus spilling out the ropes into the machine to possibly cause problems. That being the case, I recommend that you either go with a zip-shut bag or reinforce your snap-shut bag with a large safety pin.

I've had it recommended to me that you can also wash your ropes in a washing machine by first knotting the rope into a chain. I've tried this, but I've had the ropes come unchained in the machine. I'm also dubious that all of the rope gets properly cleaned with this approach. Thus, while

I'm not going to condemn the "chain" approach, I will stick with recommending the use of a lingerie bag.

Ropes can vary a surprising amount in their degree of washability, so I recommend that you not buy too much of any given type of rope until you've had a chance to test it in this regard. In general, any type of rope manufactured with the expectation that it will be used in a "wet" environment – typically an outdoor environment – will do well in the washability department. With other types of ropes, you might get a nasty surprise.

The following types of ropes usually wash well: many types of twisted ropes, boating line, tubular webbing, solid-braid ropes, accessory cord, sash cord, ropes whose cores have been removed, and braided ropes whose outer sheath and inner core are both made entirely of cotton.

The following types of rope may not wash well: Any rope that is not sold with the intention that it will be used in a "wet" environment. This would include many braided ropes with cores not made of cotton, as well as many ropes sold in hardware stores and/or variety stores, unless they are of the type previously specified as being likely to wash well. (Note: Unsuitability for washing often becomes much more than obvious the first time that the rope is washed. Be sure to use a lingerie bag.)

A few supplemental washing instructions:

- Blood can stain some types of materials if exposed to hot water. Therefore, washing away blood with cold water is advisable. Also, blood cells exposed to water of any temperature for more than about a minute can swell up, burst, and also stain the surrounding material with their cellular contents. Therefore, when removing blood from your ropes, hold them under cool, flowing water (the cold water coming from your bathroom or kitchen sink should work just fine) until the blood is washed off, then launder as usual.

- Most rope manufacturers recommend against using bleach when washing ropes.

  Fabric softener can be used as an adjunct to your washing to make your ropes softer. Your local supermarket or variety store may even sell a roughly baseball-sized ball that can make doing this easier. Just be sure to not use too much.

Note: I found that ropes which had been washed in ordinary detergent (without using fabric softener) a few times often became just as soft as rope that had been washed with fabric softener. Thus, unless you are already routinely using fabric softener in your laundry anyway, you might find it just as easy to simply run your ropes through a few more washings.

I also found that some types of sealants used on the ends of ropes, such a liquid rope whipping, did not stand up well to repeated washings with both detergent and fabric softener, but did stand up well to repeated washings with detergent alone.

- I should note in passing that washing your ropes in a standard washing machine along with the rest of your clothes does subject the ropes to a significant amount of stress and wear. Thus, while you should wash your ropes "as necessary," it is probably not necessary to wash them after every usage. You should probably wash your ropes if you have good reason to believe that they might have become stained with something like semen, blood, or vaginal fluid. You should also wash your ropes before using them on a second person (especially if you have reason to believe that they might have the first person's body fluids on them).

Stronger disinfection methods. What if I think I have significant reason to wonder if my ropes do have an infectious substance on them?

This is an interesting topic. As of this writing, I know of no cases in which it has been seriously alleged that a disease has been transmitted from one person to another by contact with a contaminated rope. Still, the possibility is there, so let's consider how one might go beyond the ordinary cleaning of a rope to disinfecting it.

Here is a very important aspect of infectious disease to remember: In order to get any infectious disease from a bacteria, virus, fungus, etc. (herein after referred to as "the bugs"), one must first be exposed to what's called an "infectious concentration" of the bugs. It most definitely does not take just one bug. Actually, it often takes several million of them.

Therefore, we don't usually don't have to sterilize our bondage gear (sterilize meaning to remove all forms of life on it). Rather, simply disinfecting it (disinfecting meaning to reduce the number of bugs down below the "infectious concentration" level) will usually do just fine.

There are two basic ways to disinfect a rope (or anything else): physical removal of the bugs or chemical inactivation of the bugs.

The usefulness of the physical removal option is often under-appreciated. For example, a good handwashing (fifteen seconds of vigorous lathering, followed by fifteen seconds of rinsing) can eliminate as much as 97% of all the bacteria on one's hands. Your ropes can benefit from a similar treatment. Certainly running your ropes through a cycle in your washing machine will physically remove a lot of bugs. (Exposure to the detergent will not make the bugs happier either.)

Let me be candid here: While you are certainly free to take further steps if you wish, as of this writing I know of no cases in which it has been seriously alleged that a disease was transmitted by a rope that got contaminated with infectious materials from one person on it but was run through a standard washing by a standard washing machine (even if cold water and a very mild detergent was used) before the rope was used on another person.

Realistically, the "washing machine option" seems to offer us a very great deal of protection in this regard. In almost all cases, the level of protection provided is probably much more than adequate. This is particularly true if such washing is combined with allowing the ropes to dry thoroughly afterwards. (See below.)

Also, let us consider that, most of the time, rope is applied to unbroken skin, and unbroken skin is resistant to many bugs. Exceptions, of course, would apply to ropes applied directly to the mucous membranes of the vulva, ropes used as gag straps that go into the mouth and thus come into contact with saliva, and ropes applied to skin that has had welts or other breaks caused in it by abrasions SM play. Also, skin that is initially unbroken sometimes becomes broken by the ropes themselves. Still, it's my experience that most rope is applied to unbroken skin and removed from unbroken skin.

If you want to go further, you can consider these additional steps.

Many bugs need a moist environment to survive, so simply allowing your ropes to dry out for several hours (as in, say, overnight) will kill large numbers of them.

(Note: most of the disinfecting methods I describe here will kill just about all bugs except for a very few special bacteria that have already formed a hard outer coat called a spore. Spores can survive many harsh treatments, including exposure to boiling water. However, about the only "spore former" that we need to worry about, at least in an SM context, is the bug that causes tetanus. Um, your tetanus shot *is* up to date, right?)

Many bugs cannot survive more than a few seconds of exposure to the ultra-violet light contained within sunlight. (Most bacteria in soil are found down in the soil, away from sunlight.) Therefore, exposing your ropes and other toys to direct sunlight (not sunlight that has passed through glass, plastic, etc., but direct sunlight) for several minutes will deactivate many types of bugs. Please note that sunlight does not penetrate well, so for the bugs to get zapped they will need direct exposure to the sunlight.

If you want to go further, you can:

- Soak your ropes in a solution of one part chlorine bleach to nine parts of water for twenty minutes. This will kill virtually everything. Please note that many rope manufacturers recommend against exposing their ropes to chlorine bleaches on the grounds that the chemical effects of such bleaches will weaken the ropes. Please also note that chlorine bleaches may decolorize some ropes.

- Soak your ropes in a solution of 70% isopropyl alcohol or ethyl alcohol for a few minutes. Most of the bug killing will be done by the end of the first minute that the rope is in this solution.

- Boil your ropes. Prolonged boiling is not necessary. By the time the water starts to boil, you can safely bet that every bug that can be killed by boiling (all but the spore-formers which have already formed their spores, and a few bugs from fecal material which are unlikely to cause problems) has been killed by then. *Warning:* Ropes made of synthetic materials may melt if exposed to boiling water.

Note: It's now possible to be immunized against both Hepatitis A and Hepatitis B. The first is a two-shot series and the second is a three-shot series, both given over a roughly six-month period; my medical consultant tells me that the two immunizations will soon be available in a combination injection. I recommend that all SM players (and virtually everybody else) get immunized against these very serious diseases.

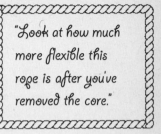

"Look at how much more flexible this rope is after you've removed the core."

Drying your ropes. Ropes made entirely of natural fibers, such as pure cotton rope or sisal rope, can usually be dried in your clothes dryer along with the rest of your clothing. (Be sure to keep them in the lingerie bag.)

On the other hand, ropes made of synthetic materials, such as nylon, polyester, and polypropylene, should probably not be placed in the dryer (unless, maybe, you turn your dryer's heat down to a very low level). This is because the heat generated by such a dryer at its typical "dry ordinary wet clothing" setting can cause ropes made of synthetic materials to melt, filling your dryer with an icky plastic-like goo that could be very difficult to remove.

Simply letting such ropes air-dry should work fine. I've found that ropes made of synthetic materials frequently come out of the washing machine feeling almost dry already, so a relatively short amount of air-drying time is often sufficient. (Please also remember that a significant period of drying, such as overnight, can be a fairly effective disinfectant.)

Given their relatively high surface-to-volume ratio, most ropes tend to dry fairly quickly. However I have found that ropes made of natural material, such as cotton or sisal, take noticeably longer to air-dry than do ropes made of synthetic materials. I also note that ropes made of nylon tubular webbing seem to take longer to air-dry than do more conventionally shaped nylon ropes.

Storing Your Ropes

Once you're done preparing your ropes, you'll want to store them until it's time to use them. As always, there are a number of ways to do this.

First, it's probably not a great idea to simply dump a tangled mass of ropes into the drawer of your nightstand table, dresser drawer, or toybag, thus creating what many folks call a "rope salad."

It can be a subtle warning flag when an SM person, particularly a dominant, dumps out a ragged assortment of toys, including a mass of tangled ropes, just prior to playing. It can indicate sloppiness, carelessness, or cluelessness – none of which are good qualities in a potential play partner, particularly one to whom you're considering making yourself very vulnerable. On the other hand, the sight of a clean, well-organized toy collection can be reassuring. It can also be, in its own way, deliciously scary.

It generally works well to separate out each piece of rope and then coil or otherwise organize it for storage and ease of use.

By the way, I recommend that you wait until a rope is completely dry after being washed before coiling or storing it. Rope, especially rope made of natural materials, that is put away damp, particularly if put away into a dark place where there is poor air circulation, can become a good "growth plate" for bacteria, mold, etc. Do not underestimate the value of keeping your ropes dry as a means of keeping them free of bugs that can transmit disease. This applies to your other SM gear as well.

There are a number of ways to coil and store rope, including what I call the Flat Coil, the Round Coil, the Bighted Round Coil, the Figure-8 Coil, and the Hanging Coil.

In general, for routine storage of ropes in dresser drawers, toy bags, and so forth, the Flat Coil, the Round Coil, and the Bighted Round Coil all work well. They can also work well for hanging ropes on hooks, pegs, and so forth.

The Flat Coil. A flat coil is very quick, easy, and simple to make. In my opinion the Flat Coil is the most generally overall useful way of storing bondage ropes. By the way, I call it the Flat Coil because rope that is stored in this manner shows more of a tendency to "lay flat" than rope stored in a Round Coil.

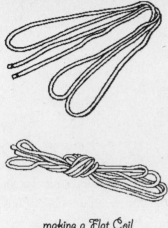

As I said, a Flat Coil is very easy to make. Simply fold your rope in half (this is also called "bighting the rope"), then fold those halves in half, and repeat until the rope becomes difficult to fold further. A six-foot rope will typically take about two such folds, while ropes in the twelve-foot to 24-foot range will typically take about three such folds. Once you have reached this point (at which time ropes in the twelve-foot to 24-foot range will be folded to eight "widths" in thickness), tie the entire coil into an overhand knot, and you're done.

making a Flat Coil

A 50-foot rope will typically take about four such coils and be 16 "widths" in thickness. This amount of width can make creating the final overhand knot something of a challenge, but it can be done. A 100-foot rope will typically take about five such coils and be 32 "widths" in thickness. Making the final overhand knot in this case can even more challenging, but possible with practice.

A refinement: If you want to make the ropes a bit easier to store and to handle while they are coiled in a Flat Coil, tie the overhand knot out towards one end as opposed to near the middle.

Another refinement. If you are folding a somewhat long rope – say, 24 feet or longer – you may find that rope storage is easier if you tie an overhand knot near both ends of the folded rope.

The Round Coil. A Round Coil is also easy to make and can work very well for either six-foot or twelve-foot lengths of rope. I've also found that it can work acceptably, if not optimally, for lengths of rope up to about 25 feet long.

It's very quick and simple to make a Round Coil. If you're right handed, place one end of the rope in your left palm with its tip at the little-finger edge Then simply wind the coil in a clockwise direction (as you look down at your fingertips) around your left palm and fingers until you have about six inches of rope left, then run the final end over the left hand side of the coil, bring it back through the coil, and tie it into an overhand knot.

Round Coil

If you are using a very long rope (say, 24 feet or longer, you can simply wind the rope around your upper arm instead of your palm.

The Bighted Round Coil. A very simple variant on the above technique is to simply bight the rope, then wind it into a round coil as described above, starting with the tails and finishing with the bight. One interesting feature of this technique is that it leaves a small loop in the end, which can be hung on a hook.

The Figure-eight Coil. The Figure-eight Coil tends to work well for ropes that are at least twelve feet long. (Shorter ropes don't easily stay in the figure-eight configuration.) One of the major benefits of storing braided rope in any variant of the Figure-eight coil is that doing so greatly reduces or eliminates "the twists" in rope. More on this later.

To store your rope in a Figure-eight coil (assuming that you're right-handed), grasp the tip of the rope in question in your left hand with its tip just slightly protruding from your fist. Now flex your elbow joint into the "make a muscle" position. (How much you must flex your elbow joint will depend on a number of factors, including your size and the length of the rope. How much flex is needed will be discovered with practice.) Wind the rope in a figure-eight pattern over your outer forearm, then around your elbow, back over your forearm, and through your left palm. Continue until you run out of rope, knot the tail around the strands on the palm side of your rope as you would if making a Round Coil, and you're done.

Figure-eight Coil

As a minor variant, if you have a bit too much rope left over, bend the surplus back into a bight and use that bight to make your final knot.

The Bighted Figure-eight Coil. This is a simple variant on the standard Figure-eight Coil, and tends to work best in ropes that are at least 18 feet long. It is a simple coil to create once you've learned how to make a regular Figure-eight Coil. Simply bight the rope and proceed as above.

The Hanging Coil. If you want to store a coil of your rope by hanging it on a peg, hook, or bedpost, you can create what can be called logically be called a "hanging coil" of rope. As always, there are a number of different ways to do this. The various books on knots in the Bibliography describe a myriad of techniques.

One very useful and relatively simple method of tying a hanging coil is to loop the rope as you would for a Round Coil, but make the loops at

Hanging Coil

least twice as big. (The longer the rope, the larger you should make these coils.) When you get to the end, fold the tip of the tail back over the coil to create a bight. Then wrap this bight of rope around the coils and run it under itself to create an overhand knot, like you did for the Bighted Round

Coil. Finally, bring the bight back over the top portion of the coil, wrap it under the coils, and tuck it under itself to create a handy loop for hanging the finished coil.

The Bighted Hanging Coil. Another method of forming a hanging coil that is especially useful for bondage purposes is to bight the rope, then wind this bighted rope into coils, starting with the tails. Create the final finishing loop in the same way that you did for the Hanging Coil.

This technique creates a very tidy- looking hanging coil that can be quickly employed for bondage purposes. To use it, simply remove it from its peg, take out the midpoint, stretch out the ropes through your fingers to remove the twists, and you're ready to deal with the twists in your rope.

Storing Ropes on Hooks, Pegs, Bedposts, etc. Bondage fans sometimes want to store their ropes in a place where the ropes are readily visible and ready to use. This can be fun, but must be approached with some caution. For on thing, if one's relatively "vanilla" friends, business acquaintances, landlords, and so forth go into one's bedroom, the sight of all those ropes may bring on unwanted attention. For another thing, having all those ropes in plain sight may scare people who are new to the idea of bondage. While keeping ropes stored in a visible and ready-to-go condition may work well in a formal SM playroom such as the "dungeons" used by professional dominatrixes, it would be wise to think twice before setting up one's bedroom in this way.

Shorter ropes, such as six-foot and twelve-foot ropes, can often be stored quite nicely by simply hanging them in Lark's Head knots (see p. 139) from the bed railings.

If you want to get even more blatant about it, you can hang a towel rack by your bed and put your ropes up on that. One friend of mine went to a boating supply store and bought what's called a "line hanger" to use. This line hanger very neatly holds four coils of rope ready for use. (Of course, my friend, being the discreet type, put up his line hanger inside his closet, thus keeping his gear stored in a more low-profile manner.)

Finally, while there are a number of "formal" techniques for folding a rope so that it can be hung on a peg, keep in mind that the Flat Coil , the Round Coil, and the Bighted Round Coil can often work just fine for this purpose.

Dealing with the twists. Many methods of coiling a rope for storage, particularly storage techniques such as the Round Coil, also impart some twists to the rope. You can see these when you uncoil the rope. For example, hold a six-foot rope up off the ground by one end and you may see the other end spin as it untwists itself. It may even form loops.

Twists can be a nuisance in the erotic bondage context. For longer ropes (fifty feet or more) they can be distinctly irksome. In more serious real-world usages, such as rescue work, twists can create life-threatening problems.

There are several strategies for dealing with twists. The first strategy is to simply live with them. As I said, in erotic bondage, twists typically aren't all that great a problem, particularly with the shorter ropes that we generally use, and you can simply let the rope uncoil naturally.

A second strategy, my personal favorite, is to "milk out" the twists just before you use the rope. This can work especially well for relatively short ropes in the six-foot to twelve-foot range. One good method of doing this is to uncoil the rope, hold it by the midpoint in one hand while you "milk out the twists" in the two parts of the rope with the other hand – one part going between your thumb and index finger and the other part going between your index and middle fingers. This can sometimes be done with a wicked "domly" flourish – just be careful to not get too melodramatic.

A third strategy is to coil your braided ropes in Figure-eight Coils. These have been described above and often work very well indeed.

A fourth strategy is what can be thought of as "counter-twisting." To do this, give each coil of the rope a half-twist in the counter-clockwise direction as you use your right hand to coil it into clockwise loops onto your left hand – as is done in creating the Round Coil. It seems easiest to give the rope this twist at the top of each coil. Practice this with a six-foot length of rope and you should pick it up easily enough.

To see if you added counter-twists properly, coil the six-foot rope, then hold it up slightly over your head by one end and drop the coil. An inadequately counter-twisted rope will have loops appear in it as it falls and/or its free end will spin. You may even have to shake the rope a bit to get it to entirely untwist. An adequately counter-twisted rope will fall pretty much straight down, with little or no looping or spinning.

To test this with longer ropes, try holding one end and either dropping the other end down something like a stairwell or throwing it "lifeguard-style" down a hallway. An inadequately counter-twisted rope will come up short in a tangled heap. An adequately counter-twisted rope will play out much more freely.

BASIC KNOTS

"I'm not any good at tying knots!"

I long ago lost track of how many times I have heard this particular lament from bondage novices – and even from a fair number of people who are no longer novices. Indeed, one of the more common reasons why BDSM practitioners resort to using formal bondage equipment such as leather cuffs has to do with "I'm not any good at tying knots."

Take heart, Gentle Reader, for the truth is that you probably already know enough knots to successfully begin your bondage career. Indeed, even the humble and much-derided Granny knot can play a very worthy role in our nefarious deeds. The trick is to take a closer look at how to effectively use the knots that you already know how to tie.

Question: Why do we need to know how tie any knots at all?

We need to know how to tie at least a few knots because if we wrap our ropes around the bottom without securing them in some fashion the ropes may simply drop off. If this happens, the bottom may scamper away across the landscape, filling the air with mocking laughter as they gleefully race to tell all their fellow bottoms about what an inept top you are. OK, maybe it won't be quite that bad, but it will probably be a problem nonetheless.

Let's take a closer look at the first sentence in that last paragraph. Particularly that word "securing." One definition of "to secure" is "to fix in place" (i.e., immobilize) – and that is exactly what most knots do. They immobilize at least some part of a rope. This frequently means joining the two ends of the rope together, but can also apply to joining one end of a rope to another object, or to immobilizing some inner segment of the rope.

Definition time: A knot can be defined as the arranging of part of a rope to another rope, another object, or back to itself in such a way that the specified portion of the rope is held in place by friction. The concept that "a knot is held in place by friction" is a key concept, and it will influence a great deal of how we consider knots.

Another definition: Ropes vary tremendously in how much friction they generate when they slide across a given surface. Because this friction can feel like the rope is trying to "bite into" the surface, referring to this property as its "tooth" can be useful. Thus, rope with a relatively rough outer surface, such as cotton rope, can be said to have "a lot of tooth" while ropes with very smooth outer surfaces, such as many types of nylon rope, can be described as having "very little tooth" to them. Run a few different types of rope through your hand with this in mind and the concept of "tooth" will likely be immediately clear to you.

OK, so we need to know how to tie knots so that we can hold the ropes in place (and thus, hopefully, also hold the bottom within those ropes in place). Fine. What knots do we need to know in order to accomplish this?

Just remember that there are only three basic knot-related tasks, and that almost all knots are used to accomplish one of these three tasks. The three tasks are:

1. To tie two rope ends together.

2. To tie one end of a rope to a non-rope object (such as a bedpost, a wrist, a dockside cleat, etc.).

3. To arrange a non-end part of a rope, frequently the middle, in a desired configuration such as a loop.

Now for some good news. Most of the bondage-related knots that you really need to know in order to accomplish the techniques in this book involve only end-to-end knots (known as "bends" in ropespeak), and only a very few of them. If you can tie either a Square knot or a Granny knot you know enough knots to do effective bondage without having to learn more – if you use those knots intelligently.

SOME BASIC KNOT VOCABULARY

One of the problems associated with researching and writing this book is that there is no single, unifying language associated with rope-related matters.

One problem is that a given knot may be referred to by two or more terms. For example, the knot I will be referring to as the Lark's Head in this book is referred to in other books as the Ring hitch, the Girth hitch, the Barrel hitch, the Cow hitch (don't tell this to the female submissive who you're tying up with this knot until she's very securely bound), and even the Lark's Foot knot.

Another problem is that one term may be applied to several knots. For example, several different knots are represented as the Lover's knot.

Nevertheless, when we start wrapping ropes around various items – limbs, bedposts, the rope itself – we need to establish a clear terminology in order to

> "It's really interesting to talk to someone when you're tied up and they're not.'"

communicate what we are doing. For example, if I ask you to loop a rope around a bedpost, what have I asked you to do? Should you simply run the rope behind the post and then bring it back? Should you wrap the rope around the post and then continue to extend it in the same general direction? Should you wrap it all the way around the post? If so, how many times? As you can see, it gets confusing. Guess what? As one of my favorite teachers used to say (rather gleefully) "Don't worry. It only gets worse."

In "ropespeak" we hear of bights, turns, loops, and round turns. Unfortunately, the usage of these terms is not entirely standardized. (In fact, while researching this book, I found some knot books that used some of these terms in entirely different ways than others used them. Confusion results.

By the way, "rope people" frequently refer to knots used to tie two ends of a rope together as "bends." Knots that tie a rope to a non-rope object are frequently called "hitches." Arrangements in an inner portion of a rope are sometimes called "loops." (Although some "rope people" might grumble about how I'm using that last term, muttering about the differences between "bights," "loops," "turns," "round turns," and "crossing turns," and also muttering about "authors who couldn't be bothered to make the differences clear.") Don't worry, I'll explain as necessary while we go along.

Fortunately, some terms are almost universally agreed upon. For example, virtually all authors agree that a "bight" is a section of rope in which the end of the rope is folded back alongside the rest of the rope for a relatively short distance. If the bight is extended back until the rope is effectively folded in half, this can be called "bighting the rope" – a very useful term for our purposes.

Also, virtually all authors agree that a "round turn" is a section of rope that is looped around something (such as a post) one and a half times, forming a turn of 540 degrees.

In an optimistic attempt to lend some standardization to this, I will primarily describe the rope turns, loops, and so forth in this book in terms of degrees. For example, if a length of rope is simply run behind a post and then returned back in the same direction that it came from, it seems obvious and intuitive to refer to that as a "180 turn." (AKA a turn or a "simple turn").

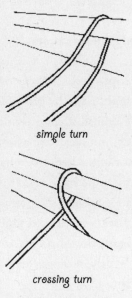

simple turn

crossing turn

If the rope is looped once entirely around an object and then continues in its original direction, that will be called a "360 turn." This is sometimes called a "crossing turn" in ropespeak.

If a rope is looped once entirely around an object and then brought back so that it returns in the direction it came from, that will be called a "540 turn" (AKA a "round turn").

Thus, we could also have "90 turns," "270 turns," "450 turns" (360 plus 90), and so forth.

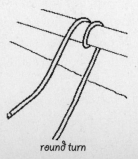

round turn

Indeed, this terminology allows us to accurately describe almost any type of turn.

Locking Round Turns: In the case of a typical 540 turn, the turns made around the object lie side by side. This allows them to move somewhat freely. However, it is also possible, when applying a 540 turn to a post, to place the second turn "over the top" of the first turn before running the end of the rope back in the direction from which it came. This creates what can be thought of as a Locked Round Turn. (Note: this is a nonstandard term.) A Locked Round Turn can place substantial pressure on the first turn, particularly if both ends of the rope are then placed under tension. This pressure can virtually lock the first turn into place, greatly reducing how freely it can move. We will be making use of Locked Round Turns in some of the techniques in this book.

Turns versus loops. When people describe how to use rope, they refer to "turns" and "loops" almost as interchangeable terms. However, it can be useful to draw a distinction.

"She's really good at highly immobilizing bondage."

For the purposes in this book, we can think of "turns" as sections of rope that wrap around an object such as a limb, a bedpost, or another section of the rope itself. (For this reason, they can also be thought of as "wrapping turns.")

Loops, on the other hand, can be usefully thought of, at least in this book, as turns which do not wrap around an object. Thus, a bight could be thought of as a "180 loop." Thus there would also be "360 loops," "540 loops," and so forth.

Loops can be further described in terms of "overhand loops" and "underhand loops." In general, an "overhand loop" is a loop in which the shorter section of the rope is on top of the longer section of rope (when viewed by the tyer). In the case of an "underhand loop" the opposite is true, and the longer section of the rope is on top from the tyer's point of view.

overhand loop

You can learn to appreciate the difference between overhand loops and underhand loops by attempting to tie a Bowline knot first with an overhand loop and then with an underhand loop. If you tie the Bowline with an overhand loop, it will set into place quite nicely and properly. However, if you try to tie a Bowline with an underhand loop, it will collapse into a Slip knot, or an Overhand knot, or some sort of unrecognizable mess, or it may simply come apart altogether.

There are a few more terms used specifically in relation to discussing ropes, bondage and knots that are very useful to understand. Those terms are, in chronological order, "initial application," "dressing," "setting," and, if you want to be really complete, "post-setting dressing."

"Initial application" is exactly what it sounds like. This is the phase in which the top first applies the bondage to the bottom's body and gets it generally into its final position.

"Dressing" can be thought of as the "getting ready to pull the knot tight" phase. In this phase, you have applied the ropes so that they are generally where you want them to be, and are now working them (by moving them, taking up the slack, and so forth) into their final position. Please note that dressing is frequently done not only to the final ends of the ropes, but also to the bondage as a whole. (Experience putting on a few body harnesses and you'll learn a lot about dressing ropes.)

"Setting" can be thought of as the final "pull it tight" maneuver. This is the final tug you give to secure a knot in place. Please note that it is usually unnecessary, and can actually be dangerous, to set a knot really, really tightly when doing bondage. I have a motto: "Don't restrain them with the knots. Restrain them with the ropes."

"Post-setting dressing" refers to any adjustments you make to the bondage after setting the knot but before moving on to other fun activities. This can refer to moving or smoothing out some ropes, further loosening or tightening the bondage, making final adjustments in a knot, and so forth.

In many ways, this process is very similar to putting on a pair of pants. There is the "initial application" (putting on the pants), the "dressing" (adjusting them so that they feel right), the "setting" (zipping and buttoning the pants, tightening the belt) and the "post-setting dressing" (moving the pants into their final position).

Another definition: The ends of the rope that are left over after the knot is tied can be usefully referred to as the "tails" of the rope.

MORE USEFUL KNOT TERMINOLOGY

"Initial knots" and "final knots." In a great deal of rope bondage, particularly when using longer lengths, we often tie two different knots in a given length of rope. For example, if I am going to tie a bottom's ankle to a corner of my bed with a twelve-foot length of rope, I will often first wrap several turns of the middle of the rope around their ankle and then secure those turns in place with a knot that I'll call the "initial knot."

Depending on what technique I used, I will then usually be left with two "tails" of rope, with each tail being somewhere between two and five feet long. I then often run these two tails together out to some point of attachment well out of the bottom's reach, and tie their ends together in what I'll call the "final knot."

"Intermediate knots." Sometimes, especially when I am using a relatively long length of rope, additional knots may be involved. These knots can be meaningfully referred to as "intermediate" knots. In most circumstances, only one intermediate knot is involved, but on those rare circumstances where more than one knot is involved, they can be numbered. Thus, when describing a rope that is tied in a series of four knots, you could refer to the initial knot, intermediate knot #1, intermediate knot #2, and the final knot.

KNOT CHARACTERISTICS

First of all, let's start by listing some characteristics that bondage-related knots do not have to be:

* *Bondage knots do not have to be elaborate.* While bondage enthusiasts may learn how to tie a great many knots (at one point, I knew how to tie more than three dozen) the truth is that very simple knots will do nicely for almost all of our basic needs.

- *Bondage knots do not have to be esoteric.* While it may be enjoyable to learn how to tie uncommonly known knots such at the Turk's Head, Spanish bowline, or Monkey's Fist, bondage fans can almost always accomplish what they need to accomplish by using much more common knots. As I mentioned, if you're smart about how you use it, you can get by quite nicely with only a Granny knot.

- *Bondage knots do not need to be pulled really, really tight.* It's a common mistake to believe that knots used for bondage need to be pulled especially tight. Actually, pulling a knot so that it's set really tightly can be a very bad idea. Keep in mind that the top may need to free the bottom quickly in the event of an emergency, and a knot that has been set so tightly that it jams will hinder this. Knots adequate for bondage usually really need only a firm but relatively light tug to be set with very satisfactory tightness.

- *Bondage knots do not need to be tied in a rope that is under significant tension (in ropespeak: under load).* It can be very difficult to properly tie a knot, particularly a two-ends-together knot (in ropespeak: a bend), in a rope that is under tension. Therefore, it's wise to apply your bondage in such a way that the final ends are not under a great deal of tension. I'll explain some ways to do this later in the book.

What bondage-related knots do have to be, in one word: *inaccessible.* As a good basic rule, assume that any knot (or unlocked buckle) which a bottom can reach with a finger, a toe, or a tooth will eventually be untied. Thus, it's good bondage practice to simply place your final knots somewhere that the bottom cannot possibly reach them – especially with their fingers. Stay alert on this point, though. Some bottoms are very clever at figuring out how to move themselves closer to the knots, or how to move the knots closer to them.

One good way to keep the final knots inaccessible is to start your bondage with the midpoint of the rope and work your way out toward the ends as you apply the bondage. A typical example of this approach would be to use a twelve-foot length of rope in such a way that the middle two feet are used to actually tie a wrist, thus leaving the top with two tails, each roughly five feet long, that they could then run these tails out to a place where the bottom could not possibly reach them. The top would then finish off the bondage by using a firm but not overly tight knot. I will share many examples of "start at the midpoint" bondage techniques in this book.

In summary, a bondage knot should

- Be relatively quick to apply.

- Not be too difficult to learn.

- Hold the rope(s) involved securely.

- Be relatively easy to untie after the scene is over or in the event of an emergency.

The Square knot. Most adults seem to have at least heard of the Square knot (sometimes called the Reef knot) even if they're somewhat unsure of how to tie it. Many people think of it as the classic tie-two-ends together knot.

The Square knot can be an excellent knot for bondage purposes, but it is a good idea to keep some of its major strengths and weaknesses in mind.

The strengths of the Square knot are that it is fairly widely known and fairly easy to learn. If it is set properly, it will usually hold two rope ends together satisfactorily.

The weaknesses of the Square knot include the following: It sometimes does not work well when joining ropes of significantly different thicknesses. (Many knot experts recommend using a knot called the Sheet bend in that situation.)

One of the more widely advertised properties of the Square knot is "the harder you pull on it, the tighter it gets." There is considerable truth to this saying. Applying substantial load to a Square knot can jam it down really tightly, making it difficult or perhaps even impossible to untie. For

Square knot

our purposes, this is a very bad idea.

Another potentially very serious flaw in the Square knot is that it is possible to "capsize" the knot, causing it to come apart completely. This is done by applying a pull to one of the free ends (tails) in a direction roughly perpendicular to the main axis of the knot. Doing so can cause the knot to "capsize" and thus quite readily come entirely apart if the rope is under tension. (If you observe the process closely, you'll see that the unpulled-upon section of the knot "flips over" into a type of knot often referred to as a Lark's Head. The Lark's Head can actually play a very useful rope in bondage – just not in this capacity. I'll explain more about the Lark's Head knot a bit later in this chapter.) Try this yourself with a loosely tied Square knot and you'll see what I mean.

The Surgeon's knot. The Surgeon's knot can definitely be a handy knot for use in bondage situations. It holds even more securely than the Square knot, and is somewhat less prone to both capsizing and to jamming when pulled tight. (By the way, this knot is called the Surgeon's knot because surgeons use it when tying sutures in place.)

two Surgeon's knots

The basic application of a Surgeon's knot is quite simple. When performing the first "right over left" wrap of the traditional square knot, simply add an additional "right over left" wrap and proceed. You can finish the Surgeon's knot by doing either one or two "left over right" wraps.

The Surgeon's knot can be especially useful when working with ropes that have an especially smooth outer sheath, such as nylon rope.

The simplicity and additional benefits of the Surgeon's knot make it one of those "you really should learn how to tie this" knots.

The Granny knot. Tie those Granny knots proudly!

That's right. You heard me correctly. Tie those Granny knots proudly! (Hey, don't stare like that. After all, you knew I was a pervert when you started reading this book.)

OK, I know that some of you are thinking something along the lines of, "Wiseman, have you lost your mind? I spent a lot of time learning how to avoid tying a Granny knot. I live in fear of being caught tying a Granny knot. Why in the world are you recommending them?" Let me explain…

In Praise of the lowly Granny knot. I, Jay Wiseman, feel that the much-derided Granny knot can play a very useful role in erotic bondage, and is in some ways even superior to the Square knot because…

- Virtually everybody already knows how to tie it.

- Under most "join two ends together" usages, it works perfectly well for our purposes.

- A Granny knot cannot be capsized, whereas a Square knot can be capsized.

- A Granny knot can be significantly less prone to jamming tightly when placed under heavy load than a Square knot. I've consistently

been able to work loose Granny knots that have become pulled very tight with much less effort than I've had to use to work loose equally tight Square knots.

Granny knot

The Granny knot does have a few disadvantages. It can sometimes be a bit harder to dress or set than a Square knot can be. Also, it sometimes does not hold as tightly under load as a Square knot can hold. Thus, it's commonplace for a Granny knot to slip at least a little bit more than a Square knot before it sets into place with adequate firmness. In fact, if you're working with rope that has a very smooth outer surface (very little "tooth" to it), such as some types of nylon rope, applying a substantial load to the rope may even result in the knot pulling loose entirely.

Note: When I'm using polyester boating line, tubular webbing, rope with a braided cotton outer sheath, or other rope with a significant "tooth" to it, I do not encounter this slippage problem with significant frequency or severity.

Of course, in this book, I recommend that the top apply the ropes in such a way that the knots, particularly the final knots, not be placed under heavy load.

This "excessive slipperiness" problem that sometime occurs when a Granny Knot is tied in very smooth rope can sometimes be adequately dealt with by making a double-wrap in the first pass of the knot, thus creating what might be called a "Surgical Granny" knot.

Securing the tails to the rope with overhand knots can also mitigate the problem. This usually suffices, but might make the knot unacceptably slow to untie in the event of an emergency.

The Figure-eight Knot. The Figure-eight knot can be used in almost every situation as the simpler Overhand knot, but the Figure-eight knot is much less prone to jamming. The elegance, simplicity, and usefulness of this knot put it into the "you really should learn how to tie this" category.

To tie the knot in its most basic form, simply fold back about a six-inch bight of rope from the end and pass first in front and then behind the main rope. Now bring the free end down through the bottom loop thus created and pull it through. Pull tight and you're done.

There are two useful variants of this knot:

First, fold the entire rope in half (bight the rope) and tie a Figure-eight knot out towards the midpoint. This is a very simple way of creating a loop of fixed size in the rope.

Second, bight the rope as before, but this time tie the Figure-eight rope out towards the tails. This has the effect of creating two opposable ends that can be used for a number of bondage purposes.

Figure-eight knot

All told, this is an easy to learn and very versatile bondage knot.

What is a "Slippery" knot? "Slippery" is another ropespeak term. A "slippery" (or "slipped") knot refers to a knot that can be mostly or entirely untied very quickly, usually even if the underlying rope is under load. Simply pulling on a free end of the knot usually does this. Such a "quick-release" factor can be provide good additional safety, and also reduce the chances that the top will have to cut the bottom free in the event of an emergency.

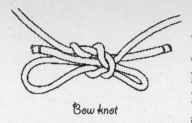

Bow knot

The common Bow knot, frequently used to tie shoelaces, is a good example of how a standard (unslippery) Square knot can be converted into a slippery knot. Many other knots have a "slipped" variant, and books on knots will often show examples of them.

In a bondage context, using a slippery knot is something of a trade-off. If only the top can reach it, tying the knot in its "slippery" variant can offer substantial additional safety with no significant loss of security. Also, when the bondage play is over, the players may not want to take a long time to release the bottom from their bondage. If slippery knots were used, the time necessary to release the bottom can be very greatly reduced. However, if the bottom can reach a free end of a slippery knot (and the little imps can be very cunning in devising ways to do this), they can almost instantly free themselves.

For our purposes, the common Bow knot will often work just fine as a slippery knot.

The Lark's Head. The Lark's Head knot, also known by a number of names including the Ring Hitch and the Cow Hitch, is my personal absolute favorite bondage knot. I use it in almost all the bondage that I do.

The Lark's Head can be used for both the beginning and the ending of the bondage. As a beginning knot, known as the Starting Lark's Head, it can work excellently for tying two wrists or two ankles together. As an ending knot, it can work excellently for securing the two ends of the rope around a bedpost or something similar. Thus, learning how to tie a Lark's Head knot can add a great deal to your bondage skill.

This knot is frequently used for bondage, and is typically started at the midpoint of the rope. To tie it, fold the rope in half (thus creating what is known as a "bight" in ropespeak), then

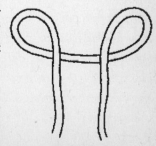

Lark's Head

fold the loop made by this half about six inches back over the rest of the rope. Raise the top of the loop so that the two folded-back halves drape over the outside of the rope, and you've made your Lark's Head.

The "Finishing Lark's Head" knot is very useful for the final securing of the two ends of a rope. For example, if you were to use the middle

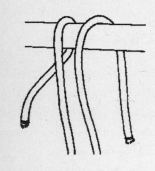

section of a rope to wrap around a wrist, you could then use the "Finishing Lark's Head" knot to secure the remaining ends to a bedpost.

The knot is quite simple to tie. Simply drape both of the free ends together over the top of post, then bring the two free ends up on opposite sides of the draped rope. This creates two tails that can easily be secured together with a Square Knot, Surgeon's knot (although this degree of extra security is usually not needed here) or Granny knot. If you wish to make the knot "slippery" for quick-release purposes, an ordinary Bow knot can work just fine here.

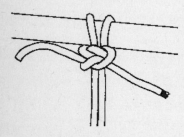

Finishing Lark's head

In summary, if you know how to tie either a Square knot or a Granny knot, you can get by just fine for most bondage purposes. However, if you know how to tie those knots, it is usually fairly simple to also learn how to tie the Surgeon's knot, the "Surgical Granny" knot, the Figure Eight knot, and the common Bow knot. Add in the Starting Lark's Head and the Finishing Lark's head, both of which are relatively easy to learn, and you have a very nice "bondage knot tool kit" for your play.

If you would like some additional illustrations, please note that your household dictionary or encyclopedia probably has several knots illustrated. You may also, of course, consult some of the resources listed in this book's Bibliography.

SINGLE-LIMB BONDAGE

n classic single-limb rope bondage techniques, we wrap some turns of rope around the limb in question to create what can be called a "cuff." We then use an initial knot to lock the cuff, and finally secure the tails of the rope to some relatively fixed object, such as the frame of a bed, with a final knot. The goal, of course, is to keep the limb stretched out, thus at least somewhat immobilizing that limb and exposing part of the bottom's body.

Note: In describing the single-limb bondage techniques in this chapter, I shall assume that you are tying a bottom spread-eagled to a bed. However, the techniques I will describe can be easily adapted to other positions. Please keep in mind that a spread-eagle position involves a rather advanced degree of immobilization and vulnerability. That being the case, you should definitely think twice about letting someone tie you up in this manner. I would only permit someone to tie me up to this degree if I knew them very well, had negotiated carefully, and had previously done less immobilizing bondage sessions with them and had good results. (See the "Who? What? When? Where? Why?" chapter for more information.)

How many wrapping turns should I apply? One of the first questions that gets asked about applying erotic bondage is "how many times should I wrap the ropes around the wrists/ankles/etc. that I want to bind?"

The answer to this question depends on a number of factors, including the width of the rope, the "hardness" or "softness" of the rope, the body part in question, the condition of the bottom's skin, how much tension the limb will be under after the bondage is applied, and so forth. However, I have encountered many fewer problems when the total width of the wrapping turns is at least 1/2" wide. In the real world, the width of restraints varies quite a bit. Police handcuffs are only about 1/8" wide at their narrowest point, while most hospital restraints are at least two inches wide.

"Hold out your wrist!"

Using the "you need at least half an inch" approach, you would thus apply at least two wrapping turns when using rope that was 1/4"-3/8" in width. For rope that is thinner than one-quarter inch, such as 3/16" ropes, you would thus need to apply at least three wrapping turns.

Note that, in order to distribute the pressure and thus reduce the probability of problems, you should lay the wrapping turns parallel to each other on the skin as much as you can, instead of "stacking" them in layers.

Most bondage using rope in the "average thickness" range (1/4"-3/8") can be done very effectively, and with relatively few problems,

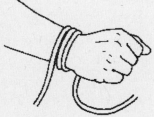

arm with three wrapping turns

if two to four wrapping turns are applied. Applying only a single turn of any rope has significant potential to concentrate the pressure of the bondage in a way that causes problems. One possible exception is tubular webbing, which lies flatter on the skin and usually comes in widths of at least one half of an inch.

Note: To help me make sure that I've applied at least 1/2" of wrapping turns, I've noted that the distance from the base of my fingernail to the tip of my left index finger is almost exactly 1/2". Thus, as a quick "rule of finger" I can hold up my fingernail and use it to measure the width of the wrapping turns. I've found this trick to be surprisingly useful.

More wrapping turns can, of course, be applied (I've seen some tops apply more than a dozen), but these turns seem to be done more for the visual effect – "look at how tied up this bottom is!" – than for avoiding problems or increasing the degree of immobilization. It's also worth noting that the more wrapping turns you apply, the harder it becomes to avoid "stacking" them. In general, in a monitored situation and using rope of average thickness, I've consistently found that using two to four wrapping turns will do the job nicely. Applying more than about six wrapping turns can start to become cumbersome, with no noticeable further reduction in problem frequency or increase in immobilization.

How tightly should the top apply the wrapping turns? The basic answer to this question, in an erotic bondage context, is that the top wants to apply the wrapping turns (and the rest of the bondage) tightly enough that the bottom will find it either very difficult or impossible to escape from the bondage, but not so tightly that the bondage damages the bottom.

Applying bondage so that it is within this narrow range of tightness can be challenging. Furthermore, there is not much readily available instruction in how to do this, because in many cases of "real world" bondage the goal is simply to make sure that the bound person stays tied. This is often done by applying the bondage as tightly as possible, with little or no regard for the person's well-being, or even an active desire to torture them.

In many ways, erotic bondage is similar to the porridge that Goldilocks found at the house of the Three Bears. There is too-tight (too hot) bondage. There is too-loose (too cold) bondage. Finally, just like Baby Bear's porridge, there is bondage that is "just right" in tightness. In fact, when applying bondage, the top tries to get it to the "Baby Bear" point and the bottom may aid this process by calling out "Baby Bear" when the degree of tightness has reached that "just right" point.

(For more information on tightness, refer back to the chapter on "Warning Signs and What They Mean.")

Single-limb bondage technique #1: The Wrap-Tie-and-Tuck cuff. This is a simple, relatively easy-to-learn, bondage technique that nonetheless is very powerful and effective, and will work well in a wide variety of single-limb-bondage situations. Furthermore, in learning how to tie this technique you will learn a number of principles that will be very useful to you as you learn other bondage techniques. I therefore strongly recommend that you become very familiar with how to apply this technique. Fortunately, because it builds strongly on knowledge that you already have, this technique is relatively easy to learn.

There are literally hundreds, if not thousands, of bondage techniques. In deciding which ones to include in this book, I kept in mind that it was for beginners and thus decided to limit the techniques that were relatively easy to learn and could be used in a wide variety of situations. This technique, because it builds on knowledge that you almost undoubtedly already know, is a good example of such a technique.

OK, so let's say that you want to tie someone spread-eagled to a bed. How might you do that? (Hint: Go get four lengths of rope, with each length being about twelve feet long.)

So now here you are, with a willing bottom, a bed, and four lengths of twelve-foot rope. What now? (Note: If you don't have a bottom, you can learn this technique quite nicely by applying it to your leg just above your knee.)

Have the bottom lie on the bed so that they are on their back with their head located at the top center portion of the bed. Then have the bottom stretch their arms and legs out towards the four corners of the bed. (Place pillows under their head, knees and/or hips as needed for comfort.)

There are three steps to the "Wrap, tie, and tuck" technique.

• *Step one – the wrap.* Take a rope, find its midpoint (which, dutiful bondage fan that you are, you have already conveniently marked) and place it on the palm side of the bottom's wrist. Then wrap the rope around their wrist in both directions and bring the ends back to their palm side (see illustration on p. 142). Wrap the rope firmly, but not really tightly. (You'll learn the difference with practice.) You have now made two "wrapping turns" of rope around their wrist. If you are using rope of typical thickness – one-quarter inch to three-eighths thick – this has a good chance of being enough wrapping turns; however, if you wish, you can wind the rope around again to create a total of four wrapping turns. This is almost certainly enough.

- *Step two — the tie.* At this point, simply tie a Square knot in the rope close to the wrist. (A Granny knot will also often work just fine here.) You have now created a basic limb rope cuff.

Many people would think that you have now reached a logical stopping point regarding tying the wrist and can now use the tails to secure the limb in place. In many cases, they are indeed correct. I know of many occasions in which a limb has been effectively secured to a bed with no problems after being tied in this manner.

However, let's take a moment to learn a truly major point of erotic bondage. Take both tails in your hand and pull on them in a

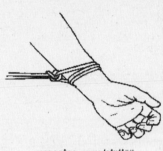

wrapping constriction

direction perpendicular to the bottom's wrist. Notice how the remaining wraps tighten around the bottom's wrist while the wrap that you are pulling on can be pulled away from the wrist to a significant degree. I call this "wrapping constriction" and it is something you should learn to spot. (You may also note how the knot you tied separates somewhat. I call this "load spreading" and will discuss it later.)

Wrapping constriction is not always a bad thing. In fact, I would say that it is usually not a bad thing, but it certainly has the potential to become a bad thing. Wrapping constriction has the potential to become damaging to the bottom because it causes an increase in tightness. It also has the potential to become annoying to the top because the loosening of one turn may make it possible for the bottom to slip that turn over their wrist, thus creating enough looseness to make further escape quite easy.

Obviously, it would be a good thing if the top could apply the bondage in such a way as to either greatly reduce or even entirely eliminate wrapping constriction.

In handcuffing, there is a principle called "double-locking" the cuffs. This involves fixing the cuffs in place, usually by pressing a small pin against a certain location on each cuff, so that the cuff can neither loosen nor tighten further. This is a good safety feature and many police departments require that handcuffs always be double-locked after they are applied.

Wouldn't it be great if we bondage fans had a way of double-locking our ropes in much the same way so as to achieve much the same benefit? Guess what? We do!

- *Step three – the tuck.* To "double lock" your rope cuff, take the two tails and tuck them under the wrapping turns in opposite directions, running them all the way through. This may be easier to understand if you intentionally tie a Granny knot instead of a Square knot at this point, because the tails of a Granny knot will "naturally" want to run in the desired directions.

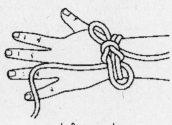

tucked square knot

These "tucking turns" (more simply referred to as "tucks") simultaneously accomplish five things:

- Tucks "double lock" the rope cuff, thus often entirely eliminating wrapping constriction.

- Tucks prevent "load spreading" of the rope cuff's knot.

- Tucks absorb much of the stress as the bottom squirms and struggles in their bondage. This means that relatively little of such stress is absorbed by the cuff's knot. Therefore, the knot is considerably less like to be pulled so tightly that it jams. This is a significant safety benefit.

- Tucks keep the initial knot under some tension, thus making it considerably more difficult for the bottom to untie.

- As a happy side effect, tucks also "fill in" some of the space that will be created when the bottom pulls on the cuff after it is tied in place. This can make the bondage much more secure and difficult to escape from. In fact, if the top wishes, they can use tucks to fine-tune the tightness of the bondage.

Caution #1: I call this type of tuck "the basic tuck" and it usually works very well, as long as the two tails are tied off in the same general direction such as to the same bedpost. If the tails are split and run off in different directions, problems could arise. I recommend using the basic tuck only if you plan to run the tails off in the same direction. Another tucking method, which I will describe later, can be used much more safely and effectively if you want to separate the tails and run them in different directions.

"I just go totally limp when I feel the knots pulled tight."

Caution #2: The "wrap, tie, and tuck" cuff can work very effectively, but it is elaborate enough that it could not be removed quickly in the event of an emergency. If such an emergency arises, the top would need to free the bottom by either releasing the final knot in the tails (this can be facilitated by tying the final knots in slipknots) or by using EMT scissors to cut through the ropes. If you must cut, then cutting the tails of the ropes close to the cuff would work well here.

Caution #3: If the basic rope cuff (or any of the other techniques described below) is tied so tightly that you cannot slip the rope ends under the wrapping turns to create the tucks, there is a good chance that the wrapping turns have been applied to a dangerously tight degree. (This is comparable to the classic bondage teaching that usually goes something like "you should always be able to slip a finger under the wrapping turns.")

Single-limb bondage technique #2 – The Obi Knot cuff. This is a simple knot that can work very well for single-limb bondage. Like the wrap-tuck-and-tie, it is relatively easy to learn and avoids the problem of wrapping constriction. This knot is already known to a large number of people, as it is the standard knot used to tie the belts that martial artists wear around their waists. In this case, we simply tie it around a wrist or ankle instead of around a waist.

To apply the Obi knot, place the midpoint of the rope on the bottom's wrist and wind the tails around the wrist in opposite directions to create what will look like three wrapping turns, with the two news turns both on the "outside" of the initial wrapping turn. Make sure that the rope coils lay flat on the skin and are not stacked.

Next, take one of the two outside wrapping turns and lay its tail across the other two wrapping turns.

Now tuck the tail of this wrapping turn under the other two wrapping turns.

Finally, fold the two tails up so they meet, dress the cuff down to the desired tightness level, and tie them together in either a Square knot or a Granny knot.

Now grasp the two tails in one hand and lift straight up. You will see that this tie avoids wrapping constriction. (Note: Some load-spreading may also be visible. Load-spreading in this context may not be a problem, *per se,* but it might look unesthetic. You can eliminate load-spreading by using basic tucks to run the tails in opposite directions under the wrapping turns.)

You can now run the tails to a secure point and tie them off. Remember that if you secured the ends with basic tucks you should run both tails off in the same direction.

In summary, the Obi knot is an excellent knot for single-limb bondage. It is relatively easy to learn, both quick and simple to tie, and works very well.

Single-limb Bondage Technique #3: The Split Lark's Head Cuff. This technique is one that has been "discovered" by a large number of bondage fans. It can work

Obi knot applied to a knee

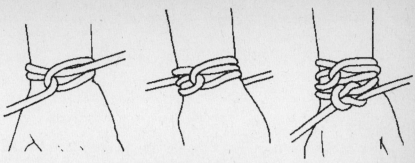

Split Lark's Head cuff

relatively well, especially if combined with basic tucks.

To apply this technique, wrap a Lark's Head knot around the limb, then separate the two tails and wrap them in opposite directions around the limb as well. This will create four wrapping turns of rope around the limb. At this point, tie the tails together in a Square knot (which may result in a better-looking cuff) or Granny knot, then run the tails under the wrapping turns in opposite directions using basic tucks.

This creates a nice-looking, secure cuff with four full wrapping turns.

Single-limb Bondage Technique #4 The Tucked Lark's Head Cuff. This technique is so simple that it is almost difficult to see it as a single-limb technique, but it can work very well, and it is another demonstration of the usefulness of the basic tuck.

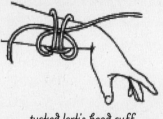

tucked lark's head cuff

To apply this technique, simply wrap a Lark's Head knot around the limb, as in Technique #3 above. Obviously, this is not a suitable stopping point, because at this stage the knot both tightens and loosens with ease, thus making it both dangerous and not very secure. You can make it much safer, and much more secure, by simply separating the tails and running them in opposite directions under the Lark's Head with basic tucks. Note: The wrapping turns may try to loosen as you apply the tucks. You can prevent this by placing the finger of one hand on the tails as they cross under the arch of the Lark's head while you work the basic tucks into place with your other hand.

This is a quick, simple single-limb tie. It might work loose somewhat if tied in a rope that has very little tooth, but when tied in a rope with a lot of tooth it secures nicely in place and can work very well. You can also increase its security by applying another basic tuck to each tail.

Single-limb Bondage Technique #5: The Looped Lark's Head cuff. This is a very simple, very effective single-limb technique and is

looped lark's head cuff

very similar to the Tucked Lark's Head. To apply this technique, drop a Lark's Head over the limb, tighten the tails as usual, then tuck the tails back under the arch of the Lark's Head, being careful to run the tails "inside" the wrapping turns. Note: As with the Tucked Lark's Head Cuff, you may need to pin the tails of the Lark's Head in place with a finger as they pass under the arch in order to prevent loosening. You can, if necessary, increase the security of this cuff by tucking the tails back through the arch a second time.

Single-limb Bondage Technique #6: The Cat's Paw cuff. I confess that this technique is my personal favorite when it comes to single-limb bondage. It is a very effective, very quickly applied bondage technique. Its tightness can be very easily adjusted after it is applied – much more so than is true for some of the other techniques. The Cat's Paw is also usually significantly easier to remove after the session is over than the other techniques are. This is a "you really should learn how to tie this" technique.

By the way, the Cat's Paw is a fairly well known "mainstream" knot and is both described and illustrated in numerous knotcraft books.

To apply the Cat's Paw Cuff, start by making a Lark's Head but do not (yet) apply it to the bottom's limb.

There are a number of ways to make a Lark's Head "in mid-air" but a simple one is as follows:

Stand up. Hold out your own left hand so that it is palm down. Bend your left elbow so that your hand is just a few inches from your chest.

Place the rope over your left hand with the midpoint lying on the back of your own wrist and the tails hanging down.

Bend your left wrist and grasp the rope with your left hand.

Reach over with your right hand and grasp the midpoint of the rope.

Pull the midpoint of the rope down over your left hand – thus creating a Lark's Head.

Note: This technique can be accomplished very quickly, as in within two seconds, once you learn it.

Now, to create the Cat's Paw…

Hold your newly made Lark's Head with one loop in each hand with your thumbs pointed away from you and the arch towards your body.

Now give each loop a single inward twist so that your thumbs first point towards each other and then towards you. (At this point, you have created a Cat's Paw.)

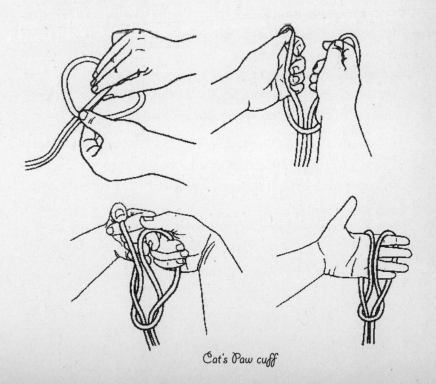

Cat's Paw cuff

To ready the Cat's Paw for use, tuck your thumbs back inside the loops so that they are touching, slide both loops over one thumb, and withdraw the other hand entirely. (This may seem cumbersome at first but becomes quite simple with only a bit of practice.) You can then either pull on the tails to tighten the Cat's Paw or pull back on the midpoint to loosen it.

The Cat's Paw can work very well for single-limb bondage. Drop it over the limb, then slide it down to the tightness you want. Once it is set where you want it, it is very unlikely to further tighten, to loosen, or to jam.

Note: The Cat's Paw sets very well if you're using rope that has some tooth to it, but may slip (and dangerously tighten) if you're using very slippery rope that has very little tooth to it. You can mitigate this danger by giving both loops an additional twist as you're forming them. It's my experience that, even when using very slick rope, usually only a single additional twist is necessary to accomplish this.

Note: It is possible to run the tails under the Cat's Paw in basic tucks. This will gain you some extra security but make the knot harder to remove. I have generally found it neither necessary nor useful to use basic tucks in conjunction with the Cat's Paw.

Caution: The tails of the basic Cat's Paw are not suitable for being separated and dangerous tightness can result if they are separated. Be sure to run them both off in the same direction for final securing.

Single-limb Bondage Technique #7: The Pre-Fab Lark's Head cuff. The pre-fab Lark's Head cuff can also be thought of as "the optimist's cuff" because, unlike other bondage techniques, it can be mostly set up ahead of time. Thus you can put it into position on your bed or a similar location in anticipation of good times to come. This cuff can also be very useful to use if it is difficult to reach sections of the frame or bedpost of your bed.

This bondage technique has two phases, the initial set-up phase and the application phase.

To initially set up the bondage on your bed, fold the rope in half ("bight the rope" in ropespeak) and apply a Lark's Head (or Prussick

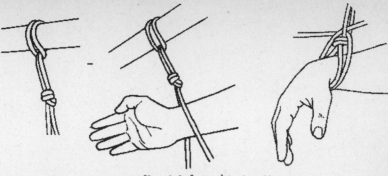

Pre-fab Lark's Head cuff

knot, which is described on p. 161) – the initial knot – around a sturdy section of the bed's frame near a corner. Run the tails out together onto the bed, determine the approximate location of where the wrist or ankle of the bound person will likely be, and tie the two tails together at that location in a Figure-eight knot. Both tails beyond the knot should be about eighteen inches long. (Note: do not set this knot tightly because you probably will have to adjust it later.) This completes the set-up phase.

To apply the actual bondage, stretch out the bottom's limb so that it is as extended as you want it to be, then place their limb between the two tails where they join the double-overhand knot. You may have to "slide" the overhand knot up or down the rope to get it to the proper location. (Now aren't you glad that you didn't set it tightly?)

Wrap the tails around the limb in opposite directions, then continue to run the tails in opposite directions between the ropes that are above the double-overhand knot. You will typically end up with two wrapping turns of rope around the limb. Now tie the tails together in a final knot. This creates a tidy looking cuff with no wrapping constriction of the limb or load-spreading of the final knot.

(This technique also provides a good review of bondage terminology, using the terms initial knot, intermediate knot, final knot, wrapping turns, load-spreading, and tails.)

Single-limb Bondage Technique #8: The Bowline on a Bight.
This is a bondage-related application of a well-known knot that is described in many knotcraft books: the Bowline on a Bight. It can be a good knot for bondage because it allows the top to wrap two turns of rope that will

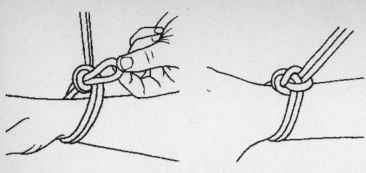

bowline on a bight

solidly lock into place around a limb. This knot can also be significantly easier to untie after the session is over than some of the other techniques in this section are. However, it can be a bit trickier to dress this knot to the "baby bear" point than it is with other single-limb techniques, so in this respect this may be a better technique for legs than for arms. Still, once you get the hang of how to adjust it properly (and that's usually not too difficult), it can be a very effective technique for both ankles and wrists. Note: This technique works significantly better in supple ropes than in stiff ropes.

To tie this knot, simply bight the rope, then make an overhand loop near the bight. Pass this bight around the bottom's wrist or ankle and then through the overhand loop in the classic "snake comes out of the hole" maneuver associated with tying a Bowline. Hint: adjust the position of the overhand loop so that the arch of the bight just barely emerges from it. Finish the knot by passing the tails through the arch and setting the knot.

Single-limb Bondage Technique #9: The French Bowline on a Bight. This technique is a simple yet innovative combination (thought up by me) of two well-known knots: the French Bowline and the Bowline on a Bight. It shares many of the benefits of the Bowline on a Bight in terms of security and ease of untying, particularly if used with supple rope. Big hint: The description of how to tie this cuff may appear complicated, but if you learn how to apply the Bowline on a Bight as a rope cuff (technique #8), this technique is very quickly learned as it involves only a single change.

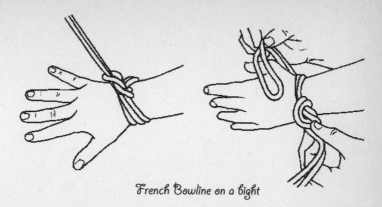

French Bowline on a bight

To tie this knot, simply bight the rope and make an overhand loop as you did with the standard Bowline on a Bight, but make this loop significantly farther away from the bight. Now wrap the bight in a 180-turn around the bottom's wrist or ankle and pass it though the overhand loop as you did in technique # 8. (OK, here's where it gets interesting.) Now wrap the bight once again in a 180-turn around the bottom's wrist or ankle as you did before. Finish the knot by running the bight through the overhand loop so that it is just barely protruding, dress the knot to the baby bear point, pass the tails through the arch of the bight to lock it into place, and you're done. You now have a limb that is bound with four wrapping turns very securely tied around it. Among other things, this distributes the pressure quite a bit — a distinct advantage if you've got a bottom who likes to struggle.

The Basic tuck and the Hitched tuck. In all of the techniques described above, I have mentioned using basic tucks. Basic tucks generally work well but they have one big drawback: the tails of a basic tuck are not suitable for being separated after they are tied. Given that most single-limb bondage involves tying off a given limb to a given bedpost, and that the tails are therefore usually run off towards the same post for final securing, this is generally not a problem. However, occasionally the top might want to separate the tails and secure them to different posts. The Basic tuck is not suitable for this, and may even be dangerous. Fortunately, we have a good "Plan B" for this situation. I call it "the Hitched tuck."

A hitched tuck is very simple to
create: After you have made a basic tuck,
simply run the tail back under the portion
of the rope that lies between the knot and
the beginning of the tuck. Dress this down,
and you're done. Repeat with the other tail.
It is possible to form the hitched tucks on
the same side of the cuff or on opposite
sides. These tails are now much more
suitable for separating.

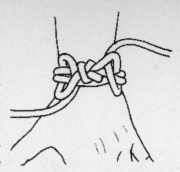

Basic tuck on left,
Hitched tuck on right

Note: It generally works better if the
tails are separated in the same general axis as the rope cuff itself. If the
tails are rotated more than about ninety degrees to this axis, a potentially
dangerous deformity of the rope cuff may be noted. This deformity is
typically quite obvious.

I've found that the Hitched tuck works well with the wrap, tie, and
tuck technique (#1), the Obi knot (#2), and the Split Lark's head (#3).
They work adequately with the Tucked Lark's head (#4) and the Looped
Lark's head (#5). It is possible but awkward and of questionable benefit to
do with the Cat's Paw (#6). Hitched tucks are possible but awkward and
often don't work well with the Pre-fab Lark's head. (#7). They are possible
but often not necessary with the Bowline on a Bight (#8) or the French
Bowline on a Bight (#9).

In summary, if you know that you will want to separate the tails after
you tie the basic rope cuff, I suggest that you go with techniques #1, #2,
or #3 as described above if you want to tie Hitched tucks. If you want to
separate the tails without doing Hitched tucks, try techniques #8 or #9.

SECURING THE TAILS

Once you have applied any of the single-limb cuffs listed in the previous chapter, with the exception of the Pre-fab Lark's Head, you will have two tails coming off of the cuff which should probably be secured somewhere – unless the sight of the bottom doing jumping jacks after you have tied rope cuffs to their wrists and ankles turns you on. (What are you, some kind of pervert?)

Logically, of course, you should secure the tails to some sturdy portion of the bed. Let's take a closer look at that.

Beds obviously come in a very wide variety of sizes, shapes, and designs. What you are looking for as you examine the particular bed in question is a sturdy point around which two tails of a rope can be passed and then tied together. Common points for this include corners of the frame, the legs of the bed where they run from the frame to the floor, and very strong posts of the bed at its corners. (It's come to my attention that, for reasons I'll bet you can guess, some bed manufacturers are now discreetly selling beds with "reinforced" frames.) Some bondage aficionados of my acquaintance increase the accessibility of the bed frame and legs by adding strong loops of rope, tubular webbing, chain or other low-stretch materials to them.

For the sake of ease of explanation, I'm going to assume that the bed you've tied your bottom to has a sturdy vertical post at each of the corners and also has a sturdy bar running horizontally just slightly above the mattress at both the top and bottom edges. (If your bed lacks these features, the legs that hold the frame up off the floor often provide excellent alternatives.)

Tail-securing method #1: Separate and Tie. This is probably the easiest and simplest method of securing two tails. This technique works especially well if the tails are not under tension at the time you tie the knot. Simply run the tails out toward the securing point (which I will call a post), separate them, run them on opposite sides of the securing point, tie the tails together in an overhand knot, adjust the tension as wanted, and tie the

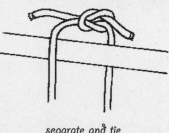

separate and tie

tails together in a final knot. For a quick-release variant, tie them in a Half-bow or Bow knot.

(Note: I found that this to one of the few situations in which the Granny knot worked distinctly poorly. The Square knot, Surgeon's knot, and Surgical Granny knot, and their slipped variants such as the Bow and Half-bow, all worked significantly better than the Granny knot in this situation.)

> "Keeping him tied up in the bedroom is almost like having the house all to myself."

Tail-securing method #2: Separate, Wrap, and Tie. The above technique will probably work just fine in the majority of cases. It's simple, tidy, and easy to adjust for proper tightness. However, it does have three potential drawbacks.

First, when the bottom pulls on the rope after the final knot is tied, this pulling can lead to extra pressure on the final knot. This pressure may cause the knot to become pulled so tightly that untying it could be a problem. In the event of an emergency, this could be a very serious problem.

Second, when the bottom pulls on the rope, such pressure may cause the knot to slip. This can be especially true if the ends have been tied in a Granny knot. This slippage can lead to undesired looseness in the tails which allows the bottom more movement than the top desires. (If the rope has very little tooth, and the pressure is very great, the knot may even pull completely apart.)

Third, the "separate and tie" method can be distinctly difficult to do, and possibly even somewhat dangerous to the top's fingers, if the tails are under tension when the top attempts to tie the final knot.

You can solve these problems in two ways, and these ways can be used either separately or together.

Your simplest solution to both problems may be to simply wrap the tails in opposite directions all the way around the post in a 360-turn (a crossing turn) before tying them together. This simple technique keeps a great deal of tension off of the knot itself, thus making it much more

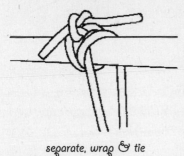

difficult for the knot to loosen or to slip. Try this yourself and you'll see what I mean. Note: one such turn is usually quite adequate to accomplish what you want, but you can wind more turns if you wish.

One very nice aspect of this "wrap before you tie" approach is that as you

separate, wrap & tie

make your two turns (which may seem a bit of a challenge if the tails are under tension, but is actually not all that difficult) you can usually easily wrap them so that one turn will "lock" over the other one as they cross each other (in fact, doing so may be difficult to avoid), thus relieving most of the tension on the tails. This locking allows the top to finish off the final

knot in an almost leisurely manner and to make sure that it sets very cleanly.

A second solution, particularly to the tightness problem, is to simply tie the tails in a Bow knot. This knot, of course, lends itself to quick release even if the knot has been pulled especially tight. There is a potential problem with the bottom being able to escape if they can reach the tails,

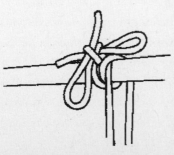

separate, wrap & tie with bow

but I'm sure that as a skillful top you've

been careful to locate these tails someplace where the bottom cannot possibly reach them.

If you combine these approaches, wrapping the tails all the way around the post at least once and then tying them in a Bow or Half-bow, you will likely have a very secure, and yet very quickly released, final knot. A nice touch.

Tail-securing method #3: The Finishing Lark's Head. This is another very easy to learn and very useful method of securing the tails, particularly if they are not under tension. We discussed it earlier in the "Basic Knots" chapter. To apply this technique, simply pass both tails together

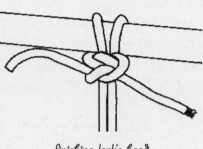

finishing lark's head

over the top of the post and back in a simple turn (a 180-turn), pull on tension as appropriate, and separate the ends. Then bring the ends over the top of the tails, tie the two ends in an overhand knot, further fine-tune the tension as needed, and tie off in a Square knot or Granny knot. Surgeon's knots, Half-bow knots, or Bow knots can also be used here. The result is a very quickly applied technique that usually works just fine.

Tail-securing method #4: The Crossed Finishing Lark's Head. When applying the Finishing Lark's Head as described above, it can be useful to keep in mind that the tips of the tails (in which the final knot will be tied) will end up on the same side of the post that the tails were initially wrapped around. This can sometimes be a bit inconvenient; however, this inconvenience is easily remedied. Simply cross the tips of the tails, continue the crossing until the tips are where you want them, and tie them together. This can also help if you are tying the tails while they are under tension. One such crossing is usually adequate, but you can make more of them if you wish. As is true with the Finishing Lark's Head, you can use a Square knot, Granny knot, Surgeon's knot, or Bow as a final knot.

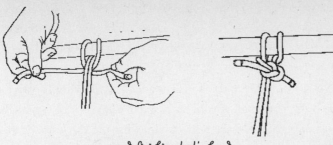

crossed finishing lark's head

Tail-securing method #5: The Finishing Prussick Knot. This variant of a well-known climbing knot can be used as a somewhat elegant means of securing the tails. If the tails are under tension, it can be easier to secure them by using this knot than by using either of the Lark's Head knots. The Finishing Prussick knot also "grips" the post much more firmly when under tension, and greatly restricts how much lateral motion is possible. (This is why this knot is so popular with climbers, who frequently use Prussick knots to help them on their main climbing ropes.) Finally, as

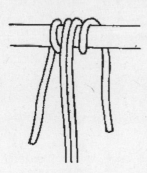

is true with the "separate, wrap, and tie" technique, this technique does a lot to prevent the final knot from either becoming dangerously tight or slipping too much when the bottom pulls tension on the tails.

To apply the Finishing Prussick, wrap the tails together around the post, separate the ends, wrap them entirely around the post a second time (laying these wraps to the outside of the initial wraps), bring the tips up on opposite sides of the tails as you did with a Finishing Lark's head, and tie them together.

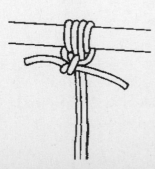

As is true with the Finishing Lark's Head, a wrapped variant of this knot can also be done.

The Prussick knot, in all of its variants, is a very useful bondage knot, and employing it can add a nice touch of sophistication to the

Prussick knot   scene.

Tail-securing method #6: The Double Half-hitch. This is a classic means of tying a rope to a post and is illustrated in numerous knotcraft books. It can be tied easily in both a single rope and a bighted (doubled) rope.

To tie this knot, simply wrap the tips around a post in a simple turn (a 180-turn), take up slack and pull tension as wanted, then run the tips back over the tails and through the space between the post and the loop. (If the tails are under tension, you may have to hold them in place with one hand.) Then once again wrap the tips over the tails and you're done. Be advised that a small amount of tension may be lost here as the knot settles into place.

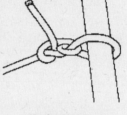

double half hitch

Note: As you tie this knot if, after going around the post, you first pass the tips over the tails (which you pretty much must do) and then once again pass them over the tails – in what can be called the "over and over" approach – you will have created the classic Double Half-hitch knot. Sharp-eyed, knowledgeable bondage fans will note at this point that the tips of the tails are configured in a Clove Hitch position.

An alternative approach is to tie the knot using an "over and then under" approach. This results in the tails forming a Lark's Head knot, and helps make it clear why the Lark's Head is also widely known as the Ring Hitch.

Caution #1: Please note that the Double Half-hitch, in either variant, is a slip knot and cannot be double-locked. If placed under tension, it can constrict very tightly and may not loosen significantly once the tension is removed. For this reason, I recommend that you avoid tying this knot around tissue. It can work well when used on bedposts or other inanimate objects, but keep it away from living flesh.

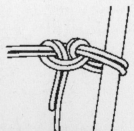

double half hitch on a bight (Ring Hitch)

Caution #2: A Double Half-hitch can be very difficult to untie if the tails are under tension. In the event of an emergency, you would have to

slipped double half-
hitch (on a bight)

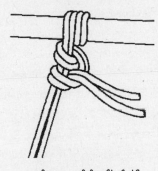

round turn and double half-
hitch (on a bight)

cut this rope. Alternatively, you can tie a Slipped Double Half-hitch that comes apart very easily even under tension. Be advised that it may come apart more slowly in a bighted rope than in a single rope. (See the safety advisory at the end of this section.)

Tail-securing method #7: The Round Turn and Double Half-hitch. This is a simple variant on method #6. The only difference is that the tips are wrapped around the post in a 540-turn (aka a Round turn) before the Double Half-hitch is tied.

As is generally true with using 540-turns, the extra turn puts more of the tension on the rope and less on the knot itself. This both makes it easier to tie the knot if the tails are under tension and lessens the chances that the knot will jam — two nice advantages.

Tail-securing method #8: The Taut-line Hitch. This is a well-known knot in camping circles (particularly among those people whose who still use low-tech tents that require tent pegs). It is illustrated in many knotcraft books. The Taut-line hitch is used on a tent guy line to keep the line tight. This knot is a good knot to use to adjust the tightness of a spread-eagle tie once you have it in place. It works significantly better in ropes that have some tooth to them.

This knot can be tied in either a single rope or a bighted rope. I will describe how to tie it in a bighted rope. To tie this knot, make a 180-turn around the post and tie a single half-hitch, just as you did to start tail-securing method #6. Now run another 360-turn around the tail inside of the half-hitch. Run the tail up above the initial turn, make another half-hitch, and you're done. This knot can also be tied by making the original turn around the post a Round turn (540 turn) instead of a Simple turn

(180 turn). It can also be tied in a slipped variant but this doesn't qualify as a quick-release variant.

Tail-securing method #9: The Clove Hitch. The Clove hitch is another well known knot, illustrated in almost every book on knotcraft, that can function well as a final knot in securing the tails. It can be tied in either a single rope or a bighted rope. This knot can work particularly well if the tails are not under tension as you tie it.

To tie it in a bighted rope, run the tails around the post in a Crossing turn (360 turn), passing the tails over themselves as you complete it. Continue wrapping the tails around the post in a second 360-turn (Crossing turn), passing the tails under the crossing section. (Try this mnemonic: First wrap it over, then wrap it under.") Set the knot, and you're done.

Note that the knot may "unwind" about one-quarter turn when tension is applied to the tails. This is usually not a significant problem. If it does become a problem, you can usually mitigate or eliminate the problem by adding an additional half hitch around the post.

An excellent variant of this technique is to tie the Clove hitch in a slipped version. This combines the features of a knot that sets up very well, withstands both constant strain and intermittent yanking very well, and yet almost always functions as a true quick-release knot. I highly recommend this variant.

clove hitch (on a bight)

Safety advisory regarding "quick-release" knots. A number of knots can be tied in what is often called a "slippery" or "slipped" version that supposedly enables them to be released very quickly even when under tension. Example of such "slipped" knots include the Half-bow (sometimes also called the Slipped Square knot), the Bow knot, the Slippery Sheet bend (not shown in this book but commonly described in the knot books in the Bibliography), and the Slipped Double Half-hitch.

One of the more eyebrow-raising facts that I discovered while researching this book was that these knots did indeed usually function quite well as "quick-release" knots, provided that they were tied in a single rope. When they were tied in a bighted rope, these knots often jammed after slipping part of the way loose when I attempted to quick-release them. I strongly invite you to discover the truth of this for yourself. The one major exception to this was the Slipped Clove hitch tied in a bighted rope.

Also, adding a Crossing turn or a Round turn to a knot consistently seemed to increase the probability of a jam occurring when I attempted to release it under quick-release conditions. Again, please check this for yourself. For example, compare the quick-release performance of the Slipped Double Half-hitch versus the Slipped Double Half-hitch with a Round turn when they are tied in a bighted rope.

"I thought of this really neat bondage technique!"

I think the take-home message regarding this is "a quick-release knot may not." Therefore, it only makes sense that the top should not automatically assume or presume that a quick-release knot will function as planned. Watch it to make sure that it has indeed released itself as wanted. If this didn't happen, work it completely loose. (Caution: remember that the tails may be under tension and may spin around and hit you or the bottom when they are released.) If the knot fails to completely release in a real emergency, grab your EMT scissors and cut the ropes.

Remember: "A quick-release knot may not."

DOUBLE-LIMB BONDAGE

TECHNIQUES. A great deal of bondage involves tying one roughly "cylindrical" body part to another. For example, arms are often tied to arms and legs are often tied to legs. Because these techniques very frequently involve tying a part of one limb to a part of another, they can reasonably be referred to as "double-limb bondage" techniques. Please note that many of these techniques can also be used to tie a body part such as a wrist or ankle directly to something such as a bedpost or chair leg.

Because many double-limb techniques are applied at or near joints, it is common to refer to things like "tying the wrists together" or "tying the ankles together."

The principles of double-limb bondage build upon those principles that you learned regarding single-limb bondage. As with single-limb techniques, it usually works well to make at least two wrapping turns (around both body parts to be bound) and to make sure that these wrapping turns total at least half an inch in width. The same general rules about proper tightness and knot inaccessibility also apply.

Note: for ease of description, I will assume that the top is tying the bottom's wrists together in front of the bottom's body. I'll make suggestions regarding other bondage positions later on in this chapter.

Double-limb bondage technique #1: The Simple Wrap and Tie Double-cuff. This technique is simplicity itself, and it can work well in a large number of situations. To apply it, simply wrap a few turns of rope

around the body parts in question and tie off the
ends in a basic knot such as a Square knot or Bow
knot.

**Double-limb bondage technique #2: The
Wrap, Cinch, and Tie Double-cuff.** This is a
simple bondage technique that introduces a very
powerful, very key concept of bondage: the
cinching turn. (Note: a cinching turn is called a

wrap & tie double-cuff

frapping turn in many knotcraft books.) To apply this technique, start at
the midpoint of a rope, apply a few wrapping turns, bring the tails to a
point in between the limbs, twist them until they run over each other at
right angles to the wrapping turns, run them in between the wrapping
turns a few times, and tie them off.

Ropes that have been run in between items that have had wrapping

turns placed around them
(such as a pair of wrists or
ankles) are commonly
referred to as "cinch loops"
and the process can be
referred to as "cinching."
Cinching is a very useful
tool for making the
bondage both properly
secure and properly tight.
This is a widely used and
very powerful bondage
technique.

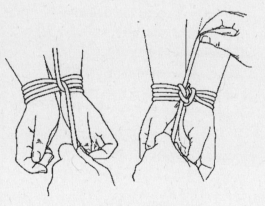

wrap, cinch & tie double-cuff

**Double-limb bondage technique #3: The Cinched Lark's Head
Double-cuff.** This is a widely useful, very quickly applied double-limb
bondage technique and I highly recommend it. It's one of my personal
favorites.

To apply it, make a Lark's Head, then pass it over the two body parts
to be bound. Adjust so that the arch of the Lark's Head is in between the
two body parts. Major point: Leave about a finger's-width of distance

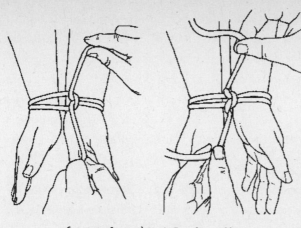

between the two body parts; do not pull them tightly together. Now separate the tails and run them in opposite directions through the space in between the body parts. Finish the technique by tying the tails

Cinched Lark's Head Double-cuff

together in an Overhand knot, adjusting to the Baby-bear point (you and the bottom may have to work together to dress the bondage down properly here) and tying off the tails in a Square knot, Bow knot, or something similar.

The result is a tidy-looking bondage technique that works very well in a wide variety of situations.

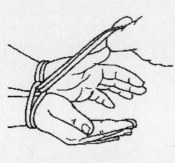

Double-limb bondage technique #4: The Continuing Lark's Head Double-cuff. Once both the Lark's Head knot and the principle of cinching are understood, this technique is often quite intuitive. To apply it, simply wrap a Lark's Head around the body parts as described in technique #3, again being sure to leave

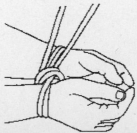

Continuing Lark's Head Double-cuff

about a finger's width of distance between the two body parts and to position the arch between the two body parts. Now, instead of separating the tails, run them both together in cinching turns around the wrapping turns and adjust the tightness to the Baby-bear point. The top can accomplish this with only a single cinching turn or may make an additional one or two such turns. (More are usually not necessary.) The technique is finished by separating the tails and running one on each side of the wrapping turns for final knotting off.

Double-limb Bondage Technique #5: The Figure-eight Double-cuff. This is an effective bondage technique that combines a high degree of security with a high degree of safety. This technique holds very well but is difficult to apply so that it is dangerously tight.

To apply the Figure-eight Double-cuff, hold the rope so that its midpoint is in between the two body parts and perpendicular to them. Now, starting from the midpoint, wrap a turn around each body part, going in opposite directions. (Note: it looks more elegant, and sometimes

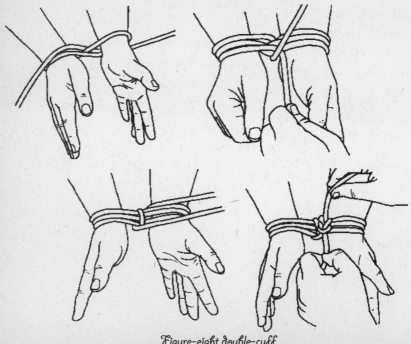

Figure-eight double-cuff

works better, if these wrapping turns are made on opposite sides of the initial wrapping turn.) After you have made two to four such wrapping turns, bring the tails back together at the "X" made by the turns and give them a 90-degree twist (with both tails on the same side of the "X"). Then run them on opposite sides of the "X" once or twice and tie them off in a Finishing knot.

Double-limb Bondage Technique #5A: The One-end variant of the Figure-eight Double-cuff. One end variant of this cuff is simple to tie, and may be a bit clearer for some people to understand. To tie it, simply hold one tail under both limbs with about six inches of rope hanging down freely. Then wrap the other end around the limbs in a figure-eight pattern. Finish the tie with the wrapped end on the opposite limb. Twist the ends together, wrap them in opposite directions around the "X" as needed, and tie off in a Finishing knot.

Double-limb Bondage Technique #6: Texas Handcuffs on a Bight. One of the very few bondage techniques that can be found in the "straight" books on knotcraft is the knot known as the "Texas Handcuff knot." Interestingly enough, it's the knot shown on the front cover of the Ashley Book of Knots.

The routinely shown Texas Handcuff knot is often not a particularly good knot for erotic bondage because it is usually shown with only a single wrapping turn around each body part. As I have mentioned earlier, unless you are using especially wide rope, such as half-inch tubular webbing, this approach has a very good chance of being too narrow, and thus exerting too much pressure, for our purposes. However, I have found that if you first bight the rope and then tie this knot, it can work very well.

Also, this double-cuff, when tied in a bighted rope and pulled tight, seems to go almost automatically to the baby-bear point. In particular, it is very difficult to apply this cuff so that it is dangerously tight. (Not impossible, you understand, but very difficult.) I really like this double-cuff.

To tie it, bight a six-foot length of rope and then fold the bighted rope in half. Hold the bighted rope up so that about the middle eight inches of rope are held horizontal. Now twist the rope with each hand so that it

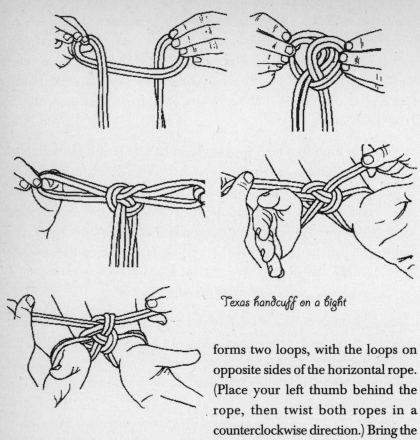

Texas handcuff on a bight

forms two loops, with the loops on opposite sides of the horizontal rope. (Place your left thumb behind the rope, then twist both ropes in a counterclockwise direction.) Bring the resultant two loops together and stack them so loop in your right hand is above the loop in your left hand. This will result in the tails assuming a Clove Hitch configuration. Then pull the inner portions of each loop through the outer portions of the other loop and dress it down neatly. The result will look somewhat like an upside-down Bow, but will not be identical to it.

To apply the bondage, slip one body part through each cuff, pull the tails down to the baby-bear point, and tie them together in an overhand knot.

DOUBLE-LIMB BONDAGE POSITIONS

Wrist-to-wrist bondage. For many people, tying the bottom's wrists in some fashion is the essential attribute of bondage. While exceptions certainly exist, in the minds of many people if someone's wrists are bound then they are bound, and if their wrists are unbound then they are unbound.

We covered various single-limb bondage techniques in a previous chapter, and many of these work well for tying wrists out by themselves. Here, we will deal with the various approaches involved in tying the two wrists together.

There are five basic positions that the wrists can take with one another regarding bondage are: parallel, reversed parallel, slightly crossed, perpendicular, and anti-parallel.

- In the parallel position, the fingers of each hand are pointing in the same general direction, the palms are facing each other and are either very close together or actually touching. The forearms are more or less parallel, although in many positions the bottom's elbows will of necessity be further apart than their wrists.

- A variation of this position, used with some frequency, is with the backs of the bottom's hands facing each other or touching instead of the palms. This can be thought of as the "reversed parallel" position.

- In the slightly crossed position, the bottoms' hands are, of course, slightly crossed at the wrists with their palms facing in the same direction (usually).

- In the perpendicular position, the bottom's wrists (or lower forearms) are crossed at a distinctly right angle to one another. As with the slightly crossed position, the bottom's palms will usually be facing in the same direction.

- In the anti-parallel position, the bottom's wrists are placed side-by-side with the fingertips of each hand pointed in opposite directions, and their palms facing in the same direction.

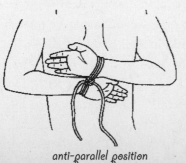

anti-parallel position

• In one variation of the anti-parallel position, the bottom's hands are "stacked" so that the palm of one hand is resting on the forearm of the other with both palms facing to the rear.

- In another, the bottom is told something like "grab your forearms." The palm of each hand is resting on the forearm of the other.

Positions of bound-together wrists in relationship to the bottom's body. A bottom's bound-together wrists can be put into one of five basic positions: in front of their body, under their chin, overhead, behind their neck, and behind their back. I will discuss each in turn.

- *Wrists bound together in front of the bottom's body:* If the purpose of bondage is to immobilize body parts, this position often doesn't accomplish all that much. A bottom whose wrists are bound in this position can often do just about everything, including juggling and checking their e-mail. Thus, this type of bondage is not much used, except for bondage done as part of a ceremony or in cases where the bottom either doesn't want to be bound very much or has some physical difficulty that prevents putting them into more restrictive bondage.

- *Wrists bound together under the bottom's chin:* In this position, the bottom's wrists are bound together and then fixed in place under their chin in some manner, usually by either attaching the bondage to a collar that the bottom is wearing or by tying a rope around the bottom's neck. (Note: I have heard no reports of problems regarding this technique.)

  This position is not generally used very much, with one significant exception: When the top wants to tie the bottom's wrists together in front of them, but does not want the bottom to be able to touch their own lower body, especially their own genitals, this bondage position can work well.

- *Wrists bound together over the bottom's head:* This technique is a fairly widely used bondage technique. It is most frequently used when the bottom is in standing bondage, and as a variant on the classic spread-eagle bondage position with the bottom lying either face-up or face-down. Its usage in the latter case has been described in the section on spread-eagle bondage.

  Safety advisory: One of the limits of this book is that I'm not going to teach or describe (at any great length, anyway) the principles and techniques of bondage that involves vertical ropes under tension. In other words, I'm not going into much detail at all about subjects such as suspension bondage or bondage in which the bottom is standing on the floor with their hands tied over their head. However, there is one matter that is very important, and the cause of many vertical-rope-bondage problems, so I am going to take a moment to address it here.

There has been a huge number of reports of bottoms fainting while being bound in a standing position. This is commonly believed to be due to two factors: (1) the bottom was standing with their hands over their head and (2) the bottom was standing with their knees locked. I think that both beliefs are at least somewhat inaccurate.

Regarding the first belief, that having one's hands over one's head increases the risk of fainting, I have never read any evidence in the medical literature to support this idea. The primary cause of such fainting is a decrease in the amount of blood returning to the heart, and raising the bottom's arms would actually increase the amount of blood returning to the heart by a significant degree, so I doubt that arm position is directly contributory. (However, I will admit that, because having one's arms over one's head for any length of time can become uncomfortable, the discomfort caused by this might increase the bottom's stress level. Thus it is at least hypothetically possible that the arm position might contribute to the problem, but not for the reasons commonly thought.)

The second belief, that having the knees locked causes the bottom to faint by cutting off their circulation, is somewhat closer to the mark but, again, not for the reasons commonly thought. People who are walking rarely faint, and people who are lying flat and being very still rarely faint, while people who are being very still while in a standing position frequently faint. The reason is that muscular contractions in the legs greatly enhance the return of venous blood to the heart. When venous return back to the heart is inadequate, there is not enough blood to adequately oxygenate the "uphill" portions of the body, especially the brain, and the person faints. Thus, it is the lack of muscular contractions that is being caused by those locked knees that causes the fainting, and not the locked knees themselves.

The problem can therefore be prevented by simply having the bottom move their legs, and thus contract their leg muscles, from time to time. I don't think that anybody has any good information on how frequently this should be done, but I speculate that somewhere between once a minute and once every five minutes would be about right. Actions could include having the bottom briefly stand on their tiptoes, briefly raise each knee, and so forth. Basically, anything that would involve the bottom moving their legs should be adequate.

- *Wrists bound together behind the bottom's neck:* This can be an interesting bondage position. The wrists can be tied in this way in any of the five basic positions, with parallel probably being the most common and anti-parallel the next most common.

    The wrists may be secured to the bottom's collar or the rope may be wrapped around their neck and tied, but this is a very controversial approach. (I discuss neck loops in the "Hogties" chapter.) A much less controversial approach is to use one of the arm harnesses discussed in the "Harnesses" chapter.

    This very vulnerable bondage position creates a great deal of accessibility to the front, sides, and rear of the bottom's torso. Their back, buttocks, anal area, inner thighs, genitals, chest, breasts, and nipples are all highly exposed and accessible. Because it shifts the position of the bottom's arms in an unusual way, this position often creates a subtle feeling of being off-balance in a bottom who is standing or sitting. Depending on how they are tied, the bottom may be able to perform oral sex and/or participate in any kind of intercourse.

"Have we got another six-foot length around here somewhere?"

    Some bottoms, particularly older bottoms or those with prior neck problems, may start to develop "bad pain" in their neck after being tied into this position for a while. The top should stay alert for this and adjust the bondage as necessary before the pain becomes worrisome.

- *Wrists bound together behind the bottom's back:* This is, of course, the classic "tie 'em up" position for the hands and wrists. There is fairly good reason for this. In this position, the hands are immobilized fairly well in a relatively out-of-the-way place, where it is often difficult or impossible for them to be used for anything useful. The head and front of the body are very exposed.

As with the other positions, the hands can be placed behind the back in any of the five basic positions (depending on the size, flexibility, and overall health of the bottom) – parallel, reversed parallel, slightly crossed, perpendicular, and anti-parallel.

- *The parallel position:* The parallel position is often used as a preliminary tie when the top intends to tie the bottom's elbows together. Indeed, it can be a difficult and awkward tie if it is not supplemented with some type of elbow bondage.

- *The reversed parallel position:* The "reversed parallel" position can be a

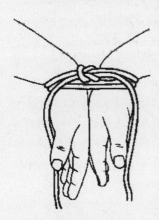

reversed parallel position

very good hands-behind-the-back tie. It also places less strain on the bottom's arms and shoulders than some of the other behind-the-back positions do. This bondage is relatively simple and easy to apply, and often accomplishes its desired task very well even when the simple "wrap and tie" approach is used. (Indeed, you can immobilize someone to an amazing degree by having them sit cross-legged and tying their wrists behind their back in the reversed parallel position followed by using a second rope to tie their ankles in an anti-parallel position.)

One bit of caution regarding tying the bottom's wrists into the reversed parallel position. In this position, the nerves and blood vessels going into the hand are relatively exposed. This means that is can be easy to apply bondage so tightly that it cuts off circulation and presses unnecessarily tightly on nerves. Stay alert for this and adjust the tightness as necessary.

- *The slightly crossed position:* The "slightly crossed" position is a bit less stressful on the bottom's arms and shoulders, especially their wrists. Indeed, it somewhat resembles the hands that soldiers put their hands in when they assume the "parade rest" position. In this position, the hands are basically in an anti-parallel position except that the front of one wrist is resting mostly on the back of the other, with both palms facing towards the rear.

- *The perpendicular position:* Tying the wrists behind the bottom's back in a perpendicular position is a very classic thing to do, and there are many depictions in movies, TV shows, comic books, and so forth of wrists being tied into this position. It is a fairly simple tie to accomplish, and the wrists can be bound into this position using either a square lashing or a diagonal lashing (see the books in the Bibliography for more information on these techniques) with cinching turns added as needed to either.

- *The anti-parallel position:* All the above "hands behind the back" positions have one major drawback: A bottom will often find it difficult to lie on their back if their hands are tied in any of those ways. This is due in large part to the fact that the hands will be compressed between the bottom's back or buttocks and the surface on which they are lying. Also, in the slightly crossed position and in the perpendicular position, the wrists and/or hands will also be compressing one another to some degree. For some bottoms, particularly lightweight bottoms who are lying on a very soft surface, this is not a significant problem, but for most bottoms it rapidly becomes a significant problem.

    The anti-parallel position frequently offers an excellent remedy for this problem. In this position, the bottom's hands and wrists usually rest in the natural, inner curvature of their lumbar spine. Being thus shielded from their own body weight, many bottoms can lie on their back with their hands tied behind them into this position with no problem. If the top places a pillow or some similar item under the bottom's hips, thus elevating their buttocks a bit, even more relief from the pressure can usually be obtained. This position often works very well, and offers the greatest versatility of any "hands behind the back" bondage tie.

- *Variant #1: The "stacked" position:* This position is an especially popular one with "Japanese bondage" fans. In this position, the bottom places one forearm in the small of their back and places the other forearm on top of the first so that the front of the first forearm is touching the rear of the second with both forearms roughly parallel to the ground. Obviously, in this position, the forearms will compress one another if the bottom lies on their back. However, because this pressure is distributed over a relatively wide area and usually not pressing directly upon any major blood vessels or nerves, this may not be a significant problem. Experiment and adjust as necessary.

- *Variant #2: The "grab your forearms" position:* I've noticed with interest how many bottoms reflexively grab their forearms when they are told to put their hands behind their back. There seems to something of a tendency to think that this is how hands and wrists should be placed for tying, and the position does have significant merit.

To assume this position, the bottom places their arms behind their back and with each hand grabs as high up as they can on the opposite forearm without straining too much. The forearms are perpendicular to the spine and the wrists are often brought nicely into opposition for tying. Note that wrists placed in this position are often bound in place nicely by using a simple wrap-and-tie technique here. Some tops enjoy using a Clove Hitch as an initial knot for this bondage position.

Most of the major nerves and blood vessels of the wrist are relatively protected from direct pressure by the ropes in this position. However, the branch of the radial nerve that crosses from the front of the wrist to the back of the hand over the thumb side of the wrist is exposed. (Tap on the side of your forearm just above your thumb and you may feel a slight tingle as the skin just over this nerve is struck.) Be careful to avoid dangerous levels of pressure on this nerve.

There are two possible drawbacks to this position:

- Some bottoms may find it difficult to lie on their back. (Try putting a pillow or something similar under their buttocks.)
- Bottoms with relatively wide torsos may not be able to grab very high up on their forearms.

Tying the elbows together. Once the wrists are tied together behind the back in a parallel position, it occurs to many tops (and a few bottoms as well) that tying the bottom's elbows together might be a really neat idea.

The idea has much to recommend it. For one thing, tied-together elbows are essentially impossible for the bottom to untie. The bottom is certainly not going to reach that bondage with their teeth, fingers, or toes. For another thing, such bondage juts the chest, breasts, and nipples forward in what can be a very inviting way. Thus you have a combination of very high security combined with a high degree of exposure of some of the bottom's most inviting body parts.

Additionally, immobilizing the elbows, in one way or another, does a very great deal to help keep the bottom's wrists securely tied together. If the bottom can't move their elbow joints, it's much more difficult, and often entirely impossible, for them to free their wrists. On the other hand, if the bottom's elbows can move, they can twist and turn their wrists so vigorously that almost no kind of bondage, other than bondage which uses something like metal handcuffs, can hold them for very long. This leads to a bondage aphorism: "If you want to keep their wrists tied, immobilize their elbows."

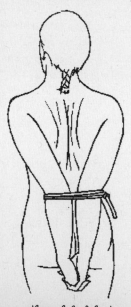

Unfortunately, this otherwise often highly appealing bondage position has one very great drawback. In almost all cases, it will be impossible for the bottom to lie on their back when tied this way without risking very serious injury. The possible exceptions to this usually involve very lightweight, very flexible bottoms who are lying on a soft surface. Even then, it's rare that the top

elbows behind back

can climb on top of a bottom who is tied this way for something like missionary position intercourse.

The basic bondage is simple to apply. First, the bottom's hands are often tied together behind their back in a palm-to-palm position. Then the top can use a simple wrap-and-tie technique to secure the elbows in place. The top can also use the Split Lark's-head technique is order to first draw the bottom's elbows together and then secure them in place. If the elbows can be placed directly against one another, there is frequently no need for cinch loops.

Unfortunately, for the most part, only very slender, very flexible bottoms can have their elbows bound together behind their back for any length of time. Probably the main problem is that, as the elbows are brought close together, the tissues of the inner, upper arm are compressed between the main bone in the bottom's upper arm (the humerus) and the side of the chest. Some of the most important tissues in this regard are the brachial artery, which supplies most of the blood to the arm, and both the median and ulnar nerves, which supply both sensory and motor functions to a great deal of the arm.

"I figured out a way to get loose."

When the upper arm is drawn against the side of the body and forcefully drawn back, the brachial artery is frequently pinched shut and blood flow to the limb is essentially eliminated. (Indeed, the early edition of "Gray's Anatomy" describes a variant of this maneuver that is used as an emergency bleeding control procedure.) If you feel the bottom's radial artery with one hand as you bring their elbows close together with your other, you may clearly feel the moment in which the blood flow to the limb stops. This stopping of blood flow can be frustrating. I know one female bottom who loves being tied this way, but the moment when her elbows touch is exactly the same moment at which her radial pulse disappears. Thus, she can't be tied in this way.

There is also the problem that if the elbows are drawn too closely together, some of the major nerves in the upper arms will be unduly pinched, with resultant tingling and numbness below that point.

There is a third problem in that many people, particularly those of us who are not young, thin, and very flexible, often rapidly develop very significant amounts of pain in the joints and muscles of our shoulders when our elbows are drawn towards each other behind our back.

Undue compression of the nerves and/or arteries, or compression and/or stretching of the bones, joints, and muscles of the shoulder girdle, is often painful, and, as I've mentioned before, such pain correlates very closely with post-bondage problems. If the bottom reports that their elbow bondage is, for any reason, becoming painful, it's definitely best for the top to loosen this bondage until it's no longer painful. That often involves removing such bondage entirely.

There is an alternative approach that can work well for a large number of people. With this approach, the top draws the bottom's elbows as close together as they can without causing undue pain, circulation loss, or compromise of nerve function, and then lashes the elbows in place. This is frequently done by making several wrapping turns around the elbows, usually just at or above the elbow joint itself, and then "filling in" the space in between the elbows with cinching turns.

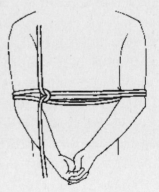

Another approach, which allows the degree of tightness to be regulated to a very close degree, is to lash the elbows together with a Lark's Head and draw them closely together, perhaps feeling the pulse in one arm as you do so. Keep the arch of the Lark's Head close to one elbow. When you reach the desired degree of tightness, separate the ends much as you would for a Cinched Lark's Head tie,

lashing the elbows

wrap the ends in opposite directions around the ropes running between the elbows, and tie off in a finishing knot.

In general, elbow bondage can work very well in increasing the inescapability of the bondage, and can present the chest, breasts, and nipples in a very inviting way. Just be sure to keep the limitations of this technique clearly in mind.

Knee-to-knee bondage. When you wish to immobilize the legs, tying the knees together can be an effective technique. The knees can be tied together in addition to tying the ankles together, or they can be tied together with the ankles left free. Tying both the knees together and the ankles together can greatly increase the "Hey, I'm really tied up" feeling in the bottom's mind. Here are a few points to keep in mind:

Knees which have been tied together have much less range of motion than knees which have been left free. For example, untied knees may have a range of motion of more than 150 degrees, while bound-together knees may have less than a 90-degree range of motion.

In general, it seems to work best to apply the bondage slightly below the knee joint itself, in the area just below the knees and just above the swelling caused by the calf muscles. This point often becomes very clear if the bottom is stood up and told to attempt to walk. In such a case, bondage that has been placed higher on the knees will often drop down, making its looseness very obvious.

A person whose knees have been bound together but whose ankles have been left free often retains a surprising degree of mobility. They may even be able to go up or down stairs if they turn to the side as they attempt this. Thus, if the top is looking for a way to "hobble" the bottom, this technique is worth a close look. Remember that the bottom is at above-average risk for falling, so stay very close to them.

Bondage which was applied "baby bear" tight when the bottom's legs were relatively straight, such as they were when the bottom was standing or lying on a bed, may become painfully tight, or even dangerously tight, if the bottom's legs become bent at the knees. Thus, be careful when doing something like tying the bottom's knees together while they are in a standing position and then ordering them to kneel.

When tying a man's knees together, be certain to bring his testicles forward so they are not pinched in between his thighs. Such pinching could be painful or even damaging. If you decide to sit on his penis while he is tied face-up with his knees together, be careful to avoid putting undue pressure on his testicles while they are trapped in this rather exposed position.

Ankle-to-ankle bondage. Once the bottom's wrists have been tied together, it often seems only natural to add to the bondage by tying the bottom's ankles together.

The ankles are, in general, probably the easiest joints to tie together. The heel on each foot forms a natural wide point that makes binding the ankles relatively easy. It is only the loosest of ankle bondage than can be slipped over these heels, particularly if the bottom is tied in such a way that their hands cannot assist in this process. (Be advised that the bottom can sometimes rub their ankles together in a way that can greatly help them slip out of ankle bondage.) Also, their toes cannot reach the knots on their ankles.

There are four main positions in which the ankles may be bound together: parallel, crossed, perpendicular, and anti-parallel.

Note: If the ankles are bound with bondage that uses cinch loops, these loops can often act as something of a pivot point or hinge, allowing the ankles to move relatively freely between the four positions.

- *Tying the ankles into a parallel position:* Tying the ankles so that they are parallel (side-by-side) is probably the most common way that ankle bondage is portrayed. Obviously, the bottom's legs are substantially immobilized when their ankles are tied this way. They can't walk in any sort of ordinary way (although they may be able to take tiny "baby steps") and they certainly can't run, kick, and so forth. Please note very well that a bottom standing with their ankles tied together is in a very unstable position and is at greatly increased risk for falling. The top should accordingly stay close to them or otherwise secure the bottom in place so that their risk of being hurt in a fall is greatly decreased. Note that bondage which was applied

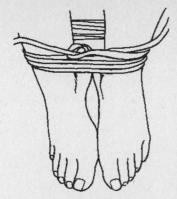

ankles in parallel position

baby-bear tight to the ankles when the bottom was not bearing weight on their feet may become too tight when they stand up.

When the ankles are tied in a parallel position, the bottom can usually kneel with at least some degree of stability, although the tightness of the bondage may increase as they sit back on their heels. This increase in tightness may or may not be a problem.

Tying the ankles together in a parallel position obviously limits access to the female genitals, except if the woman is bent at the waist, in which case her genitals may be accessed somewhat from the rear. Missionary-position penis-vagina intercourse is impossible if a woman's ankles are tied this way. Missionary-position penis-vagina intercourse may be possible if a man's ankles are tied this way, but if his hands are tied behind his back then much of his body weight will rest on the woman, and many women find this unacceptably uncomfortable. "Doggie style" vaginal or anal intercourse is sometimes possible, with the bottom either bent over in a supported position or lying on their side.

Access to a man's genitals and anal area remains pretty good if his ankles are tied in this manner. If he is on his side, he may be able to participate in anal intercourse, either as one who is penetrated or as the one who is doing the penetrating. If he is on his back, he may be able to be the (somewhat passive) penetrator during anal intercourse.

"Would you please tie my ankles together?"

- *Tying the ankles into a slightly crossed position:* To tie the ankles into this position, simply cross one over the other so that the bottom's knees remain fairly close together. If you want to make it harder for the bottom to move their ankles from this position, use a simple wrap-and-tie technique and avoid cinch loops.

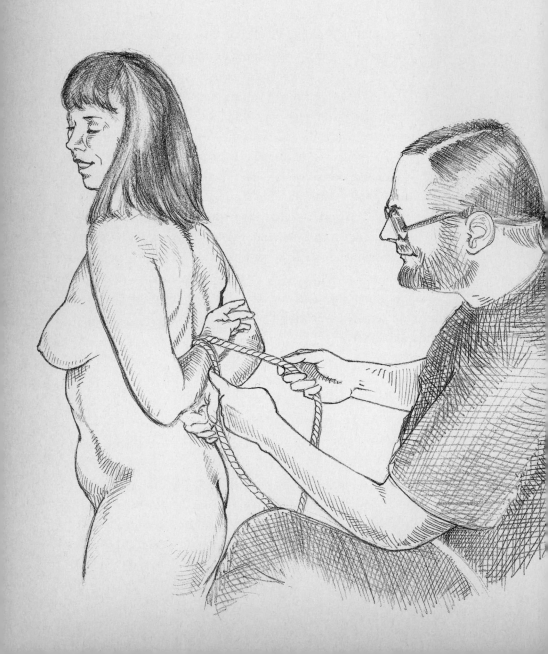

This is something of an interesting position because the bottom cannot stand if their ankles are bound this way, thus their degree of immobility is significantly increased. A bottom can usually still kneel, although they may be a bit less stable. This position otherwise shares many of the pluses and minuses of the ankles-tied-parallel position.

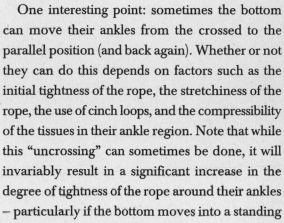

One interesting point: sometimes the bottom can move their ankles from the crossed to the parallel position (and back again). Whether or not they can do this depends on factors such as the initial tightness of the rope, the stretchiness of the rope, the use of cinch loops, and the compressibility of the tissues in their ankle region. Note that while this "uncrossing" can sometimes be done, it will invariably result in a significant increase in the degree of tightness of the rope around their ankles – particularly if the bottom moves into a standing position and/or if cinch loops were not used. Thus, many bottoms will re-cross their ankles after a brief time.

ankles in slightly crossed position

- *Tying the ankles into a perpendicular position* (for more information on these bondage techniques, see pp. 253-255): This is an interesting position in that the ankles are kept at more-or-less right angles to each other with the knees spread somewhat apart.

There are a number of ways to tie the ankles into this position.

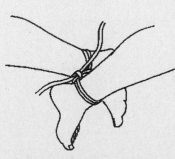

Possibly the easiest way is to simply take the midpoint of a rope, wind about four turns of rope across the ankles, twist the ends, repeat the process in the perpendicular axis, and tie off in a finishing knot. For those of you who want descriptions of more formal, classic techniques, consult the knotcraft books under "square lashing" and "diagonal lashing" for more information.

ankles in perpendicular position

When their ankles are spread in this position, the bottom can assume most positions except standing. They can usually kneel in an upright "standing on their knees" position with relative comfort, but the bondage may become unacceptably uncomfortable and tight if they try to sit back on their heels. (Some bottoms can assume this position for longer periods of time than others.)

Missionary-position intercourse may be possible if the female has her ankles tied in this position, and because of the accessibility and vulnerability it offers, can be a very powerful emotional experience.

I have not observed this particular ankle bondage position being used very frequently.

- *Tying the ankles into an anti-parallel position:* I confess that this is one of my personal favorite positions for ankle bondage.

  To tie the ankles into this position, have the bottom sit down or lie down on their back, then have them spread their knees far apart and cross their ankles. For the greatest immobility, tie their ankles into this position using a simple wrap-and-tie *without* using cinch loops.

  When the ankles are tied in this position, the bottom absolutely cannot stand up. They also cannot bring their knees closely together (although that can vary with how tightly the rope was applied and how many wrapping turns were used). Access to the genitals is usually excellent. Missionary position penile-vaginal intercourse is frequently possible if a female bottom is tied this way (although the man will usually have to "climb" in between her legs and her torso). Anal intercourse in a missionary position may be possible, but is often awkward. If a male bottom is tied this way, woman-on-top penile-vaginal intercourse may or may not be possible, depending on the bodies of the people involved.

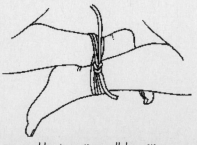

ankles in anti-parallel position

The bottom is often able to lie on either side without too much difficulty. They frequently find it very difficult, and there may even be significant risk of serious injury, if they try to lie face-down while their ankles are tied in this way. Kneeling may be possible, but is often both awkward and unstable.

Special Note: There is a special position, usually used for penile-vaginal intercourse, known in tantric sex as the "yab-yum" position. This position is used for prolonged intercourse and can be very intense. In the basic yab-yum position, the man sits cross-legged and the woman sits in his lap facing him with his penis in her vagina. For our purposes, this can be done with either partner in bondage.

Caution: If one person in the yab-yum position has their hands tied behind them, they obviously will have difficulty holding themselves (and, of course, their partner) upright. Therefore, some means of external support for them, such as having them lean back against the head of the bed, should be provided – or the unbound partner will have to hold them up.

SUPPLEMENTAL DOUBLE-LIMB BONDAGE POSITIONS

While most double-limb bondage positions involve tying identical joints together (wrist-to-wrist, ankle-to-ankle, and so forth), some bondage positions involve tying non-identical joints together. While virtually any joint can be lashed to any other joint if the bottom is flexible enough (for example, I'd be interested in seeing a bottom in ankle-to-elbow bondage), I'll describe some of the more common techniques below.

Supplemental double-limb technique #1: Wrist bound to knee. If a female bottom lies on her back with each wrist bound to the same-side knee (usually bound to the outside of the knee), missionary position intercourse works quite well. In fact, she can often be bound into this position while the act is in progress. It is not a highly secure position in terms of inescapability because the bottom can often reach the knots once the top moves out of position, but as long as the top stays in place (or otherwise keeps the bottom's knees separated) it can be very secure.

In addition to being on their back, bottoms can sometimes be placed on their side in this position, with rear entry of their vagina or anus often possible. The security of this position can be enhanced by tying the bottom's knees together and also by tying their ankles together.

Caution: Some bottoms can be placed in a face-down, knee-chest position after being tied this way, but both the top and the bottom must stay very watchful to make sure that this position does not create undue strain, especially on the bottom's neck. Placing a thick pillow or something similar between the bottom's chest (probably just below their collarbones) and the surface they are lying on may help a great deal. Stay alert for "bad pain" and immediately adjust as needed.

It's possible to tie the bottom's wrists together, then tie their knees together, and finally secure their wrists to the front of their knees. If this is done in such a way that the bottom cannot reach the knots and is otherwise secure, this can be a very low-stress bondage position that nonetheless offers a fair amount of accessibility.

Supplemental double-limb technique #2: Wrist bound to ankle. Like the wrist-to-knee bondage position, this position can allow the bottom to lie face-up, on their side, or (with the precautions described in the wrist-to-knee position) in a knee-chest, face-down position. Access to their genitals can be especially good.

This is often not an especially secure bondage position in terms of inescapability, especially if their ankles are not kept well separated. However, its inescapability can often be greatly increased by tying the bottom's elbow/upper-arm area to their knee-thigh area.

Supplemental double-limb technique #3: Wrist bound to thigh. This can be a good bondage position, particularly for bottoms who cannot bring their hands behind their back very well. The bottom's wrists are tied to the outside area of each upper-thigh region.

The bottom can frequently stand, sit, kneel, lie face-up, face-down, or on their sides. Thus, it is a very versatile position. However, the bottom may find it difficult to lie on their side, and the precautions noted above should be taken if the bottom is placed in a knee-chest position.

This is not highly inescapable position, but its security can be enhanced by tying the bottom's elbows to their sides. Its security can often be greatly enhanced by tying the bottom's ankles widely apart.

Supplemental double-limb technique #4: Wrist bound to elbow. Some bottoms, particularly very flexible bottoms with relatively narrow torsos, can place their forearms into an anti-parallel position and have their wrists bound to their elbows. This can be done with the hands either behind their back or in front of their chest, with the former being, of course, the more challenging. If tied in front, the arms can be either left in place at the lower front of the chest or they can (flexibility permitting) be drawn overhead

"I picked up some more braided nylon rope today."

and secured into place to create a surprising degree of exposure and vulnerability.

A bottom may be able to lie on their back if their hands are secured behind them this way, particularly if a pillow or something similar is used to elevate their hips.

Supplemental double-limb technique #5: Ankle bound to knee. This can be a very highly immobilizing position, but it can only be safely done on particularly flexible bottoms.

In this position, the bottom crosses their legs in a lotus position and each ankle (or foot) is bound to the opposite knee. This can create a very high degree of immobility to the bottom's lower torso. Depending on their flexibility, a bottom may be able to sit in this position or may be able to lie face up. Intercourse may be difficult or even dangerous, but the high degree of both access and immobility makes their genitals very open for whatever combination of pleasure and torment the top feels like administering.

Supplemental double-limb technique #6: Elbow bound to knee. In this position, the bottom's elbow is bound to their knee. This can be done either with each elbow bound to the same-side knee or with the knees and elbows all brought together (in front of the bottom's body, of course). Either can be a relatively low-stress bondage position, but the knees-and-elbows-together position can be very easy to endure, particularly if the bottom is placed on their side.

This is not a particularly secure position if the knees and elbows are bound separately; if the bottom can move their knees, they can usually slip the ropes downward over their calves or hands to escape the tie. But if the knees and elbows are all bound together with the knots inaccessible, it can be very secure.

SPREAD-EAGLE BONDAGE

W hen many inexperienced people think of doing erotic bondage, they commonly think of tying someone stretched out "spread-eagle" – which is to say, lying face-up with their arms and legs stretched out and bound to the four corners of the bed. This can be a perfectly wonderful bondage position but, because of its unique aspects, it deserves special consideration.

I always turn a little pale when I hear someone propose something along the lines of: "Let's try a little bondage. Nothing heavy. I'll just tie your wrists and ankles to the corners of the bed." My reasons for feeling that way are as follows:

The spread-eagle position, because it involves single-limb bondage techniques, can be very secure. As a general rule, it is much easier to apply bondage that is essentially inescapable if you bind only a single limb out by itself than if you bind two limbs together. This is especially true of wrists. Thus, even an inexperienced bondage top may find it relatively easy to bind someone (such as you) in this way so as to make getting free essentially impossible.

The spread-eagle position involves a very high degree of immobility. If you are tied to a fixed object, especially something as heavy as a bed, your degree of immobility is very high. If things start to get crazy or abusive, your ability to do anything effective to protect yourself is basically nonexistent. Obviously, you want to think twice, and then think again, before you make yourself this vulnerable to someone.

My personal general rule is that on a first bondage date with someone
I'm just getting to know, I will let them tie my hands behind my back, but
that's it. I won't let them tie my legs in any way, I won't let them blindfold
or gag me, and I won't let them tie me to any heavy object such as a chair,
post, or, of course, a bed. I will also, of course, have a silent alarm in place

and will diplomatically let my partner know
that it's in place before I arrive at their
house (and I will suggest that they have
one set up as well).

"Want to see how you
look in bondage?"

OK, so let's assume that you are a top,
that you have done at least two previous
bondage sessions with someone, and that
those sessions went well. You and your
bottom have now decided to do a spread-eagle bondage session and have
negotiated it adequately. How might you proceed?

Well, first you have to answer a few questions. Actually, you have to
answer three: (1) Do you want the bottom to lie face-up or face-down? (2)
Do you want the bottom's wrists tied spread apart or tied together? (3) Do
you want the bottom's ankles tied spread apart or tied together? In the
classic spread-eagle position the bottom is tied face-up with both their
wrists and their ankles tied apart. However, those of you who are
mathematically inclined may have realized that these possibilities present
the top with four basic face-up positions and four basic face-down positions
– and that's not even counting the deviations!

Each spread-eagle position has its advantages and its drawbacks. Let's
look at each one in turn.

**Spread-eagle position #1: Bottom tied face-up with both wrists
and ankle tied apart (the classic spread-eagle tie)**. As I've mentioned,
this is the classic spread-eagle tie. It offers excellent access to the bottom's
genitals, inner thighs, and perineum. Regarding their upper body, it offers
excellent access to the front and sides of their chest, and to their breasts,
nipples, and armpits. Thus, this position often lends itself very well to "tie
and prolonged tease" types of bondage scenes.

A woman who is tied into this position is often capable of missionary position intercourse, and indeed her vulnerability to this very act is a large part of this position's appeal to many people. (Note: she may need a bit of slack in the ropes attached to her ankles. Experiment and adjust as necessary.)

"Classic" spread-eagle

A man who is tied into this position may or may not be able to perform penetrative vaginal or anal intercourse, depending on a number of factors including the bodies of the people involved, the softness or firmness of the surface he is lying on, and so forth.

A bottom who is tied face-up (in virtually any of the spread-eagle positions) is generally not capable of too much receptive anal play. However, there is a variant that is described later in this chapter that can lend itself very well to anal play.

A bottom who is tied into this position can often perform cunnilingus or analingus, and can frequently do so for a very long time, if the top kneels astride their head. (This kneeling can be done with the top either facing towards the bottom's feet or facing away from them.) Fellatio, however, is often relatively difficult for them to perform, except perhaps in the "69" position.

A bottom tied in this way is, of course, very available for having either cunnilingus or fellatio performed upon them, and/or for being masturbated. Indeed, prolonged masturbation scenes are very commonly done when the bottom is tied this way. Note: many men find it difficult to reach orgasm, no matter how skillfully they are stimulated, if their legs are tied apart. This fact is sometimes used with mischievously delightful results by some tops.

Note: Because the general advantages and limitations of the face-up spread-eagle tie have been mentioned in describing this spread-eagle position, I will henceforth mostly only describe how those vary for the following face-up spread-eagle bondage positions

Spread-eagle position #2: Bottom tied face-up with wrists tied apart and ankles tied together. This position often does not work all that well if the bottom is female, because it substantially limits access to her genitals. (A variant in which the bottom's knees are tied apart but their ankles are tied together can solve this problem.) If the bottom is male, this position can be a very good one.

"Man, I can't move at all."

Regarding a male bottom, access to his inner thighs and perineum is limited, but access to his genitals remains good. A male bottom is often much more capable of participating in penetrative vaginal or anal intercourse if he is tied with his legs together. (This bondage can often be nicely supplemented by tying his knees together as well.) Furthermore, his genitals are usually still more than adequately accessible for any pleasures or torments that the top might care to administer.

Two cautions: His testicles may be subjected to increased risk of not-fun injury if he's tied into this position. Therefore:

Make sure that you draw his testicles forward, clear of his inner thighs. This can be especially important if you tie his knees together. Otherwise, his testicles may be dangerously pinched between his thighs.

If you decide to have the bottom penetrate your vagina or anus with his penis while he is tied into this position, be mindful of where his testicles are. Carelessness here could result in his testicles being dangerously pinched in between your two bodies. This is usually not a problem, but take a moment to make sure that you, as the top, know where his testicles are before you get too carried away with any rocking or thrusting motions. The bottom will usually be more than happy to help keep you adequately informed on this point. (Trust me on this one!)

Spread-eagle position #3: Bottom tied face-up with wrists tied together and ankles tied apart. This position usually contains no particular advantages over the classic spread-eagle. Furthermore, because it typically draws the bottom's upper arms close to the sides of their head, it can limit access to the bottom's face – thus hindering their ability to perform cunnilingus or analingus. However, it does have some major fans. Tying the wrists close together like this can lead to an even greater sense of being exposed and vulnerable. One delightful female bottom of my acquaintance absolutely loves to be tied into this position. It's her favorite.

Spread-eagle position #4: Bottom tied face-up with wrists tied together and ankles tied together. This position shares many of the disadvantages of the legs-tied-together and wrists-tied-together spread-eagle ties, but it has one major advantage: When a bottom is tied into this position, it is often relatively easy for them to move from lying face-up to lying face-down – and back again. (Just be sure that when they go to move back into the position which they came from that they turn back in the same direction. Otherwise, their bondage can become "wound up" in an awkward and potentially dangerous matter.) This allows the top access to almost all of the bottom's skin, both front and back. The potential here is delightfully obvious.

A few general comments about face-down spread-eagle bondage positions:

All variants of face-down spread-eagle positions are generally good if the top wants to do things to the bottom, but are often relatively poor positions regarding having the bottom do things to the top.

Caution: In all face-down spread-eagle positions, the bottom will often have difficulty keeping their head in a face-forward position and will thus have to turn their head to one side or the other. How well the bottom will be able to tolerate this position depends on a number of factors, including the bottom's overall health, any history of neck problems, the softness of surface that the bottom in lying on, and so forth. If the bottom is lying on a very soft surface, there is a chance that they might sink into this surface far enough to make it difficult for them to breathe. This is usually almost immediately obvious.

The various difficulties associated with face-down bondage can often be substantially lessened by placing something such as a pillow or towel under the bottom's chest and/or under their forehead. A little experimentation here is usually very revealing. Just remember the difference between "good pain" and "bad pain." If you as a bottom are holding your neck in a position that is causing "bad pain," let your top know about this sooner rather than later. I know some bottoms that didn't, and they ended up with long-term neck problems as a result.

Spread-eagle position # 5: Bottom tied face-down with wrists tied apart and ankles tied apart. This is another classic spread-eagle bondage position, often associated with the bottom being whipped. This position exposes almost all of the bottom's backside and a fair portion of the sides of their trunk and legs as well.

"This would work better if you would loop it under that bar."

In this position, the bottom's body is very well exposed for various types of whipping and spanking. Access to their back, buttocks, and upper thighs is usually quite good. Their inner thighs can often be reached adequately as well. Access to their genitals is often only fair, and vaginal intercourse is often so difficult as to not be worth attempting. (Putting a thick pillow under a female bottom's pelvis may help.) The male genitals can often be drawn back so that they are at least somewhat accessible.

As I mentioned, the ability of the bottom to do things to the top is typically very limited in all forms of face-down spread-eagle ties. If the top were to sit or lie at the bottom's head, it might be possible for the bottom to perform oral sex on the top, but this is often a somewhat cramped, uncomfortable position for both partners (experiment with adjusting the wrist bondage; more length may help here). Because they must use their neck muscles to hold their head up while performing oral sex, many bottoms find that they cannot do so for long periods – at least not without risking a serious neck strain.

On the other hand, anal play is often very possible in this position, and many bottoms love to be tied into this position and then get anally penetrated by a top's penis or strap-on dildo.

Spread-eagle position #6: Bottom tied face-down with wrists tied apart and ankles tied together. This position greatly reduces access to the genitals, and significantly reduces access to the inner thighs. Vaginal intercourse becomes essentially impossible, and anal intercourse may become significantly more cumbersome due to the decreased ability of the bottom to move their body in order to assist the process.

One advantage of this position is that a male bottom's genitals, particularly his testicles, are almost invariably entirely covered by the upper thighs as they are held together. This covering allows the top to spank/whip/etc. the bottom's buttocks with the chances of an accidental blow to the bottom's testicles being essentially eliminated.

Note: As with the face-up version of this bondage position, this position can be enhanced nicely by tying the bottom's knees together.

Spread-eagle position #7: Bottom tied face-down with wrists tied together and ankles tied apart. This position generally allows the same excellent access to the bottom's buttocks and inner thighs as the classic face-down spread-eagle position. Furthermore, tying the bottom's wrists together can increase their feeling of exposure and vulnerability. Binding the bottom's wrists together may limit their ability to turn their head from side to side, but this is usually not a problem. (If it becomes a problem, the bottom should advise the top.)

Spread-eagle position #8: Bottom tied face-down with both wrists and ankles tied together. This position limits access to the bottom's genitals and inner thighs, but it can be a very good position for spanking, whipping, and so forth. As mentioned earlier, it is often possible for the bottom to move from the face-down position to the face-up position when tied in this way.

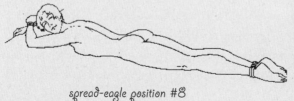

spread-eagle position #8

FIVE MODIFICATIONS

There are a number of variations to spread-eagle bondage. Five in particular come to mind.

Variant # 1: Bottom tied face-down with hands tied behind their back and ankles tied apart. This position can be a good one for spanking and whipping the bottom's buttocks, but care must be taken so that their hands don't reflexively move down in an attempt to cover their buttocks. Using one of the arm harnesses described in the "Harnesses" chapter can be useful in preventing this problem.

When a bottom is tied into this position, it may be possible for them to perform oral sex for at least a moderate period of time before their neck starts to experience "bad pain." Furthermore, anal play, including anal intercourse, may be possible. Just watch out for the bottom's hands. You don't want to injure those hands by lying on them too heavily, and occasionally a bottom will try to use their hands in a mischievous manner.

Variant #2: Bottom tied face-down with their hands tied behind their back and their ankles tied together. This can be something of an intense position, and can lend itself to having the bottom experience a real "I'm being held captive" feeling. As with variant #1, oral sex and anal play may be possible. It is also often possible to turn the bottom over to a face-up position without too much difficulty.

Caution: A bottom tied into this position could conceivably wiggle themselves over toward the side of the bed and potentially even partially fall off. Doing so would put them into a painful, awkward, and even dangerous position. (It could become difficult for the bottom to breathe if they were kept in this position too long.) That being the case, the top should use this bondage position only in a closely monitored situation. Alternatively, the top could run a rope from under the bottom's armpits to the head of the bed so that the bottom's lateral movement is restricted.

Variant #3: Bottom tied face-up with their hands tied behind their back and their legs tied apart. This can be a very good bondage position. It combines excellent access to the bottom's genitals, inner thighs, and so forth along with fairly good access to their chest, breasts, and nipples.

This position can also often lend itself well to missionary position intercourse, and the experience can be a very powerful one for both parties.

When a bottom is tied into this position, their head is very accessible for sitting astride. Therefore, cunnilingus and analingus are often possible, and because the bottom is not using their muscles to hold their head in position, can often last for a very long time.

(I know one lady top who ties her bottom into this position, or into a similar position, and then sits astride the bottom's face, facing away from them. She then bends forward so that she can rest her torso on a large pillow that she has positioned for this purpose. Thusly positioned, she can relax and enjoy herself for a very long time.)

Caution: In all cases in which a bottom has had their hands tied behind their back and are then made to lie face-up, their hands, wrists, and forearms will invariably be compressed to at least some degree in between their torso and the surface that they are lying on. Depending on a number of factors, including the size of the bottom and the softness or hardness of the surface they are lying on, sometimes this is not a problem, but sometimes it is. The top needs to monitor this aspect of the bondage closely. The problem can often be lessened to an acceptable degree by placing a pillow or something similar under the bottom's hips, thus elevating their hips slightly and taking much of the weight of their torso off their hands, wrists, and forearms.

Variant #4: Bottom tied face-up with their hands tied behind their back and their ankles tied together. As with the spread-eagle version of this tie, a male bottom is often capable of participating in penetrative vaginal or anal intercourse when tied this way. This ability, when combined with the superior accessibility to his head for cunnilingus or analingus, and the fact that he can often be turned face-down and returned to a face-up position with relatively little difficulty, can make this a genuinely excellent position to bind a male bottom into.

Caution: As with variant #2, a bottom tied into this position could conceivably have their head and torso fall off the side of the bed while their feet are still tied to the footboard. Thus, monitor them closely and/ or tie a rope from the torso to the head of the bed to prevent this.

Variant #5: Bottom tied face-up with their wrists tied apart and their knees tied elevated and spread. This position can be a truly excellent position for either vaginal or anal intercourse. Access to the bottom's genitals, perineum, and anal area can be very good, and access to their buttocks for spanking can be much more than adequate. Access to their chest, breasts, and nipples is

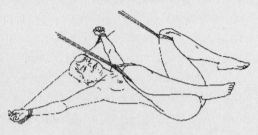

Spreadeagle variant #5

usually at least acceptable. However, access to their head for oral sex can be very difficult, and often not worth the bother.

This position is often very secure by itself, but the top may sometimes want to add a bit of security and/or stability by running a rope from around the bottom's rear waist down to the center of the bed's footboard or frame.

Caution: Being tied into this position can occasionally cause bottoms to develop some difficulty in breathing. This difficulty may be increased if the top gets on top of the bottom for vaginal or anal intercourse. Fortunately, this problem usually takes time to develop and (unless the bottom is intoxicated or their ability to feel is otherwise impaired) the bottom will be able to notice and report these difficulties long before they become dangerous, and the top will be able to modify the position and/or activity as needed.

Another Caution: Be careful about tying a bottom into this position, especially if you get on top of them for intercourse, if the bottom has a history of back problems. If they report feeling any "bad pain," modify the bondage position and/or the activities as necessary.

Yet Another Caution: It is possible to tie a bottom so that they are face-up with their hands tied behind their back and their knees are tied to the head of the bed in an elevated and spread position. However, this position often strongly compresses the bottom's hands, wrists, and forearms between their torso and the surface that they are lying on. This position works for some people, but in general I have found that it creates so many pressures and stresses, in so many places on the bottom's body (especially on their hands and lower back), that I mention it here mostly for the sake of completeness. Try it (carefully, please!) if you wish, but don't get your hopes up.

Spread-eagle Variants

The One-arm-semi-free Variant. This is an interesting variant that can be useful for prolonged bondage scenes and in other types of play.

In this variant, the bottom's ankles are tied apart in the usual way and one of their wrists – let's say their left wrist – is also tied to the bedpost in the usual way. Their right wrist is tied on a much longer length of rope.

In one example, their right wrist is tied to the right, lower bedpost (the same bedpost that their right ankle is tied to) by a rope that is long enough that the bottom can reach their genitals. This bondage position still immobilizes the bottom to a very substantial degree, and yet is also allows the bottom to masturbate themselves if that's what the top wants them to do. (One of my friends who contributed to this book suggests tying the bottom's dominant hand and thus making them masturbate with the "wrong" hand, evil woman that she is.)

In another example of this variant, the bottom's right wrist is secured to the right, upper bedpost but, again, with a rope long enough that the bottom can reach their genitals. Interestingly enough, this will also allow the bottom to reach their own mouth and other parts of their face. (This bondage position is similar to the one described in the Poe story "The Pit and the Pendulum.") Note that because the bottom will be able to reach their mouth with the wrist cuff, it should be of a type that the bottom cannot readily free by using their teeth.

The Double Spread-eagle. This is a very interesting and simple bondage technique that can increase the immobility of the standard Spread-eagle bondage position to a surprising degree. It usually calls for a six-foot length of rope, although in some cases a twelve-foot length will be needed.

To apply the simplest version of this bondage, imagine that the bottom is lying face-up with their ankles spread apart and lashed to the usual corners of the bed. To apply the Double Spread-eagle technique, position the midpoint of the rope at the bottom center of the bed and run each end out towards an ankle cuff. Thread the tail of the rope through the cuff and bring it back towards the bottom center of the bed. Dress this rope snugly, tie the ends together in a finishing knot, and you're done. When properly applied, this technique significantly increases the immobility of the bondage. (It can often have a strong emotional impact on the bottom.)

Alternately, the rope can be attached to the first cuff by a Beginning Lark's Head knot and to the second cuff by a Finishing Lark's Head knot. This can allow a very precise adjustment of the tension.

In some cases, sturdy O-rings or D-rings can be added to the rope cuff as it is first applied. The second rope can be threaded though these rings instead of the cuff.

When running the rope from one of the bottom's wrists to the other, make sure to position the knots so that the bottom cannot reach them.

While this tie is usually done from ankle to ankle and/or from wrist to wrist, running it from wrist to ankle can be an amusing variant.

The Super-spread-eagle. This technique can create an amazing degree of immobility. To apply it, put the bottom in a spread-eagle tie, possibly using cuffs that have O-rings or D-rings attached or threaded through them. (Attached would probably work better.) Next, apply ankle-to-ankle and wrist-to-wrist ropes to create the double-spread-eagle effect. Finally, run ropes from wrist-to-ankle on both sides of the bottom's body. Applied properly, this technique pins the bottom's wrists and ankles very firmly in very particular spots, thus making it very hard for them to move.

FACIAL BONDAGE

**LINDFOLDS.** A blindfold is not, strictly speaking, a bondage device in and of itself. It certainly does not limit the bottom's ability to move. However, a lot of bondage has to do with increasing vulnerability, and a blindfolded person is certainly much more vulnerable than an unblindfolded person.

A typical blindfold has two components, the eye covering and the head strap. Eye coverings can be fashioned from washcloths, foam rubber, fur, or other materials. Head straps can be made of leather, rope, elastic bandages, and similar materials. I've even seen various types of goggles and swimming masks whose faceplates were painted black or covered with tape used as blindfolds. (Actually, those can work pretty well.) A good blindfold should block the bottom's vision as completely as possible, but should not put pressure directly on the eyes.

It is challenging to completely blindfold a bottom by using only improvised materials. In particular, the areas just to the side of the bottom's upper nose can be hard to block.

Also, bottoms can sometimes escape from blindfolds without too much difficulty. This is particularly true if they can rub the head strap against something such as a wall, the bed's mattress, or even their own shoulder.

Many SM supply stores and erotic boutiques sell blindfolds. In addition, places like drugstores and travel supply stores sell "sleep masks" that often work very well. I have a "Bucky" brand of sleep mask that I bought at my local travel store. While it's significantly more expensive than most other sleep masks, it is well made, very comfortable to wear (it features a soft inner ridge that keeps pressure off of my eyes), and comes in very handy during my afternoon naps. It even has a small compartment for storing earplugs.

Eye patches can also make excellent blindfolds. One top I know likes to use the adhesive-bandage type of eye patches that are sold in drugstores. Such patches are relatively inexpensive and allow some light through, but entirely obstruct the bottom's vision.

It's usually best to wait until at least your second or third play date with a new partner before using a blindfold as part of your SM play. During those early sessions, when you're still getting to know one another, the top needs as much feedback as they can get from the bottom, and their facial expressions are one important source of such feedback. Also, an unblindfolded bottom is somewhat less vulnerable to unethical behavior by a top. (I have a case report of an unethical – to say the least – top who promised that he would not videotape their SM play, then blindfolded the bottom and promptly broke that promise. Last I heard, lawyers were involved.)

"This degree of vulnerability is just fascinating."

Caution: Our vision is one of three systems that our body uses to maintain our balance. A blindfolded bottom cannot see and has lost one of their three "maintain balance" systems. They are therefore at increased risk for falling. (Remember, falls are the single most common cause of serious bondage-related injuries.) If you blindfold a bottom, first position them in such a way that they are unlikely to fall. If you must move a blindfolded bottom, stay very close to them, preferably with at least one hand touching them, so that you can instantly steady them if they start to lose their balance.

Bottoms react in various ways to being blindfolded. Male bottoms may find blindfolds frustrating because they often strongly want to see what is going on. Some bottoms react with increased anxiety to being blindfolded. This can sometimes build to a panic reaction. Other bottoms love being blindfolded and drift away into an altered state of consciousness.

Some bottoms can only begin to feel truly submissive if they are blindfolded.

When one of our senses is blunted, our other senses do not become sharper, but we tend to pay closer attention to them. Thus, if they cannot see, many bottoms experience what they hear, smell, taste, and (of course) feel more intensely.

While the image of a bound, gagged, and blindfolded bottom is often seen in the movies, on TV, and in magazines, this is a fairly extensive degree of bondage that it's usually best to work up to. For example, I recommend that you do at least one session in which the bottom is only gagged, and then at least one session in which the bottom is only blindfolded, before you and they attempt a session in which the bottom is both blindfolded and gagged. Remember that increasing the intensity of the SM play too quickly is a common mistake made by inept tops, and the cause of many panic reactions.

GAGS

When considering the subject of gags, it can be useful to look at it in terms of "who, what, where, when, why, and how." Actually, for our purposes, an approach of "who, what, why, where, when, and how" might be more logical.

As to the "who" of being gagged, I would hope that the answer is fairly obvious: the bottom.

As to the "what," "where," and "why" questions, my dictionary defines the word "gag" (when used as a noun) as "Something thrust into the mouth to prevent speech or outcry." While we can go into nuances later, that pretty well basically sums up those points.

Regarding the question of when to gag a bottom, or when a bottom should let themselves be gagged, my basic rule is "not on the first play date." When a top and a bottom are just beginning to get to know each other, it is best for there to be as many channels of communication open as possible. Given that the first BDSM playdate between two people is probably the one most likely to go wrong, both players benefit from the verbal feedback allowed by unhindered speech. If the first one (or two, or three) play dates go well, then the risk level of a misunderstanding caused by the use of a gag is greatly decreased for future play dates.

(Again, while other experienced sadomasochists have different approaches, my own personal basic rule when bottoming to a top for the first time is that I will let them tie my hands behind me, but I will not let them gag me, blindfold me, bind my legs in any way, or let them tie me to any fixed object such as a bed or chair. In all my years of practicing SM, there was only one occasion when I was glad that I took this admittedly go-slow approach, but on that one occasion I was very, very glad that I had done so.)

Regarding the "how" of gagging someone...

The first thing I should make clear is that the decision to use a gag as part of your bondage play is automatically and unavoidably a decision to increase the play's risk level. The use of a gag inherently increases how vulnerable the bottom is to the top (such increased vulnerability is part of the arousal for many bondage fans) and can in and of itself be hazardous. As always, it's a matter of "what risk level do you feel comfortable with?"

(Intoxicant usage always increases the risk level. I would put a gagged, intoxicated bottom in the "extreme risk" category.)

Second, given the nature of how a human body makes sound, understand that a top will never be able to silence a bottom entirely. Given that many humming-type sounds can be made by a bottom's vibrating vocal cords (which are down in their throat) even if their mouths are entirely filled, totally silencing a bottom is essentially impossible. (Even coating their neck with layers of sound-absorbing cloth will not significantly help here.)

Third, it is actually fairly difficult to gag a bottom in a way that they cannot eventually defeat if they really want to. The muscles of the neck, lower face, jaw, and tongue are fairly strong and allow a great deal of highly coordinated movement. Thus a bottom is frequently able to spit out a gag unless it is applied with a fair amount of sophistication. Tops, don't be too surprised if your first few attempts to gag a given bottom fail. Of course, you should get better with practice.

Let's look at all the "awful truths" first, and then we'll look at how to avoid these matters and make our gag play be both as exciting and as safe as possible.

A basic gag often consists of something used for mouth-stuffing and something such as a face strap used to hold this mouth stuffing in place. If the mouth stuffing works its way too far into the back of the bottom's throat it can cause death by a number of ways, including (1) blocking the bottom's airway, thus causing death by suffocation, (2) triggering the bottom's gag reflex, thus causing them to vomit into a gagged mouth, or (2) triggering a neurological response (vagal response) in the bottom, thus slowing or even stopping their heart. There have been a number of deaths reported in the forensic pathology literature of people who have died due to one or more of these causes after being gagged.

The obvious solution to this problem is to use mouth stuffing that is attached to the face strap. Under most circumstances, this attachment should make it difficult or impossible for the mouth stuffing to work its way back into the throat to a dangerous degree. If the top decides to use mouth stuffing that is not attached to the face strap, they will need to monitor the bottom much more closely.

Almost all of the gag-related deaths that have been reported in the forensic pathology literature have involved someone who was gagged and then left alone – often by criminals who gagged the victim and then abandoned them. Other such deaths have been reported in self-bondage practitioners. (I was consulted on a death that involved someone who was placed in very restrictive bondage and gagged – whether he did this to himself or had help in doing so was somewhat unclear – and then left alone. Inescapably bound and gagged while alone, he developed a nosebleed. The clotted blood blocked his nose and he suffocated.)

The obvious solution here is to use a gag only in a monitored situation. Once again, we see the crucial importance of the presence of a sympathetic monitor.

Safety Note: I strongly recommend that a gagged bottom who is in a "loosely monitored" situation have their monitoring supplemented by some sort of electronic monitoring device such as those used to monitor babies in their cribs. There are a number of such devices on the market, and they range considerably in price and features. You can buy one-way-transmission monitors or two-way-transmission monitors (a nice touch). You can also buy monitors that have improved privacy features – they are, after all, small transmitting radios and are widely sold, so you don't want to either entertain or alarm any neighbors who have similar units. You can buy monitors that sound an alarm if the person being monitored (infant or bottom) hasn't moved for twenty seconds – as happens in "stopped breathing" cases. You can buy monitors that use a small video camera and monitor. Some of these video monitors even have an infrared light feature that allows you to see the person on the screen even while the room is dark. (I hope it goes without saying that you should not actually tape the session unless you have the bottom's express permission.) Spending some time looking over the various types of "nursery monitors" on the market can be very educational.

Plus, you may be able to adapt some of your existing equipment. For example, the cordless phone that lives by my side of the bed has an intercom mode that allows the top to carry the handset quite some distance away about fifty yards) and still communicate with a bottom tied to the bed by use of a speaker and microphone built into the base portion.

Gags can cause lesser problems as well. For one thing, any foreign body placed in the bottom's mouth will cause them to salivate. It can be difficult to swallow saliva (or anything else) if you cannot bring your teeth closely together. (To test this for yourself, put one or two fingers in between your teeth and try it.) Thus, if the bottom cannot swallow this saliva, they may either have to hope that the mouth stuffing is made of some absorbent material or to let it run out of their mouth – which they may find humiliating. (How the bottom feels about this humiliation will, of course, vary.)

For another, if the bottom's jaws are forced too far apart for too long they can suffer muscle strains, sprains of the tendons and ligaments in their jaw area, damage to their temporomandibular joint, or even, in the most extreme cases, dislocation and/or fracture of the jaw bone (the mandible) itself. Finally, although this is unlikely to cause major problems under the two-hour-maximum bondage parameter outlined in this book, it should be noted that a gagged bottom will find it very difficult or impossible to eat or drink while the gag is in place.

Additionally, given that a gagged bottom may only be able to breathe through their nose, their nose should be clear. If the bottom has any sort of runny nose, it may be best to defer using a gag until another time. Some bottoms take a spray or two of nasal decongestant beforehand as a "just in case" measure if they know they are to be gagged.

Finally, every now and then a gag will unexpectedly trigger a panic reaction in a bottom. This may come as a complete surprise to both the top and the bottom. Sometimes a bottom who can handle very extensive, very extreme types of bondage just simply can't handle one particular type of it. Sometimes a bottom will be able to handle different types of bondage individually but can't handle them in combination. Tops (and bottoms) need to keep in mind that every now and then completely unforeseeable panic reactions happen, and be ready to deal with them.

A top should keep in mind that some type of emergency may arise that may make it necessary to remove a bottom's gag within a few seconds. This could be especially important if the bottom suddenly became nauseated and needed to throw up. One thing I learned during my days of working on an ambulance is that when a patient says "I need to throw up" they don't mean within five to ten minutes – they are much more likely to mean within five to ten seconds.

(Safety precaution: While the need to vomit may become irresistible within a few seconds after it is first felt, this is usually preceded by a much longer period of time in which the person feels increasingly strong feelings of nausea. This being the case, it is vitally important that gagged bottoms (and bottoms in general) alert their tops sooner rather than later regarding any feelings of nausea they may be developing.)

One final problem with a gag is that the bottom will often find it difficult or even impossible to use conventional SM safewords. Thus, the top will have to provide the bottom with some effective alternative means of communicating. While some people use hand or finger signals (a bottom's dropping a ball placed in their hand is a time-honored non-verbal safeword) these can be difficult to do if the bottom is lying with their hands tied behind their back. I have done a fair amount of experimentation with alternative signaling methods and, after trying a number of different methods, I have come to prefer audible signals such as two loud grunts. Among other things, such grunts can be heard in the dark.

Types of Gags

- *Ordering the bottom to be silent.* This, of course, often has overtones of psychological domination to it. The top must decide how much silence they want from the bottom. For example, is speech forbidden but non-verbal moans, etc., allowed? What is the penalty for failing to keep silent? How silent is the bottom expected to remain while enduring the various "torments" that the top may choose to inflict upon them?

- *The top's hand.* Simply placing one's hand over a bottom's mouth can make for a reasonably effective gag. This can be done in either a light or a forceful manner, and often adds a nice touch of psychological domination to the scene. (Touching someone on their face is usually an act of affection or domination – or both.) It can involve anything from lightly placing a fingertip on the bottom's lips to roughly covering their mouth with one hand while painfully grabbing the hair on the back of their head with the other hand in order to pin the head in place. Do not overlook the very significant potential of this type of gag.

- *Tape gags.* Gags made of tape, either applied partially over the victim's lower face or wrapped entirely around the head, are commonly shown in various movies and television shows. Unfortunately, tape gags usually do not work very well for our purposes. For one thing, it is essentially impossible to secure the mouth-stuffing to a tape gag. For another, it can be difficult or impossible to remove a tape gag quickly in the event of an emergency (at least, without risking seriously hurting the bottom). Additionally, when tape is removed it often leaves a distinctly telltale band of reddened skin behind (and, if wrapped entirely around the head, will leave adhesive in the hair, where it can be a real nuisance to remove). Given these realities, I do not recommend the use of tape as a gag.

• *Ball gags.* The ball gag has been seen in a number of movies and television shows. In its simplest form, it is merely a rubber ball (often red in color) that has had a leather strap pierced through it. This strap, often equipped with a buckle, is then used to secure the gag in place around the bottom's head. (Some such straps have lockable buckles, but for emergency-quick-release reasons I recommend that such buckles not be locked. If the top is worried about the bottom escaping from the gag, it's better that they tie the bottom so that the bottom cannot reach the buckle.)

Ball gags can sometimes work very well. Given that the balls are not very compressible, a top may have to experiment a bit to find the size of ball that is comfortable yet effective for a given submissive. Unfortunately, it's easy for such a ball to be too large or too small.

"I figured out how to tie that."

Also, ball gags may cause the bottom to salivate, and the hard rubber ball will not, of course, absorb this saliva. Thus the hapless bottom may have to let it run down their chin.

• *Panty gags.* One common technique found in female-dominant scenes is for the dominatrix to use her own panties as the gag's mouth-stuffing portion. This can work fairly well, but the caution about attaching the mouth stuffing to the face strap should be remembered. (Some dominant women place their panties inside one of their nylon stockings and use that stocking as a face strap. This can work well provided she remembers that knots tied in nylon stockings can pull so tightly as to become impossible to untie. In such cases, she should tie knots that can be released or be prepared to cut off the stocking.)

- *Inflatable gags.* Some SM stores sell "pump gags" intended to be placed in the bottom's mouth and then inflated. These can be very effective gags, but they are probably the riskiest types of gags on the market and require the very closest of monitoring and communication. While such gags can create just the right amount of mouth stuffing, it is also relatively easy to overinflate them and block off the bottom's airway or trigger their gag reflex. In particular, the use of a pump gag in connection with any sort of hood-type device can be especially hazardous, and I have heard reports of fatalities associated with this combination of devices. I'm not saying don't use them, but stay on "high alert" if you do.

- *Foam-rubber-and-stick gags.* This is actually my personal favorite type of gag. Foam rubber is my preferred and recommended type of mouth-stuffing. It conforms to the shape of the bottom's mouth even if they increase or decrease how widely they have opened their jaws. It also absorbs both sound and saliva very well. Furthermore, it rarely fatigues the bottom's jaw muscles in the way that other, harder forms of mouth stuffing sometimes do.

  To create the mouth stuffing, use a simple piece of foam rubber. (A trip to your local foam rubber store, particularly to look through their "discards" bin, can be lots of fun.) This may be left as a rough, irregular block, or cut to (or purchased as) a more conventional shape such as a cube or cylinder. Just be sure that it has no "loose ends" that might be likely to separate from the main block while in the bottom's mouth. As a rough rule of thumb, the size of the mouth-stuffing block should be about the size of the bottom's fist.

  Some bottoms will be able to bite into foam blocks and leave lasting cuts into the foam from their teeth. They may even nearly bite off substantial sections of the foam; however, the stick generally prevents them from biting all the way through. Fortunately, the low cost and ready availability of foam makes replacing such a damaged foam block fairly simple.

The stick portion can be a metal or wooden bar pierced through the center of the foam block. This stick typically protrudes an inch two beyond the sides of the bottom's head. It is held in place with a strap of some type that runs around the bottom's head. While various types of straps and ropes may work adequately for this, I have had my best results by using slightly stretchable materials such as elastic bandages. For example: a gag made of a short stick threaded through the center of a block of foam rubber and held in place with an elastic bandage often makes a truly excellent gag in terms of its ability to muffle sound without unduly fatiguing the bottom's jaw, yet they often find it impossible to spit out such a gag.

In summary, while the decision to use a gag invariably raises the risk level of the bondage play somewhat, I have found that when the top and the bottom know each other fairly well, and neither is significantly intoxicated, and the gag is being used in a situation that is being at least loosely monitored (preferably with some type of electronic assistance for those times when the top is out of sight range), and the gag can be removed very quickly without damaging the bottom in the event of an emergency, then the overall risk of Something Really Bad happening drops to an almost nonexistent level.

EARPLUGS AND EARMUFFS

In addition to wanting to limit a bottom's ability to see by using blindfolds, many tops wish to limit their bottom's ability to hear by using various types of earplugs and/or earmuffs. (The top can also create an interesting scene by using only the hearing-limiting devices by themselves.) As is true with the use of blindfolds, when one sense is diminished we tend to pay closer attention to the messages being sent to us by the other senses. In an SM context, this is primarily the sense of touch.

Basic anatomy and physiology: While a top can completely block a bottom's ability to see by the skillful application of a blindfold, it is essentially impossible to completely block the bottom's ability to hear. This is because sound is transmitted to the bottom's brain by two different pathways: air conduction and bone conduction. Thus, even if the top were to completely fill the bottom's ear canals with 100% sound-absorbent material, sound would still reach their brain through bone conduction. However, the bottom's ability to hear can still be significantly limited, or otherwise controlled.

The three basic devices used to limit hearing are industrial earmuffs, earplugs, and headphones.

Industrial earmuffs are easy and quick to apply (just don't pinch an earring when applying them) and do a good, basic job of limiting the bottom's ability to hear. While they are not, in general, as good as earplugs in this regard, they still work pretty well. Such earmuffs can be purchased at larger hardware stores.

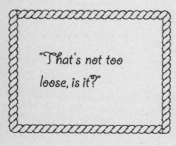

"That's not too loose, is it?"

Earplugs are probably the best devices for limiting hearing. While they are sold in hardware stores, travel supply stores, sporting goods stores, and gun stores, I have usually found the best selection in large drugstores. Most earplugs (and industrial earmuffs) come with what's called an NRR on them. This stands for "noise reduction rating." I recommend that you purchase earplugs with an NRR of at least 30. (These will usually be soft foam earplugs.)

Earplugs also come in various shapes, particularly cylinder-shaped and a type with a widened base that can be thought of as trumpet-shaped. I have found both types of earplugs relatively easy to insert. (It helps to grasp the bottom's ear and gently pull up and back as you insert; this maneuver helps to straighten out the ear canal.) However, I have found the trumpet-shaped earplugs considerably easier to remove.

Headphones. While headphones, of either the earmuff or earplug type, can somewhat limit the bottom's ability to hear, they are more suited to controlling what the bottom can hear. Headphones can, of course, be attached to various types of radios, CD players, and so forth, so that whatever the top wishes the bottom to hear can be "piped in" to them.

Caution: Because the top will usually not be able to hear what the bottom is hearing, it is important to ensure that whatever sound is being piped in to them is not so loud that it causes hearing damage (which can last for a long time or even be permanent.) Thus, it's important for the top to first test out the sound level on the device themselves, perhaps listening to it for about an hour, before using it at that level on a bottom. It is also a wise idea to make sure the volume knob is clearly marked in a way that makes it obvious at a glance if the sound level is turned up too high. Because hearing loss can be long-term and very disabling, bottoms should be advised to use their safeword sooner rather than later if they are distressed by the level of sound to which they are being exposed.

In keeping with the "build up the intensity gradually" approach, it would probably be better to do at least one scene with a bottom using only a blindfold before doing a scene with them that involved both a blindfold and earplugs.

HOODS

"Hoods" is an overall term applied to a group of bondage devices intended to fit over the entire head of the bottom in a fashion similar to the way an astronaut's helmet covers their head. Most hoods are made of leather, but I have also seen them made out of latex and spandex. They are sometimes referred to as "discipline helmets."

Hoods are advanced devices, and their inclusion in this relatively fundamental bondage book was something of a judgment call on my part. However, given that they are likely to be for sale in the same places that my readers might buy their other bondage gear, and given their strong potential for both use and abuse, I decided to include at least some basic information about hoods in this book.

Hoods do offer a significant increase in the inescapability of the bondage. While a bottom may be able to rub off a blindfold, gag, or set of hearing-restricting earmuffs, they are not going to be able to do the same thing to a hood.

The use of a hood in a bondage scene can substantially increase the risk and vulnerability level of the SM play. They often have a powerful emotional effect on both the bottom and the top.

The bottom can be emotionally affected by the very "closed-in" feeling that often accompanies wearing a hood. Some bottoms absolutely love being hooded. It allows them to enter a state of mind that could be accurately thought of as an altered state of consciousness. Other bottoms hate being hooded. Many bottoms who can easily handle being blindfolded, earplugged, and gagged nonetheless cannot stand to be hooded. Panic reactions can result.

I should note that I have occasionally seen "half hoods" offered for sale. These hoods fit over the head of the bottom in a way that covers their ears and eyes but not their nose and mouth. They are somewhat similar to the hoods that hunting falcons wear. Bottoms may find such a hood easier to cope with. A scuba-diving friend also recommends the hoods available in dive shops, which leave the eyes, nose and mouth uncovered, but cover the head, block most hearing, and convey the "closed-in" feeling enjoyed by hood-loving bottoms.

Tops can be emotionally affected by the sight of a hooded bottom in that a bottom wearing such a device has been depersonalized to a significant degree. Under these circumstances, it can be easier for a top to do more extreme things to a bottom than they would otherwise be willing to do. Given this potential, it's pretty obvious that a hood should not be used until a given top and bottom have successfully played together several times before.

Hoods have another property that both tops and bottoms need to be aware of: they can decrease the ability of the bottom to lose body heat to a significant degree. Given the rich blood supply to our scalps, we can radiate 25%-50% of our body heat out into our environment through our head. (Thus the exceptional importance of keeping one's head covered when going into very cold environments.)

Bottoms who have been hooded are more prone to becoming overheated than many tops realize. The discomfort that accompanies this overheating can cause bottoms to want the hood removed, or even to panic, long before they actually become overheated. Contrariwise, if a bottom who is in bondage and hooded begins to panic, they can often be greatly reassured by only removing the hood.

Also, if a nauseated bottom were to throw up into a hood, they could be in an immediately life-threatening situation.

Thus, one of the key points to keep in mind when considering purchasing a hood, perhaps *the* key point, is that a time may come when the bottom's very life will depend upon the top's ability to remove the hood within a matter of seconds.

Hoods are held in place with a variety of devices. Some hoods use zippers. Some use straps and buckles. Some use laces. Some use a combination of devices. Whatever type of hood you choose, make sure that the top can remove it within seconds in the event of an emergency, preferably without having to do something like cut the laces. (If you do have to cut off a hood with your EMT scissors, it may work best to cut from the back of their neck upwards, going between their ears. Try not to cut their hair, but an emergency is an emergency.)

I have seen many hoods that come with various attachment points. In general, these make me somewhat nervous. While I suppose I might feel OK about having a bottom who is lying face-up on a bed having the top of their hood secured to the head of the bed by a length of rope, the idea of a similar arrangement between a standing bottom's helmet and an overhead eyebolt makes me very nervous.

I have also seen arrangements where attachment points on the back of the hood can be used. While I suppose bottoms with healthy necks could stand to have their heads pulled back by such an arrangement, bottoms with a history of neck problems could be at risk. In particular, I feel uncomfortable regarding hogtie arrangements where the bottom's ankles are held in place by a rope or strap running between their tied-together ankles and the back of their head. The more sharply the head is pulled back, the more I worry about this arrangement. (It might actually be safer to attach the strap to their collar.)

In general, I prefer arrangements in which a hooded head is otherwise left free.

One type of hood that bondage fans should be especially wary of is the hood that comes with a built-in inflatable gag. Given the relative lack of communication between the "inside" and the "outside" of such a hood, I have heard of deaths that have resulted from the over-inflation of such a gag.

Some hoods come with detachable blindfold and gag sections that snap on and off. These can add greatly to the versatility of the hood, and I have heard no reports that they are especially easy for the bottom to remove.

Given that hoods tend to be expensive items of bondage gear, if you think that you might enjoy playing with one, you might first try to improvise a hood by using a plain cotton pillowcase. Such a pillowcase should allow adequate breathing (unless large sections of it become wet). Pillowcase hoods can be held in place by placing them under the bottom's collar or by tying a rope in place around the bottom's neck and over the pillowcase. The ends of this rope should be left free and the top should be able to pass two fingers between it and the hood without difficulty. In other words, this rope should be applied no more tightly than a strap intended for this purpose on a real hood would be applied.

In summary, keep in mind that hoods are not trivial items and that there is both significant potential and significant risk associated with their usage. As the saying goes, "hoods are heavy."

BREAST AND GENITAL BONDAGE

BREAST **B**ONDAGE. So, Mr. or Ms. Top, there you are, having a fine old time with a very nice female bottom, and you just happen to notice those lovely breasts of hers. (For the purposes of this essay, I'm going to assume that breasts are those lovely fleshy protuberances that come attached to the front of female chests. However, I'm aware that some people are of the opinion that males also have breasts, and many of my remarks below will be applicable to them as well). You furthermore just happen to have some rope handy. In such a situation, a top could have… thoughts. Thoughts involving breasts, ropes, and the delightfully lascivious combining thereof. What is a top to do in such a situation?

Well, what are the top's options? Ropes can be applied to the bottom's breasts, and to the surrounding tissue, to achieve the following effects:

- *Sensation.* The bottom may enjoy the sensations, particularly the constriction-like sensations, associated with having her breasts bound (or may "enjoy not enjoying" those sensations). The top may enjoy the fact that the bottom is enjoying the sensations, or the top may enjoy the fact that the bottom is "enjoying not enjoying" them.

- *Decoration.* Breast bondage can accent or draw attention to these lovely female secondary sex characteristics.

- *Enhanced appearance.* Some forms of breast bondage can uplift breasts that have become a bit "fallen," and/or cause the breasts to swell to a fuller shape.

- *Immobility.* Some breast bondage can hold the breast tissue in place, thus making it more accessible to whipping, clamping, etc.

Important Health Warning. In BDSM, breast play may at times become very rough indeed. Breasts may be some combination of caressed, pinched, squeezed, slapped, licked, tweaked, clamped, kissed, whipped, bound with ropes, pulled upon, adorned with hot wax, pierced with needles, shocked with electricity, and more.

Therefore…

It is very important that the bottom disclose to the top anything unusual about her breasts before any breast play is begun, and preferably before BDSM play of any sort is begun. (This is one reason of why adequate pre-play negotiations are so crucial.)

For example, if the bottom has breast implants, the top should be informed about this, along with what effect the presence of these implants might have on possible breast play.

Other things that should be disclosed include the presence of any known breast lumps, any history of breast surgery, any extra nipples (yes, some people have more than two), and if the bottom is in a phase of her menstrual cycle that makes her breasts more sensitive than usual. Any other unusual condition about the bottom's breasts should also be disclosed to the top prior to beginning any breast play. If the bottom knows, or can surmise, how this unusual condition might affect or limit the play, she should communicate that as well.

What type of breast bondage is suitable for a given bottom in a given situation will, of course, vary. (These sorts of things always vary.) Factors include the size of the breasts involved, the position that the bottom is in while the bondage is being applied (or afterwards), and what effect the top wishes to create.

Breast constriction bondage. When a top is faced with the sight of an attractive breast while said top is holding a rope, one of the very first desires that such a top might have is the desire to "tie the breast up" – i.e., to simply tie some loops of rope tightly around the breast itself. This can be a fun thing to do and can look very erotic on some women.

However, not all breasts are equally suited for such bondage. In general, larger breasts can often be bound in this way, but smaller breasts often cannot be.

The position the bottom is in while the top is trying to apply such constricting breast bondage can also play a significant role. In general, the position that usually seems to work best is for the bottom to have her torso in an upright position, and perhaps leaning slightly forward. The breasts of a bottom who is lying on her back can be difficult to bind even if she is very large-breasted. On the other hand, if a bottom bends forward at the waist so that her breasts are hanging straight down, sometimes this will allow the top to "capture" enough tissue to do effective breast constriction bondage.

What materials should be used for breast constriction bondage? While ropes in the "standard bondage thickness range" of one-quarter inch to three-eighths of an inch can be used for some types of breast bondage, these thicknesses can be awkward for use in this context. Instead, you might find narrower rope, such as 3/16" rope or 1/8" parachute cord, more useful here.

Also, shorter lengths of rope can be used in this situation. While most bondage seems to go better with lengths of rope that are at least six feet long, lengths of narrow rope that are about three feet long can work very well for constriction breast bondage.

Applying the bondage itself is usually quite easy. One technique that can work well is to simply place the midpoint of the rope at the top of the breast, wrap a turn around the breast in either direction, dress the bondage until it's snug, and tie off in a Surgeon's knot or Obi knot. (These knots seem to hold better than the Square knot in

"Want to try to copy the pictures in this bondage magazine?"

this situation.) Be careful, of course, to avoid pinching any of the bottom's skin in either the wraps or the knot.

(A note to you "knot researchers": I have tried using the Ashley "constrictor knot" in this context, and have generally been unhappy with the results. I personally have consistently had much better results using the Surgeon's knot or the Obi knot.)

How tight should the constriction be? I have found that I can be reliably guided by feedback from the bottom regarding whether the breast constriction feels "good tight" or "bad tight." In general, the top should apply the bondage so that it is tight enough to not fall off and also tight enough to create that "pleasantly unpleasant" constricting sensation, but not so tightly that the breast tissue is actually damaged.

Because constrictive breast bondage may inhibit venous return (the escape of blood from the breast tissue), the breasts may swell somewhat in size and become a bluish or reddish color. This is usually harmless unless it lasts for prolonged periods of time. (Remember that a basic parameter of this book is that no bondage will be left on for longer than two hours. That would include breast bondage.)

Danger signs that the breast bondage has been on for too long or is too tight would be a feeling of tingling or numbness in the breasts, or the appearance of an aching, genuinely unerotic pain in them. If this pain causes the bottom to feel nauseated, it's definitely time to loosen the associated bondage – and possibly all other bondage as well.

Note that breast constriction bondage alone is often not especially secure, particularly if the bottom's torso is moved into a "harder to bind" position after the bondage is applied. For example, if you apply breast constriction bondage to a bottom while her torso is more-or-less vertical, don't be too surprised if it later slips off while her breasts are being jostled as she lies on her back during missionary-position intercourse.

The breasts can be lifted if, after constricting bondage is applied to each breast, that bondage is augmented by taking a length of rope (six feet to twelve feet long, depending on the size of the bottom, the size of her breasts, etc.) and placing the midpoint at the base of the back of her neck. Bring the ends forward over her collarbones and loop them under each breast (looping in the in-to-out direction usually seems

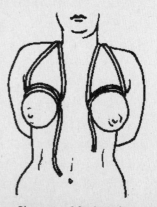

One type of bondage bra

to work better), lifting each breast as you do so. Finish the looping by bring the ropes back up the front of her chest, and tying the rope's ends together at the back of her neck.

This creates one example of a type of "bondage bra" that lifts the breasts and holds them more stationary than they normally are. Details regarding your possible plans for the breasts thus presented are, somewhat unfortunately, beyond the scope of this book – although I did provide some strong hints at the start of this chapter. (See "SM 101" and other such books for more specific information.)

Caution: Breast bondage techniques that cause the breast tissue to become less able to move, including most if not all of the techniques presented in this chapter, usually cause no particular problems in and of themselves. However, there would be at least some danger of serious injury to bound breasts if the bottom were to be placed in a face-down position in which the weight of her torso is compressing her immobilized breasts.

Therefore, if you are considering moving a woman with bound breasts into a face-down position, please do so very slowly and carefully, with good communication in place between the two of you. Be ready to move her instantly out of this position if the weight of her body upon her breasts causes her to feel "bad pain." This advisory also applies if you do anything to increase the pressure on her bound breasts, such as lying on top of her as she lies face-down with her breasts bound.

"Double-bound" breasts. This can be a fun technique to apply to larger breasts. In this technique, the rope is wrapped around both breasts at the same time and they are drawn together, like a pair of wrists or ankles. The rope is then snugly dressed and knotted. A Square knot, Surgeon's knot, or Obi knot can work well here.

The "Over and Under" breast tie. This type of breast bondage technique can work well on both larger and smaller breasts, including some men's breasts. A rope about eighteen feet long can be useful here. Simply run the ropes around the bottom's torso so that they pass both under and over her breasts. Her upper arms may be included or excluded from the wrapping turns, at the top's discretion.

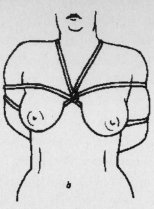

One example of how to apply this bondage technique would be to place the midpoint of an eighteen-foot rope on the center of the bottom's chest, just above her breasts. Wind the rope around the sides of her chest, across her back, and bring them together in front of her chest, just above the breasts. Now cross the rope (either with a simple overlap or by twisting it back upon itself) run the ends under her breasts, and once again wrap

one style of over & under breast bondage

the rope around her torso. Bring the two free ends once again back to the front, dress the entire bondage, and tie the ends together. A Surgeon's knot can work well here.

If you have a bit of rope left over in the free ends, the lower ropes can be joined to the upper ropes at the center of the chest. An Ending Lark's Head knot works well for this.

Note: In accordance with the "keep the knots away from their fingers" principle, if the bottom's hands are to be tied behind her back, then the final knot of this tie should be in the front of her chest.

The risk level associated with bondage that significantly constricts the bottom's upper torso is often increased if the bottom also has ropes tightly wound around their upper abdomen and/or if the bottom is lying on their stomach.

If this type of tightness is going to become a problem, it will usually become a problem over a somewhat prolonged period of time. Thus, there is almost always adequate time to loosen the bondage before it becomes seriously threatening – provided that the bottom is being adequately monitored.

Breast constriction can be added to this breast bondage by taking two additional short lengths of rope, and tying each of them to the encircling chest loops between the outer side of the breast and the arm. (The Starting Lark's Head knot works well here.) Apply the Starting Lark's Head, then slide it towards the midline of the chest, constricting the breast as you go. (Be very careful not to pinch any skin!) Compress the breast tissue as much as seems appropriate, then pull the free ends under the breast and tie them off.

Note: "Rope Purists" might want to use a Prussick knot here instead of a Starting Lark's Head.

*Major Caution:*Ropes that have been tightly wound around the bottom's upper torso, particularly low-stretch ropes, can limit the ability of the bottom's chest wall to expand, and thus hinder their ability to breathe. Under most circumstances, mild to moderate constriction of this type is not much of a problem. However, severe constriction of this type could be dangerous, even life-threatening.

These are only a few of the more common types of breast bondage. With several different lengths and thicknesses of ropes, and an amenable bottom, all sort of variations are possible. Have fun exploring!

GENITAL BONDAGE

Given that most BDSM play is, if not outright sexual, then usually done in an erotic context, it is quite understandable that the top might wish to bind the bottom's genitals in some fashion. (The bottom may also wish for the top to do this.) It is very common that, once the bottom's wrists and ankles are secured, the top then turns their attention to securing the bottom's genitals.

Binding someone's genitals is, to say the least, a highly personal, intimate thing to do. Such binding can make a very direct statement of the degree of power and control the top has over the bottom. Binding the genitals can add a substantial degree of erotic intensity, can in some cases greatly increase the intensity of the orgasm the bottom feels, and can greatly increase the security of the bondage. It can thus have a powerful emotional effect on both the top and the bottom.

MALE GENITAL BONDAGE

When binding the male bottom's genitals, the top usually needs to make a few decisions beforehand, particularly regarding the bottom's penis.

In particular, the top needs to decide how much access they will want to the bottom's penis (and with what parts of their own body). Does the top want the bottom to be capable of erection? Ejaculation? Does the top intend to masturbate or fellate the bottom, or use the bottom's penis for their own pleasure during vaginal or anal intercourse?

"I love watching you squirm around like that."

Types of Rope. Male genital bondage can be done effectively with conventional-sized rope, but many bondage fans prefer using smaller-diameter rope. Rope that is 3/16" wide is popular, and 1/8" wide parachute cord is very popular. Parachute cord that has had its core removed can work deviously wonderfully for male genital bondage. Bootlaces made of leather or nylon are also popular for male genital bondage. In most cases, it's wise to start with a length of rope that is about six feet long.

A lot of male genital bondage is something of a variant on what's called a cock ring, so we bondage fans should have at least a basic understanding of what a cock ring does.

A basic cock ring is a ring that is looped snugly around both the bottom's penis and his testicles. Many such rings are made of metal, in which case first one testicle is threaded through the ring, followed by the other, and finally by the (flaccid) penis, which is then aroused to an erect state. The idea here is to limit the flow of venous blood away from the bottom's penis, resulting in a firmer erection. While many such rings are made of metal, they are also sometimes made of leather (with snaps that allow good adjustment of the tightness) or of rubber or some other flexible material – including, of course, rope.

An additional benefit – indeed, from the top's viewpoint, possibly the major benefit – is that such a ring often pins the skin over the penis very tightly into place. This "immobilized" skin is frequently more sensitive to touch. In fact, touching it with hands can actually be painful if the area is not first lubricated. (When doing any type of male genital bondage, it usually works better to first apply the bondage and then apply the lube.)

To apply a basic bondage cock ring, the top simply winds several turns of rope firmly above the top of the bottom's penis and scrotum, often starting with the midpoint behind the scrotum and working out towards the ends, and ties the ends in place. Depending on how firmly this is done, the result can range from merely providing decoration to providing very firm or even painful pressure. I've found that it usually works best to apply the genital bondage tightly enough so that it's slightly challenging to endure.

An alternative application is to wind the coils of rope around the top of the scrotum only, leaving the penis entirely out of it. Such bondage can immobilize the testicles and present them nicely for further attention, although this technique sometimes tightens the scrotal skin to the point where clamps cannot be then applied. This bondage can merely imprison the testicles, or it can be gradually wound on so that the testicles are pressed more and more tightly within the scrotum, thus creating an interesting sensation. Note: to avoid lasting damage to the bottom, this bondage should be applied slowly and with feedback. If the bottom starts to become nauseated, or otherwise starts to experience genuine distress, it's time to loosen the bondage.

Yet another application is to first wind a few coils above both the penis and scrotum, and then wind a few coils around just the scrotum itself. If you do this, you may find it helpful to lift the penis fully upright as you pass the ropes just below it. This will prevent a frequently unwanted and often painful pinning of the skin just under the front of the penis, allowing the bottom to have a more unhindered, normal erection.

A final, classic cock and balls bondage technique is often applied as follows. You will need about a six-foot length of relatively narrow rope. While it's possible to apply this bondage to a male bottom who is in virtually any position, it usually goes on more easily if his torso is upright and his legs are slightly spread, such as when he is standing upright.

Place the midpoint of the rope on the upper, rear wall of his scrotum, then wind the tails forward in opposite directions above both his penis and scrotum, returning the tails to where you started from. Now repeat these winding turns forward, this time running below the penis and firmly

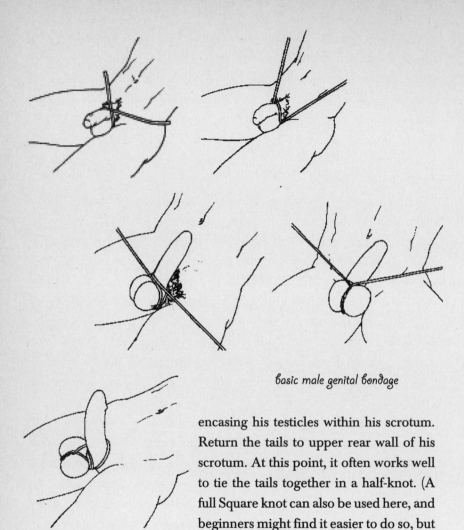

basic male genital bondage

encasing his testicles within his scrotum. Return the tails to upper rear wall of his scrotum. At this point, it often works well to tie the tails together in a half-knot. (A full Square knot can also be used here, and beginners might find it easier to do so, but if you use such a knot be advised that untying it later might be a bit difficult.)

Here's where it gets really interesting: Having secured the tails together at the upper, rear wall of his scrotum, twist them together – applying roughly one to two twists per inch of rope – as you bring the tails forward along the midline of his testicles, raising the rope as you go to slightly separate his testicles. When you reach the front of his scrotum, separate the ends, wind them firmly around the top of his scrotum until you run out of rope, and you're finished. The finished result is an emphatic binding of the male genitals that can create a very strong effect, both physically and emotionally.

A few facts regarding male genital bondage. Remember that the penis has a tube that runs down its length called the urethra. Bondage applied to the penis may either partially or completely constrict the urethra. If the urethra is partially constricted, the flow of semen (or urine) through it will be hindered. This partial constriction often results in a more intense orgasm for the male bottom. If the urethra is fully constricted and he is brought to orgasm, he will have what is called a "retrograde ejaculation" in which his semen travels back up into his bladder instead of out through his penis. An occasional retrograde ejaculation is not typically associated with lasting harm to the man in question, but I suggest moderation in this practice.

The male genitals provide an obvious anchor point for many bondage techniques, and it can be great fun for both parties to employ them in this way. However, it's especially important to keep the "what if they faint? what if they fall?" saying in mind. For this reason, I suggest that you only use male genital bondage that would not result in severe injury to the bottom if they were to faint or fall. For example, tying a bottom's scrotum to a doorknob by a short length of rope would be an extremely risky technique.

Also, it would be important to keep your EMT scissors handy so that the rope running from the genitals could be cut quickly in the event of an emergency. For obvious reasons, this is one situation in which the use of (more precisely controllable) scissors is preferred to the use of a knife.

A leash can be attached to a male bottom's genitals and used in a very attention-getting manner.

Binding the penis. Binding the shaft of the penis itself can create a very intense experience for the bottom. The classic way in which this is done is to wrap turns of rope around the shaft of the penis while it is in a flaccid state. For starters, this is often done with two short ropes, with one such winding just at the base of the penis and another just after the head of the penis.

A effective variant of this is to use a slightly longer rope for the scrotal bondage techniques described above. When one of those techniques is applied, several inches of rope will be "left over" in each tail. These tails can be crossed and wound around the penis in opposite directions and tied off. The result is a tightly bound, flaccid penis. (Sometimes keeping the penis flaccid while this bondage is being applied can be a bit of a challenge.) One extra benefit of this bondage technique is that the penis section of it can be removed later while still leaving the scrotal section in place.

As the bottom becomes aroused and blood flows into his penis, it swells and begins to press painfully against the interior of its bondage. Thus the bottom's own sexual arousal is used to cause him pain – a very devious situation. If this process is helped along by the erotic touch of the hand or mouth of the top, the bottom can be in – OK, I'll say it – a real double-bind.

Caution: While fairly strong bondage can often be wound around the shaft of the penis without causing significant damage, bondage that puts significant traction along the lengthwise axis of the penis – either suddenly or gradually – can be genuinely dangerous. Strong traction in that direction can either damage the ligament that attaches the penis to the pubic bone, or can damage the soft tissues of the penis itself. This is another good situation to consider the "what if they faint?/what if they fall?" questions.

FEMALE GENITAL BONDAGE

Given that the female genitals lack the obvious anchor points that the male genitals have, binding them can be somewhat trickier, and often does not really add that much to the immobility of the bondage. Still, when one is binding a tasty female, the temptation to run some ropes down towards or through her crotch area, possibly with a knot tightly pressed against her clitoris, can be very strong indeed, and the

basic female genital bondage

sensations thus created can have a powerful effect on both of you.

One simple but effective technique calls for a twelve-foot length of rope. This technique works better on a woman whose waist is significantly narrower than her hips. To apply it, simply press the midpoint of the rope on her lower abdomen just above the crests of her hipbones. Firmly wind the tails of the rope in opposite directions around her waist, just above her hipbones. When you get to the rear of her hipbones, run both ends down and through her crotch (either between the labia or on either side of the vulva, depending on your future plans), then bring each end back up towards the same hip that it started from. Pull these ropes tight, then wind them firmly around her waist until the tails meet and tie the tails together in a finishing knot.

The Lana White Female Genital Harness. This harness was taught to me many years ago by another bondage enthusiast: San Francisco Bay Area professional dominatrix (now retired) Mistress Lana White. It also

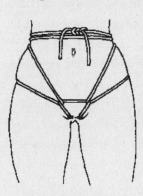

involves a twelve-foot length of rope. To apply this technique, bight the rope, and run the bighted end through her labia in a back-to-front direction. Finish with the arch of the bight about three inches in front of her vagina. (If she is in a standing position, she or someone else may have to briefly hold this in place.) Bring the tails back up over her butt cheeks and across the top of her hipbones, and pass the tails through the arch, preferably in an in-to-out direction. Finish the bondage by pulling each tail back towards the top of its respective hip, thus separating her labia and

Lana White female genital harness

exposing her clitoris. As Lana said when she taught this to me, "That gets her attention." Wind the tails around her waist until the tips meet, and tie them off in a finishing knot.

Either of these techniques may make vaginal or anal intercourse essentially impossible; thus, it is usually wise to remove them before attempting either activity.

Mini-harnesses

For those of you who want something a bit more than just genital-only bondage but something a bit less than a full body harness, here are a few mini-harnesses.

Waist-strap female mini-harness. This technique typically takes about a twelve-foot length of rope.

"I bought this great rope remnant at the climbing store!"

To apply it, position the midpoint of the rope at the small of her back and wind the tails around her waist in opposite directions until they meet on the lower front of her abdomen. Pull the tails until they are narrower than her hips and tie them together – a Surgeon's knot works well here. Now run the two tails together down and between her inner labia. (If you're feeling impish, you can tie the tails together in one or more Overhand knots or Figure-eight knots just at the point where they pass over her clitoris. You might also want to tie them a bit higher up than you think they'll need to be, because pulling the ropes snug – as will happen later – will frequently pull the knots a bit lower than you originally thought they'd be.)

Continue to run the tails together between her labia and over her anus – thus sealing in anything that you might have previously inserted into either orifice – and pass the tails over the rear of the waist loop. (I recommend using the inside-to-outside direction.) Pull this rope very snugly, then run the tails back down through her butt cheeks and through her crotch again. For variety's sake, I suggest that as you come back through you run the tails just outside of her outer labia. As you did in back, run the tails under the front of the waist loop, again in an inside-to-outside direction, and pull them snug. Separate the ends, then tuck them under the ropes coming up from her crotch in opposite directions to create two opposing ends. Tie those final ends together, typically using a Finishing Lark's Head knot, and you're done.

This creates a tie that can produce a strong, constant sensation on her genital and anal area. As I mentioned, it can also seal inside anything you have previously placed into either orifice. Finally, it is also possible to now tuck a smallish vibrator between the ropes and her genitals, where the pressures can hold it snugly in place. (Alternatively, you can tuck such a vibrator in place and tie it into position with another piece of rope.)

A further potential benefit of this tie is that the area on her back where the crotch ropes pass over the waist rope offer a potential attachment point for helping to secure her wrists and/or other parts of her body in place, or for attaching her to some object.

A somewhat quicker-to-apply variant of this technique involves bighting the rope and applying a Lark's Head knot around her waist, then proceeding in the usual way.

While this tie does pretty much seal off her vagina and anus for much in the way of further play, particularly play that would involve penetration, it can otherwise be a very effective bondage technique.

Waist-strap male mini-harness. This technique also typically calls for a twelve-foot length of rope and is applied in almost exactly the same manner as the female body harness.

The main difference is as the crotch ropes make their "initial descent" after the waist loop is applied, they are wrapped around the male's genitals. These wraps can encircle both the cock and balls, or merely the balls. Caution: It is usually best to apply this tie with the male in a standing position and with his legs slightly together. If his legs are widely spread his testicles could be pulled in between his legs in such a way that they could be injured if his legs are brought together. Once these wrapping turns are applied, the tie proceeds as with the female version. If the top wishes, the wrapping turns can be repeated as the crotch ropes return on their back-to-front journey.

A simple but surprisingly powerful variant can be done by tying a waist rope in place, then winding the midpoint of a second rope around

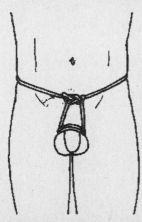

male mini-harness

his genitals a few times and pulling the tails back through his butt cheeks and tying them in place at the rear with a Finishing Lark's head.

BODY HARNESSES

The Lana White Male Body Harness. This technique was in danger of being lost, so it is my privilege to describe it here. This technique may seem a bit complicated, but it is actually rather quickly learned with a bit of practice. Depending on the size of the man, either an 18-foot or a 24-foot length of rope is needed.

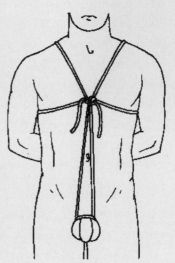

To apply this body harness, it usually works best to start with the male bottom standing in front of you. Bight the rope and apply the midpoint to the upper posterior wall of his scrotum. Bring the tails forward and cross them on his pubic bone, just above his penis, then continue to wind them around the top of his scrotum and pull the tails back through his legs.

Have him place his legs somewhat close together to prevent his testicles from being pulled back in between his legs. Now move behind him or have him turn around, then pull the tails firmly up through his butt cheeks (thus helping to seal in place any item previously inserted there). Then bring the tails up his back and drop each tail over his corresponding shoulder, just beside his neck.

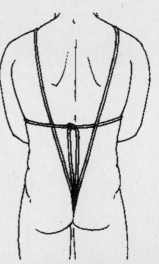

At this point, either move around to the front of him or turn him to face you. Cross the tails and run them in opposite directions under each armpit, then either

Lana White harness, front & back

move behind him or have him turn, and bring the two tails together. (This may produce a bit of pressure near where his neck meets his shoulders, but should not put any pressure actually on his neck.) Dress the rope snugly, then tie the tails together in a Square knot or Surgeon's knot.

Now run the tails back down between his butt cheeks in a very snug manner. (This will typically result in the freshly knotted section being pulled down several inches, but that is not usually a concern and often helps to further secure the harness). Move to the front of him or have him turn, and run the tails up along either side of his scrotum, continuing up the front of his abdomen and lower chest until you reach the "X" formed by the earlier rope crossing. Run the tail under the "X" and bring them out the top, then bring the tails back down onto his abdomen. Dress the entire harness very snugly at this point, adjusting as necessary. You may need to move the ropes so that they don't obstruct your access to his nipples. Once the harness is fully dressed, tuck the tails in opposite directions under the ropes just below the "X" to create two opposing ends, tie them off, and you're done.

The result is an interesting combination of genital bondage and body harness. The genital bondage can act as a quite serviceable cock ring. The rest of the body harness helps hold items inserted into the rectum in place, and significantly limits the range of motion that is (comfortably) possible for the male torso. In particular, bending forward, lateral bending, and lateral twisting can all increase the intensity of the harness. Additionally, the harness can serve as a point of attachment for further bondage. The knot on the bottom's upper back and the "X" on the front of his chest can be particularly useful in this regard.

There are a number of variants possible with this harness.

First, the initial genital wrapping can be done only with the scrotum. This variant leaves the penis freer.

Second, the initial genital wrapping can be done with two wrapping turns of both the penis and scrotum, followed by two wrappings of just the scrotum itself, thus increasing the intensity of this tie.

Third, as the tails are run up his back for the first time, a Figure-eight knot can be tied in the tails just below where the knot on his upper back will be. When this Figure-eight knot is tied, the tails can go on to be knotted together in the usual fashion and then "tucked inside" the top of this Figure-eight knot before they are run back down towards his buttocks. This can result in an even more secure harness.

The Lana White Female Body Harness. Note that, depending on the size of the woman, this harness may call for a somewhat longer rope.

To apply the basic female variant, place the midpoint of the rope at the small of her back, then run the tails around her waist. Pull the tails so that they are narrower than the width of her pelvis and knot them together. You can then proceed to apply the harness in the usual manner (omitting the male genital wraps, of course).

A somewhat more intense female variant of this harness can be applied by placing the midpoint of the rope on the front of her abdomen, just above her hips, and winding the tails in opposite directions around her lower waist, pulling snugly as you go. When the tails return to the front of her abdomen, run them diagonally down the front of her lower abdomen and then either on the outside or the inside of her labia. Continue to apply the tie in the normal fashion.

ARM AND LEG HARNESSES

ARM HARNESSES. In tying the bottom's wrists together behind their back, it is often very wise to further immobilize their arms. As is sometimes all-too-obvious, a bottom whose wrists are only tied together behind their back may still have a very great deal of movement available to their bound arms. It's my experience that if a bottom has only their wrists tied together with rope behind their back, they will almost undoubtedly be able to free themselves within a relatively small number of minutes, provided that:

- The bondage is not tied so tightly that it is dangerously tight.

- The bottom has a fair amount of movement possible in their elbow and shoulder joints. (Slender, flexible submissives whose wrists are tied together behind them but whose arms are not otherwise restrained may even be able to do things like check their e-mail and fix a meal.)

- The bottom is willing to lose a little bit of epidermis in their squirming to get loose.

In the process of researching this book, I bound a fairly large number of people and then watched them carefully as they attempted to free themselves. The results were illuminating (and the process was fun).

My basic conclusion was that the more movement a bound body part was capable of, the more likely it was to free itself from the bondage. In the case of young, strong, flexible bottoms who had their wrists bound together behind their back but whose arms were not otherwise restrained, they could often free themselves relatively quickly. (This was particularly true if they had gained some practice and experience in this regard.)

So, after a fair amount of experimentation, I came up with the saying "If you want their wrists to stay tied together behind their back, you're going to have to do something about their elbows."

Basically, the more you can limit the range of motion of their elbow joints (and shoulder joints), the more likely their wrists are to remain tied together behind their back.

The simplest way to immobilize their elbows is, of course, to simply tie them together behind their back. This is an elegant solution because it is an especially secure bondage technique. There is no way that they are going to reach the rope binding their elbows together with a finger, toe, or tooth. (OK, maybe a toe if they are really flexible, but I wish them lots of luck.)

However, as we already discussed, binding their elbows together is rarely a viable option. Many bottoms can't have their elbows brought together behind their back at all. Usually it's only very slender, flexible bottoms who can endure having their elbows tied together behind their back for any significant length of time without dangerously compressing both the nerves and blood vessels in their upper arms and also causing them severe pain.

Furthermore, even if the bottom can handle having their elbows tied together behind their back, this bondage position can be very limiting. It often seriously interferes with access to their buttocks for activities such as spanking, and only a very small percentage of bottoms can endure lying on their back while their elbows are tied together. We clearly need a different approach.

Listed below are eight different "arm harnesses" with their applications and characteristics. In the first seven of the eight cases, it is assumed that the top has started the bondage by binding the bottom's wrists together behind their back starting at the midpoint of the rope and working outward towards the tails.

Note: given that bottoms vary considerably, it is probable that some of the harnesses listed below will work relatively well and some will work relatively poorly on a particular bottom. It is important to experiment.

Arm harness #1: The Simple Waist Loop Harness. This technique typically uses a twelve-foot length of rope. It is perhaps the simplest arm harness of all, and yet is often both very effective and very comfortable. To apply it, the top ties the bottom's wrists together (usually in the anti-parallel position in the small of their back) and then simply brings the tails around to the front of the bottom's torso and ties them together there.

It is very important that this waist loop be tied fairly snugly. (Tying the tails together with a Surgeon's knot can work particularly well here.) In particular, the waist loop must be pulled tightly enough so that it is narrower than the bottom's pelvis. This will prevent the bottom from simply sliding the waist loop off as if it were a pair of pants.

Caution: Because the waist loop is tied relatively tightly around the bottom's lower torso, there is at least the hypothetical possibility that it could interfere with their breathing. I have never actually encountered this problem, nor have I ever heard of it actually happening but, at least in theory, the risk is there. If it does occur, the top should be able to correct it long before it becomes a serious problem.

If this technique is applied using a twelve-foot length of rope, typically two tails of somewhere between two to four feet in length will be left over after the technique is applied. A number of things can be done with such tails:

- They can be simply left in place, either dangling freely or tucked under the waist loop.

- If the bottom is male, they can be used to bind his genitals.

- If the tails are long enough, they can be used to bind the bottom's ankles.

- They can be brought back to the wrists and cinch-looped between the bottom's wrists and their back, thus further immobilizing their wrists. (This may leave the final knot in a position where the bottom can reach it, which may or may not be a problem. Of course, even if they can untie this knot, doing so does not affect the basic security of this tie.)

- The tails can be brought up behind the bottom's neck and tied in place there. (Again, even if they can reach and untie this knot, the overall security of the bondage is not seriously affected.)

As an alternative to all of the above, this might be one of the few situations in which using a nine-foot rope, or an even shorter rope, would result in a "cleaner" tie.

Arm harness #2: The "Military" Neck-loop Harness. This technique typically uses about a twelve-foot length of rope. I call it the "military" arm harness because it is a variant on a technique widely taught to military personnel (and to martial artists) as a method of tying enemy prisoners. This is definitely an increased risk technique, but I have found that its actual degree of risk seems to be significantly lower than frequently believed. Still, it does call for alertness and communication on the part of both the top and the bottom. (I know that a number of my readers have been taught, as a standard, basic BDSM teaching, never to tie anything across the front of a bottom's throat. Therefore they may be wondering, and may even feel a bit alarmed, that I have included such a very "politically incorrect" technique in this book, particularly given that I have a reputation within the BDSM community as something of an ultra-safety-conscious person. Let me assure these readers that I haven't lost my mind, and that this inclusion is an intentional, considered action on my part. For more information, please see my essay "The Military Hogtie" on p. 266.)

To apply the technique, the top ties the bottom's wrists behind them using the midsection of the rope, lifts the bottom's wrists so that they are as bent at the elbows as they can be without heavy straining, then runs the tails up and around to the front of the bottom's neck and ties them in place there.

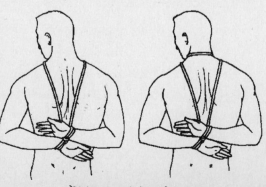

Military neck-loop harness

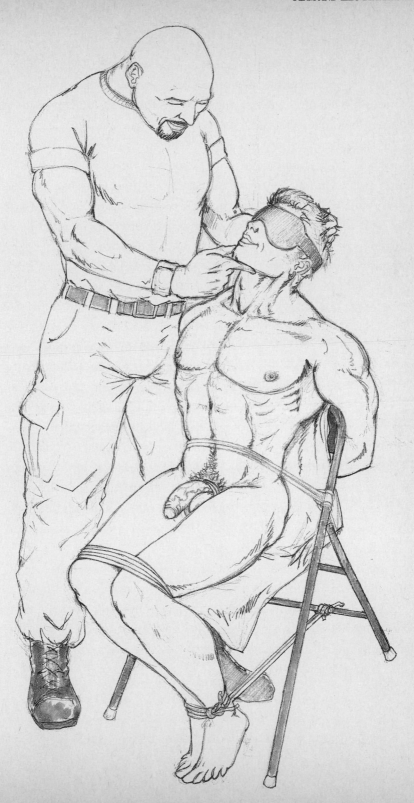

To help avoid cinching constriction, it usually works better to finish the knot, then thread the tails between the wrists so that the tails are between the bottom's wrists and their back. This is a good approach for all hands-behind-the-back arm harnesses.

Provided that the rope running from the bottom's wrists to their neck is not under significant tension (which the bottom will be able to determine almost immediately), and there is no significant pressure applied around the bottom's neck, and provided that there are no sudden, strong tugs on this rope, I have not found this to be a particularly uncomfortable or dangerous tie. This can be especially true if the bottom's wrists are left free, with no rope running down towards their ankles. However, it is a position that discourages struggling because such struggles can cause uncomfortable pressure on the bottom's throat (thus making it a form of what is sometimes called "predicament bondage"). Obviously, any severe struggling could cause an uncomfortable or even dangerous amount of pressure on the bottom's throat.

"I love the feel of nylon rope."

Because some flexible bottoms can lift their wrists and thus cause the neck loop to slip down across one shoulder, or perhaps even down over both shoulders, and thus defeat the basic construction of this harness, some tops will wind the tails a few times around the bottom's neck until they "run out of rope" and then tie off the ends. The ends are usually much less accessible to the bottom if they are tied off in front of the bottom's neck. (As a refinement, a variant of the Obi knot cuff – see the section on single-limb bondage for more information on that knot – is sometimes used as the final knot here.) An alternative approach, for those who wish only a single neck loop while increasing the security of the tie, is to wind the tails running from the wrists to the neck around each other as the bondage is applied.

Arm harness #3: The Politically Correct Arm Harness. For those of you who want most of the security of the Military Neck-loop harness without the potential risks of that tie, this technique, which I've named the "Politically Correct Arm Harness," can work almost as well. It typically takes about an 18-foot length of rope.

To apply this technique, tie the wrists as desired (the anti-parallel position is strongly recommend here) with the midsection, then lift the bottom's wrists as high as you can on their back without causing heavy straining. Thread the tails to prevent cinching constriction, then run the tails up to either side of the bottom's neck and drape them over their shoulders. Cross the tails as high as you can on the bottom's chest, then run the tails back under their arms and over the ropes running from their wrists to their shoulders. Bring the tails back to the front. Tie the tails together at that point, and you're done. This is a symmetrical arm harness that avoids putting pressure anywhere on the bottom's neck.

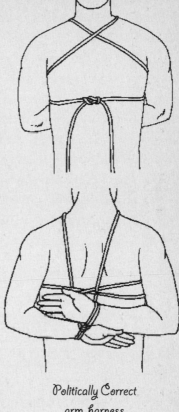

Politically Correct arm harness

Make sure that the final knot is "eel-proof" and that the bottom can't reach it with their teeth. If they can, tuck the tails out of reach or follow some similar precaution.

Arm harness #4: The Breast-Cross Harness. This is an elegant arm harness that I invented while researching this book. It takes about an 18-foot length of rope.

To apply this harness, tie the hands in the anti-parallel position with the midsection of the rope, lift their wrists up as high on the back as you can without causing heavy straining, then run the tails under the bottom's armpits, up over their collarbones, and cross them low at the back of the bottom's neck. Be sure to run the tails between the wrists after tying so as to avoid cinching constriction.

Continue to wrap the tails under the bottom's armpits and bring them together at the front of the bottom's upper chest, over their breasts. Tie the ends together here. (A Surgeon's knot may work especially well.) Now here's the interesting part: to prevent the bottom from simply being able to shrug off the ropes running across their collarbones, run a tail up and around this rope, then bring the tails back down to the chest knot and pass them through the angle thus created. This creates two opposable ends, which you can then tie off in a final knot. As with the Politically Correct Arm Harness, make sure that the bottom can't reach the final knot with their teeth, or take precautions if they can.

One interesting feature of this arm harness is the "X" formed by the ropes as they cross in the center of the bottom's upper back. This makes

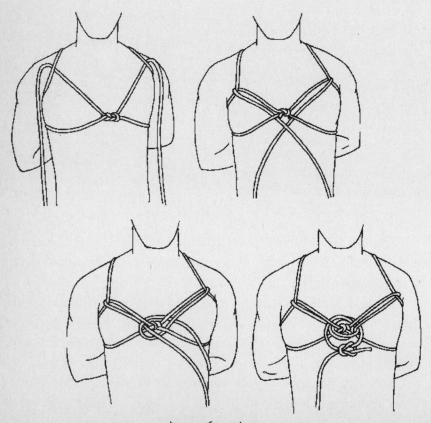

Breast Cross Harness

for a natural attachment point (which can be used for such matters as helping to secure the bottom's ankles in place).

Arm harness #5: The Japanese Arm-wrap Harness. This arm harness is a "kinder, gentler" variant of a hojo-jitsu prisoner-tying technique. It can be an especially good harness when dealing with "escape artist" bottoms. The basic idea of this arm harness is that if the bottom pulls their wrists down towards their buttocks in an attempt to escape, the arm wraps are tied in such a way that they become tighter as long as such a pull is being applied, but loosen once the pull is stopped. Depending on the size of the bottom and how the harness is applied, this harness will require an 18-foot to 24-foot length of rope.

To apply the harness, bind the wrists as usual with the midsection of the rope and take the normal precaution to prevent cinching constriction. Run the tails together up across the back to one of the bottom's arms. (This tie may be more secure if you run the tails across the back of the uppermost arm. In this case, we'll say that it's their right arm.) Wrap both tails firmly but not really tightly around their right arm by running the tails between the side of their chest and their arm and then in the natural narrowing point just above the bottom's biceps muscle in a front-to-back direction, with the tail coming back around under the initial wrapping. (If the bottom is an "eel," do a second such wrapping.) Now (key point) run the tails under the first wrapping and then through the bottom's armpit to the front of their chest. If the bottom is female, run the tails across her chest just slightly above her breasts.

When you get to their left arm, wrap the tails all the way around their upper arm by running them first between the side of the bottom's chest and their upper arm in a back-to-front direction (again, if the bottom is an "eel" do a second wrapping) and then bring the tails back over the wrapping turns. Now wrap the tails over the section of rope that runs between the bottom's chest and the wrapping turns and run it back down towards their wrists.

Wrap the tails twice around the ropes running to the bottom's right arm as close as you can to their wrists (a round turn). Finish the harness by separating the tails and running them in opposite directions around

the bottom's upper arms to the front of
their chest and tying the ends together
in a Square knot or Surgeon's knot.

Another alternative ending to this tie
(there are several, depending on, among
other things, how much rope the top has
left over after wrapping the tails off in
the final round turn) is to have the bottom
bend their ankles back toward their wrists
and finish off in a hogtie.

**Arm harness #6: The Japanese
Single-chest-wrap Harness.** This is a
basic arm harness that is simple to apply,
and very effective in its basic form. As a
bonus, it lends itself to a number of
variants. Depending on the size of the
bottom and the variant that the top wishes
to apply, this harness calls for an 18-foot
to a 24-foot length of rope.

To apply the Japanese single-chest-
wrap harness, use the midsection of the
rope to tie the bottom's hands behind
them (as before, the anti-parallel position
will probably work best). Position the tails
to avoid cinching constriction, and run
the tails together over one of the bottom's
upper arms (let's say the right arm) at
about the junction point of the top third
and middle third of the arm. Run the tails
across the bottom's chest, usually just
above their breasts. (As a variant, you
can separate the tails and run one end
just above their breasts and the other end
just below their breasts.) Continue

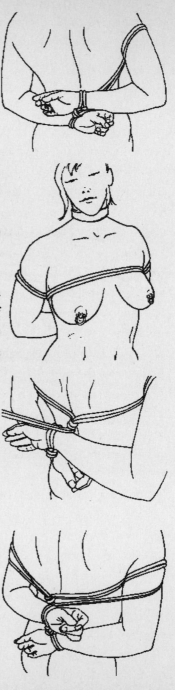

Japanese Arm-Wrap Harness

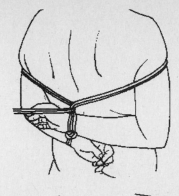

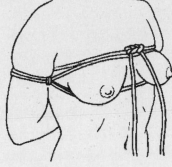

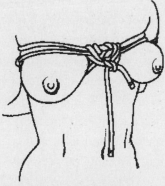

Japanese Single-chest-wrap Harness

running the tails across the bottom's chest and run them around the bottom's left arm. As before, run the ropes across their arm at about the junction of the upper third and middle third of their arm.

Run the tails back down towards the bottom's wrists and wrap them together in a simple turn (a 180-turn) around the ropes running from the bottom's wrists to their right arm. Cinch the arm harness down to "baby bear" tightness, then continue to wrap the tails around until you've completed a round turn (a 540-turn). You are now ready to finish tying this arm harness, and you have several options at this point.

The simplest option is to simply separate the tails and run them in opposite directions up over the bottom's arms until they meet at the center of the bottom's chest and tie them together.

A somewhat more secure option is to separate the tails and run them under each armpit, then tie them together at the center of the bottom's chest.

An even more secure option is to separate the tails and run them under the bottom's armpits, running them in a crossing turn over both the front and rear sections of the chest wrapping turns. Thus, when the two tails meet at the front of the bottom's chest, the top can cinch the chest wrapping turns even more securely before tying off the tails. (Be careful to avoid pinching skin when you do this.)

Finally, regarding tying off the tails, if the top separated the initial chest wrapping turns so that one tail was above the bottom's breasts and the other was below it, a breast bondage variant may be possible. To create this variant, simply tie the two tails together (a Surgeon's knot is recommended), then use any remaining rope left in the tails to join the two chest wrapping turns together. This creates a very secure, very symmetrical arm harness.

"Let's try looping that rope under your breasts."

Arm harness #7: The Japanese Double-chest-wrap Harness. This is a slightly more elaborate version of the Japanese Single-chest-wrap Harness. Depending on the size of the bottom and the variant that the top wishes to apply, this harness typically calls for a 24-foot, or even a 30-foot, length of rope. (If the top doesn't have a 30-foot length of rope, it's usually a simple matter to tie a 12-foot rope and an 18-foot rope together, although you may have to experiment a bit to make sure the connecting knot isn't in an awkward place.)

To apply this arm harness, tie the bottom's wrists behind them with the midsection and take the standard precaution against cinching constriction. Then run the tails together up over one of the bottom's arms at the top-third to middle-third junction and across their chest just above their breasts. Then run the tails over their opposite arm and loop them under the ropes running to their right arm. Take a moment to cinch this section fairly snug. Now run the tails together back over their arms, this time passing slightly below the original wrapping turns, and run the tails just under the bottom's breasts. Continue to run the tail across the bottom's right arm, again passing just below the original wrapping turns, and run them back down to the loop. Run the tails down through the loop, cinch them up a bit, and wrap the tails around the rope. The top is now ready to complete this arm harness. As before, they have a number of options.

One option especially worth exploring at this point is to run the tails up the bottom's back and across their shoulders on opposite sides of their neck. To finish this harness in a not-politically-correct fashion, tie the tails together at the front of the bottom's throat. To finish the harness in a politically-correct fashion, run the tails down on opposite sides of the

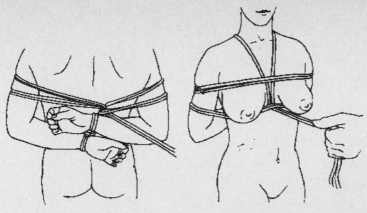

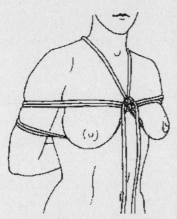

Japanese Double-chest-wrap Harness

bottom's neck, down over (or under) their upper chest wrapping turns, and then loop the tails around the lower chest wraps in either an in-to-out or an out-to-in direction. Finish the tie by bringing the tails back up to the upper chest wrappings and running them behind the ropes coming down from their shoulders to create to opposable ends. Tie the ends together, take anti-biting precautions as needed, and you're done. The end result is a very secure, fairly elaborate arm harness that can be very sexy-looking... if you're into this sort of thing.

Arm harness #8: The Split Lark's Head. This is exactly the same technique that was presented in the section on single-limb bondage techniques (p. 148), except in this case the technique is applied around the bottom's entire upper body instead of a single limb. This is a good technique for immobilizing the bottom's upper arms tightly against the sides of their body, thus often making it considerably easier to immobilize their elbows and wrists. This technique typically calls for at least a 12-foot length of rope.

To apply this technique in its most basic form, take the 12-foot rope and make a Lark's Head knot with the midpoint of the rope at the center of the knot. Now drape the entire double-loop over the bottom's upper body so that the wrapping turns go over the bottom's upper arms at about the top-third to middle-third junction, or perhaps at the midpoint of the upper arm. Make sure the arch of the Lark's Head is centered behind them on their spine. (If the top wishes, they can separate these wrapping turns so that one goes over the bottom's breasts and the other goes under the bottom's breasts.) Cinch this tightly, and perhaps lock it in place as described for the Looped Lark's Head cuff. To complete the tie, simply separate the tails, run them back around the bottom's upper arms and tie the ends off in front of them. (At this point, the bottom's forearms and wrists will still be free, so the top will have to apply additional bondage to immobilize those parts of the bottom's body.)

If the top is using a longer rope (for example, a 24-foot rope), they can go on to bind the bottom's wrists behind them and perhaps bind them even further. This can be done by tying a Figure Eight knot in the tails just after finishing locking the Separated Lark's Head in place, then binding the bottom's wrists behind them, and perhaps binding their ankles with any extra left over.

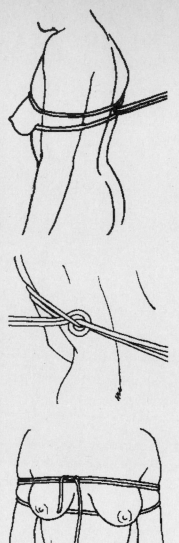

Split Lark's Head harness

Thus, we have several arm harnesses, ranging widely from the very simple to the fairly complex, and from the very politically correct to the very politically incorrect. Given the variety to choose from, the top should be able to find at least one that works very well for both the top and the bottom.

LEG HARNESSES

Binding the bottom's legs is usually significantly simpler. Among other things, because the relatively prominent heels form a natural widening point, it is usually much easier to bind ankles than it is to bind wrists.

To bind the bottom's ankles when doing a hogtie, the top has several options. In all the techniques described below, I shall assume that the top has already tied the bottom's wrists behind them by using one of the techniques described above.

Leg harness #1: The Two-rope harness. This is a very simple, and yet very effective technique that calls for two ropes, each about six feet long.

To apply this, first use one of the six-foot ropes to bind the bottom's ankles together. While the parallel, crossed, or perpendicular positions can be used, in practice the anti-parallel position often works best as it provides both a high degree of immobility and a high degree of accessibility.

Note: this is one of the few bondage techniques that often works better, in terms of rendering the bottom's legs immobile, if cinch loops are omitted after applying the wrapping turns. However, the top can certainly add them if they want the bottom to have a greater range of motion possible at their ankle joints. In particular, the bottom will often only be able to lie on either their front or their back if their ankles are bound without cinch loops, but will often also be able to kneel if their ankles are bound with cinch loops.

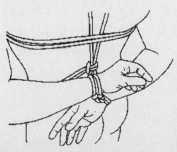

leg harness anchor point

Once the bottom's ankles are bound in the desired fashion, take the second rope and drape its midpoint around the arm harness using either a simple turn, a round turn, a Lark's Head, or an Overhand Knot. (In practice, I usually prefer using the Lark's Head.) It often works best to place the midpoint of the leg harness rope around the section of the rope just after where the wrists are tied together. While you can also place the midpoint between the bottom's wrists, this may lead to an unwanted further tightening of the wrist bondage. In the Breast Cross arm harness, you can attach the ankle rope at the rear "X" formed by the arm harness.

Now that the midpoint of the rope is secured to the arm harness, bend the bottom's bound ankles up as close as desired to their wrists, then use the tails running down from their wrists to their ankles to secure their wrists in place.

There are several ways to use the tails to secure the ankles in place. The simplest way is to merely run one tail over the ankles and the other tail under the ankles and tie them together.

As a somewhat more stringent alternative, you can wind the tails around the ankles in opposite directions using round turns and then tie them together.

If you wind the tails around the ankles together in the same direction, you can complete the bondage by tying the tails together in a Finishing Lark's Head.

In all of these ankle harnesses, you should try to tie the final knot as far away as possible from the bottom's fingers. This typically will mean tying the knot on the "toe sides" of their feet instead of the "heel sides" of their feet. Proper positioning of the knot often becomes obvious with practice.

Safety note: The large quadriceps muscles on the front of the bottom's upper legs will develop a significant amount of tension if they are highly flexed (such as when someone kneels so that they are sitting on their heels). This is, in my experience, not usually a problem if the bottom is lying on their back, but it can be a problem if the bottom is either lying on their stomach or moves from lying on their back to lying on either their side or their stomach. In such cases, the amount of tension on the rope running from the bottom's wrists to their ankles can dramatically increase.

Leg harness #2: The One-rope Harness. This harness is often both very simple and very effective. It typically calls for a single length of rope that is about twelve feet long.

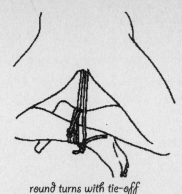

round turns with tie-off

To apply this harness, attach the midpoint of the rope just as you would for the wrist-to-ankle rope (I usually use a Lark's Head), then run the tails down to the drawn-back ankles and tie them off. As always, there are a number of ways to do this.

The most direct way is simply to wind the tails around the crossed ankles in opposite directions until you reach the ends, then tie the tails together. While this creates a sort of "open system" that could possibly loosen if the bottom worked at it a bit, in practice it usually works just fine.

You can also wind the tails around the crossed ankles together in the same direction and tie them off in a Finishing Lark's Head knot.

One fairly elegant, and very secure, way to bind the bottom's ankles is to draw their ankles up as close to their body as desired, and then tie the tail together in a Figure-eight knot just slightly above that point, thus creating two opposable ends. The top can then wind these ends around the bottom's ankles and tie them off, thus creating a much more secure "closed system" which the bottom is much less likely to be able to escape. As a refinement, the top can run the tails above the Figure-eight knot as is done for the Prefab Lark's Head wrist cuff to avoid wrapping constriction. This last technique especially shows skill and elegance.

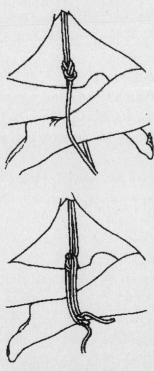

"closed system" leg harness

Leg Harness #3: The Lark's Head Waist Loop. In this leg harness, the wrists and ankles are not connected at all. Such an arrangement will permit the bottom to have a significantly increased amount of movement, particularly at the waist. Thus the bottom may find it easier to stay in a sitting or kneeling position when tied this way. This leg harness typically calls for about a 12-foot length of rope.

To apply this leg harness, the top applies a Lark's Head loop around the bottom's waist so that the arch of the knot is located in the small of the bottom's back, making sure to pull it tightly enough that it is significantly narrower than the bottom's pelvis. The Lark's Head can then either be left free or

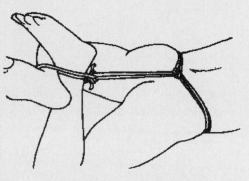

Lark's Head waist loop harness

"locked" in place as is done with the Looped Lark's Head. (While I have not had significant problems leaving the Lark's Head free, I would recommend, as a general measure, that the Lark's Head be locked. Among other things, doing so may prevent the waist loop from further tightening to a dangerous degree.)

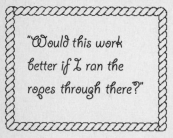

"Would this work better if I ran the ropes through there?"

Note: There is a slight possibility that such a waist loop could interfere somewhat with the bottom's ability to breathe, but this will typically become apparent fairly readily, and the top should be able to correct this well before it becomes a serious problem.

Once the Lark's Head loop is in place around the bottom's waist, their ankles can be drawn back towards their body and tied in place using the techniques previously described.

Note: A simple variant of this harness could be applied by simply applying the midpoint of the rope to the front of the bottom's lower abdomen, then running the tails around to the small of their back, pulling the tails snug, tying them together (a Surgeon's knot works well here) and proceeding as above.

Leg harness #4: Male Genitals Anchor Point. In this variant, the midsection of the rope is tied securely to the male bottom's genitals, then their ankles are drawn up and tied in place with the tails. This technique typically calls for a 12-foot length of rope, although sometimes a six-foot length can be substituted.

Note: This is obviously a somewhat riskier technique than some of the other leg harnesses, but I have never heard of an actual injury resulting from its use. Also, I have had this harness applied to me on many different occasions and, other than it being a very effective reminder for me to keep my ankles "where they belong," I have never experienced any damage or undue amount of pain from having it used on me.

To apply this technique, the top loops the midsection of the rope around the bottom's genitals (either around both the penis and scrotum or simply around the scrotum by itself) much as they might when applying a single-limb cuff, secures the loops in place, then uses the tails to tie the legs in position.

Interestingly enough, this position is often both more immobilizing and actually safer if the bottom's ankles are pulled back as closely to their scrotum as possible without causing heavy straining in their legs. It's safer because the more the legs are flexed at the knee joint, the less force the bottom will be able to generate as they try to straighten out their legs. Fully flexed legs may be able to generate only a relatively weak pull, while legs flexed only about halfway may be able to generate a very strong pull.

The scrotum and testicles can often withstand even a fairly strong pull without damage provided that such a pull is not applied very suddenly. Thus even bottoms who are thrashing about "in the throes of passion" can usually self-regulate the amount of tension in this ankle harness without hurting themselves.

However, please keep two particular cautions in mind:

Caution #1: As I mentioned, I have heard of no reports of injuries if the tension on the scrotum-to-ankles ropes is increased gradually and can be eased off readily if it becomes unduly painful. However, a sudden, sharp increase in the tension on this rope would be much more likely to cause serious injury. In particular, if a bottom tied in this way were to do something like fall off of the bed, they could be at risk for very severe injury. Make sure this doesn't happen.

Caution #2: I do not recommend tying the penis alone in this manner. While I have had no reports of damage if both the scrotum and penis, or the scrotum alone was bound in this way, I have heard reports of lasting damage to the penis if it was subjected by itself to either a sudden, sharp pull or to a lasting, gradual pull. In the first case, the bottom might suffer lasting stretching of the penile tissue, and/or damage to the ligament that helps elevate the penis during erection. In the either case, permanent stretching of the penile tissue may result, leading to long-term difficulty in maintaining a firm erection.

A "female" variant of this technique can be applied by applying clamps to the bottom's outer labia, attaching the midsection of the rope to them, and they proceeding as above. I put "female" in quotes because, of course, the same thing could also be done to the skin of the scrotum or penis.. (Caution: While I have heard no reports of lasting stretching of the genital skin from this technique, it is a possibility, so please be appropriately cautious.)

Note: Given that this book does not cover how to use clamps, the top should receive instruction in that aspect of BDSM before trying this. Please consult "SM 101" or some other good source of information before attempting this variant.

Leg Harness #5: Bind each ankle separately. In this technique, as described, each ankle is bound separately instead of being bound together. This technique typically calls for a 12-foot length of rope.

To apply this technique, attach the midpoint of the rope as described with any of the above leg harnesses, then run a tail out to each ankle and tie it in place. I suggest that you use a technique that avoids wrapping constriction for this tie. (I'd particularly recommend the French Bowline as it allows for more wrapping turns and doesn't further tighten when under tension.)

Leg Harness #6: "Frogtie" the Legs. This is an interesting variant in which each ankle is bound closely to the rear, upper thigh of the same leg. This technique typically calls for a 6-foot length of rope for each leg, although a 12-foot length can also sometimes be used. This can be a very good bondage technique as it can combine a high degree of leg immobility with a fairly good amount of access to the bottom's genitals and anal area.

leg frogtie

One way to apply this technique is to have the bottom kneel so that they are "sitting on their heels," and place the midpoint of the rope on the center of their upper thigh, then wrap the tails around the lower leg, bring them back to the top of the thigh, and tie them together. (Try to position these wrapping turns so they are not putting painful pressure on the bottom's shinbone.) It is not usually necessary to use cinch loops with this technique, but they can be applied.

Once the bottom's legs are secured, the bottom may be able to kneel, or lie on their side, back, or stomach.

A variant on this technique is to have the bottom kneel with their legs closely together and wrap the tails around both upper and lower legs, binding both legs together in a flexed position. Obviously, this can limit access to their genitals or anal area.

THE HOGTIE

The hogtie position, in one variant or another, is known to many people and is often considered a "heavy duty" bondage tie. Furthermore, it is a relatively controversial position and can be somewhat risky – particularly some of its variants. A number of deaths have occurred after a person was hogtied. However, essentially all of these deaths occurred under very specific circumstances that are fairly easy to avoid. I'll describe them later.

As you already know, the subject of bondage is a very far-ranging one, and I had to make some editorial decisions regarding what I would and would not cover in this (relatively fundamental) book. Some of the more "heavy duty" bondage practices that I decided to omit were suspension bondage, prolonged bondage, and bondage applied to someone who was resisting. (Among other things, as of this writing I am not particularly educated or experienced regarding these practices. That may change.)

On the other hand, I am very well-acquainted with the hogtie position, having spent a considerable amount of time on both the "inside" and the "outside" of it. I feel I can discuss this bondage position with substantial familiarity. Given my extensive personal experience with this bondage position, and that it is otherwise consistent with the parameters of this book, I decided to include it, but many readers will consider the hogtie to be the riskiest and most intense bondage position in this book.

Because of the risks and controversies associated with the hogtie bondage position, I'd like to take a moment to refer you back to the "Risk Factors and Warning Signs" chapter, in which I discuss degrees of monitoring, risk factors, and my philosophy on risk-taking – critical context for the information in this chapter. Having reviewed such matters, let us explore the hogtie.

THE BASIC HOGTIE

In the basic hogtie position, the bottom lies face-down, their wrists are tied behind their back, their ankles are tied together, and finally their ankles are drawn back towards their wrists and tied in place. The stringency of this bondage position depends substantially upon how closely the bottom's ankles are drawn to their wrists. I've seen everything from the ankles drawn back so closely to the wrists that they were touching, to a very loose hogtie in which the ankles were just very slightly lifted off the floor.

The hogtie position, particularly if the bottom's ankles are drawn back closely to their wrists, can be very immobilizing. While the bottom may be able to wiggle around a bit, that may be about it. Some bottoms find even rolling from the face-down position onto one side or the other to be very difficult if not impossible, and most will not be able to rise to a sitting or kneeling position without assistance. Short of tying someone to a heavy fixed object such as a bed or post, the hogtie is about the most immobilizing bondage position there is.

From a BDSM point of view, the hogtie is something of a mixed blessing. While it frequently offers both a high degree of security and immobility, it can often significantly reduce access to the bottom's body – particularly if the bottom is lying face-down. Access to their back is fair at best, and access to their buttocks can be significantly blocked by their wrists, their ankles, and the rope running between them. Of course, if the bottom is lying face-down, access to their chest, breasts, nipples, and genitals is usually difficult. This being the case, the classic, face-down hogtie usually works best in a "you just lie there and be tied up until I want you for something – and that may be a while" sort of scene.

Some of the variants and modifications of the hogtie, however, offer a great deal more promise.

For example, if the bottom is hogtied and placed into a kneeling position, this exposes most of the front of their body. Their chest, breasts, and nipples are usually very available, and access to their genitals is often good – particularly if their ankles are tied in a perpendicular or anti-parallel direction. Furthermore, they can often perform oral sex while bound into this position – particularly if the rope running between their wrists and ankles is long enough to allow them to kneel. If the rope running between their wrists and ankles is long enough to allow them to "stand on their knees" (known in "SM 101" as the "kneel up" position), then they can have a nice amount of mobility – enough to greatly enhance their ability to perform oral sex – while still being securely bound.

In the sitting-cross-legged variant of this position, access to the bottom's upper chest usually remains good, but access to their genitals, buttocks, and anal area is much more limited. (Access to a male bottom's genitals may be adequate.) One benefit of this position is that the bottom may find it less stressful on their legs than they find the kneeling position, thus they may be able to stay in this position considerably longer.

If the rope running between the bottom's wrists and ankles is long enough to permit the bottom to move back and forth between a "kneel up" position and a sitting-cross-legged position (they may need assistance in this), they probably will be able to kneel, sit, and lay on their stomach, side, and possibly their back. This allows the top to position the bottom in various ways while still retaining both a high degree of security and a relatively high degree of immobility. A nice combination.

(Caution: ropes that were baby-bear tight around the bottom's ankles when they were lying down may become uncomfortably tight, or even dangerously tight, when the bottom moves to a kneeling or sitting position.)

Hogtying a bottom and then placing them on their back can create a very high degree of security along with a very high degree of vulnerability and accessibility. Furthermore, many bottoms can stay in this position for a relatively long period of time with reasonable comfort – if some thought is given to the tying technique.

It usually works best for the top to tie the bottom's wrists behind them in an anti-parallel fashion, with the bottom's wrists in the small of their back. It's often a good idea to place a pillow or something similar under the bottom's buttocks to take some of their body weight off of their wrists and hands. The bottom's ankles are then bound together (the anti-parallel position often works best for this), drawn up fairly closely to the bottom's genitals, and tied in place. This position is often enhanced by elevating the bottom's head and shoulders with one or two pillows, thus allowing them a clearer view of what's being done to them. (Of course, if the top felt like denying them that view, they could simply not place such pillows.)

Is the hogtie position intrinsically dangerous? In the criminal justice area, there have been a fairly substantial number of deaths reported after a suspect has been place in a hogtie position (also known in those circles as the "hobble" position). So we know the following: (1) the suspect was placed in a hogtie position and (2) they died shortly after being placed in such a position. The obvious question arises: what, if any, is the cause-and-effect relationship between those two facts?

There are two basic categories of hogtie-related deaths: gradual deaths and sudden deaths. Let's take a closer look at each.

• *Gradual hogtie deaths.* The primary concern in these cases seems to be the question of to what degree being placed in the hogtie position limits the person's ability to breathe. Three factors appear to play a significant role here.

The first factor is that, given that the bottom is lying face-down with their hands tied behind them, their abdominal cavity is compressed and the contents of their abdominal cavity are pressing on the underside of their diaphragm with an unusually high degree of pressure. This can limit how easily the diaphragm can move and thus make the bound person have to work harder – expend more muscular effort – to breathe. Over time, this can become a problem – how much of a problem cannot be predicted in advance. Some bottoms can tolerate this position for hours at a time, while others develop significant respiratory difficulty within a few minutes. Heavier bottoms tend to have more problems with this position than lighter bottoms have, and older bottoms tend to have more problems than younger bottoms have.

The second factor is that the standard hogtie position may in some cases limit the bottom's ability to expand their chest wall adequately when they breathe. This can be due in part to having their arms drawn tightly against the sides of their chest and in part to laying face-down with their chest directly on the surface in question.

The third factor is the surface that the bottom is lying on. In particular, if the bottom is lying on a soft bed with lots of fluffy pillows, covers, and so forth, they may sink into the bed, with the result that their nose and/or mouth may be obstructed.

In all of the above cases, the distress associated with the situation usually comes on rather slowly, with many minutes or even hours passing before the problems become significant. Thus, the bottom is able to give more than adequate notice to the top, and the top can correct these problems with relatively little difficulty – provided, of course, that there is a top present to do so. Once again, we see the crucial importance of a sympathetic monitor.

The conventional wisdom in such cases is that the gradually increasing respiratory distress associated with the hogtie position can often be relieved almost entirely by placing the bound person on their side or back (or almost any other position than face-down; sitting or kneeling can also work). Indeed, many bottoms will move into such positions on their own if they can. Police officers and ambulance crews are often taught that if 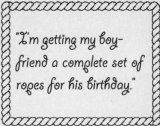 someone has been hogtied, they are to be placed in an on-their-side position (and closely monitored) while being transported to jail or to the hospital.

- *Sudden hogtie deaths.* Most of the sudden deaths attributed to the hogtie position have involved males who were being arrested. Many such men were under the influence of substantial amounts of recreational drugs that directly affect heart function, including cocaine, alcohol, and amphetamines. Furthermore, these people often had very high levels of adrenaline (epinephrine) in their systems due to their being in a "for real" fight-or-flight situation. Additionally, there was classically a period of violent struggle while they were being placed in a hogtie position, often with a police officer kneeling on their upper back (and thus further limiting their ability to breathe) during this process.

It appears that it is this combination of stressors – recreational drugs (especially stimulants), high levels of adrenaline, strong rage and/or fear, violent exercise (often in a person whose level of cardiopulmonary fitness is very poor), and unusual compression of the chest due to someone kneeling on their back – that causes almost all of the sudden deaths. It seems that these people died of what could be thought of as "metabolic suffocation." That is to say, even though they could still breathe (at least somewhat), the various stressors caused their heart's demand for oxygen to soar above their body's ability to supply it, and they died from lack of oxygen.

From the viewpoint of a consensual bondage practitioner, this is good news. It provides us with a set of fairly clear guidelines to help us avoid such mishaps. If we avoid doing things such as kneeling on the bottom's back while they are enraged and under the influence of recreational drugs, we should have many fewer problems.

THE MILITARY HOGTIE

There are several standard, "learn during your first SM teachings" aphorisms in the SM world. Commonly included among these teachings are phrases such as "SM play should always be consensual," "always play with a safeword in effect," and "never tie anything across the front of a bottom's throat."

As I've mentioned before in this book, all of the above such teachings (and virtually everything else associated with BDSM) are subject to debate, nuance, and exception. For example, there are knowledgeable, experienced

BDSM practitioners who sometimes do "consensually nonconsensual" scenes, and there are also knowledgeable, experienced BDSM practitioners who sometimes do "no safeword" scenes. These are very controversial topics, and there is – as I mentioned – a great deal of debate and discussion about them, including whether or not it is possible to do them at all. In any event, the topics of "consensually nonconsensual" scenes or "no safeword" play are definitely beyond the scope of this book – and, candidly, I breathe a sigh of relief upon contemplating that thought. (However, I will advise you to not attempt either type of BDSM play until you know your partner extremely well and both of you have BDSM experience levels that can be measured in terms of years.)

The "never tie anything across the front of the bottom's throat" issue, however, is more objective. It is certainly possible to do that type of bondage. The fact that this could be risky bondage is obvious. However, the question emerges, what is its actual risk level? Should we automatically put this type of bondage in the "extreme level of risk" category? Many knowledgeable, experienced practitioners strongly think that indeed we should.

The question is made somewhat more complex by the fact that, while this technique is hardly ever explicitly taught or used in the BDSM world (at least in public), it is very widely taught and used in the military/ martial arts world as a method of binding prisoners, and there are not numerous reports of prisoners dying after being tied in this way.

In this hogtie variant – seen fairly frequently in gay male bondage photos – the bottom's hands are tied behind their back (often in an anti-parallel position) and their wrists are then pushed relatively high up on their back, typically so that the angle of their elbow joints is less than 90 degrees. The rope is then looped around the bottom's neck – usually only once, but sometimes more than once – and then brought back down to their wrists and once again secured there. The bottom's ankles are then drawn back towards their wrists (how closely they are drawn to the wrists can vary widely) and tied in place – thus completing the tie. Because this variant of the hogtie is widely taught to soldiers as a means of securing enemy prisoners, I have named it "the military hogtie" – a phrase that is becoming more popular.

The basic idea of this hogtie position is that as long as the bound person stays relatively still, the bondage is not particularly uncomfortable. Indeed, the bound person may even be able to sleep while tied this way. However, if they struggle in an attempt to free themselves, the pressure across the front of their throat might increase to the point of significant discomfort. If they were to pull strongly, the pressure across the front of their throat might increase to the point where it could cause injury, unconsciousness, or, in an extreme case, even death. Thus the point of this tie is to discourage struggling, not to inflict unavoidable strangulation. As long as the bottom stays still, no significant pressure is applied to their neck and the bondage often feels no more uncomfortable than a slightly snug necktie.

OK, so here is an obvious example of a fairly large number of people outside of the BDSM community engaging in a bondage practice that people inside the BDSM community are commonly taught to never do. What should we make of this?

As part of researching this book, I put out a call for "Type One" and "Type Two" incidents. Type One incidents were cases in which something unexpectedly bad had occurred. Type Two incidents were cases in which something unexpectedly good had occurred (or, more precisely, cases in which the expected bad outcome did not occur.)

What I found, somewhat to my surprise, was a relatively large number of reports of Type Two incidents involving bondage that went across the front of the bottom's throat, with no problems. A surprisingly large number of knowledgeable bondage practitioners have been doing "never do this" bondage involving the military hogtie (and other methods of running a rope across the front of the bottom's neck) in their private play fairly frequently and for quite some time. Yet there was a virtually nonexistent rate of significant injury – provided that this type of bondage was done within certain parameters. What's going on here?

First, let's talk about the cases in which the bottom was harmed, or even killed, by this type of bondage. Interestingly enough, all the cases that have been reported to me as of this writing have involved either (a) cases in which the victim (and in this case I will call them a victim, not a bottom) was tied with "real world" criminal intent or (b) cases in which the bottom was in an unmonitored situation while tied into this position, either due to self-bondage or to being tied this way and then abandoned by their partner.

In other words, despite a diligent search, in numerous case reports of such usage, I have received no reports of a bottom who was injured or killed by a military hogtie provided the bottom was tied by a top who (a) had no criminal intent regarding them and (b) monitored the bottom (either closely or loosely) after tying them into this position. What should we make of this?

I believe the evidence presented to me supports the conclusion that the military hogtie more rationally falls into the "above average" level of risk category than into the "extreme level of risk" category provided that:

1. It is applied by a top who cares about the bottom's welfare in the usual BDSM sense.

2. The top monitors the bottom after the tie is applied.

3. The tie is applied in a manner that does not apply uncomfortably tight pressure to the front of a bottom's throat while they are lying still in a resting position.

A few supplemental comments. If the military hogtie was applied in such a way that the bottom had to use their muscles to relieve the pressure across the front of their throat, that would certainly qualify as "extreme level of risk."

If this type of tie is applied, it is especially important that the top have the resources necessary to release the bottom very quickly if a problem develops. (EMT scissors, or their functional equivalent, would be particularly important in this regard.)

Bottoms with a history of a seizure disorder would be an increased risk if tied this way.

There have been a number of cases in which only a few seconds of strangulation have stopped the recipient's heart. While such incidents are relatively rare, they are not unheard of. Such cases usually involve a bottom who is older and/or has a history of heart disease, and/or is experiencing significant anger or fear at the time.

There is some reason to believe that pressure applied relatively high on the person's neck (near what's called the carotid sinus bodies) was more likely to be involved in such incidents than pressure that was placed relatively low on the person's neck (away from the carotid sinus bodies). Additionally, it has been reported in the forensic pathology literature that neck pressure due to manual strangulation is significantly more likely to cause this problem than is pressure from a constricting band, since pressure from manual strangulation can be concentrated more locally upon the carotid sinus bodies. (See "Forensic Pathology," second edition, by Knight.)

"I'm a victim of macrame!"

There has been the occasional case in which pressure on the arteries in the neck, from whatever cause, have dislodged a cholesterol plaque from the interior wall of the artery, which may then travel up to the brain and cause a stroke. Such incidents are very rare, and almost all of those that do occur involve people over the age of 60.

As is true with any form of bondage, the use of any intoxicants to any degree by either the top or the bottom pretty much automatically increases the level of risk by one level. If both people are using intoxicants the risk level automatically becomes extreme.

The conventional recommendation is that if someone develops difficulty breathing from being placed in a face-down hogtie, this difficulty can often be resolved by rolling the tied person onto their side. While researching this book, we found this recommendation to be true if the person was in a conventional (nonmilitary) hogtie. However, we found that a person in a military hogtie who was rolled onto their side usually experienced an increase in neck-loop pressure, with potentially dangerous results. For people tied into a military hogtie to get relief, it was necessary to roll them all the way over onto their back. Fortunately, this was usually accomplished fairly easily, particularly if the bottom's wrists were tied in an anti-parallel position.

Interestingly enough, many bottoms reported that being on their back while tied in a military hogtie was a very comfortable position, and that they could stay in this position for the maximum bondage duration of two hours that is recommended in this book without undue difficulty. (Some bottoms needed to have a pillow or something similar put under their buttocks to help take the weight of their body off of their hands and wrists.)

Most of the pressure across the front of the bottom's throat comes from the quadriceps muscles located on the front of the bottom's upper thighs, and is transmitted to their throat by the rope running between the bottom's ankles and their wrists. Thus, if the top wanted to relieve the throat pressure as quickly as possible, it would probably be best to cut this rope first.

If the top wanted to reduce the pressure that could potentially be applied to the front of the bottom's throat, they might apply the wrist tie and neck loop, but omit running a rope from the bottom's wrists to their ankles. One of several playfully wicked variants of this technique, used especially on male bottoms, is to apply the wrist tie and neck loop with one rope, and then use one or more additional ropes to tie the bottom's ankles together and then draw them back and tie them to the bottom's genitals. (Refer back to the "Harnesses" chapter for more ideas.) As with the standard military hogtie, this technique seems to be an above-average level of risk technique but not an extreme level of risk technique.

In summary. As I mentioned earlier, one of the main purposes of this book was to advance the body of knowledge regarding bondage, and to re-examine its teachings and aphorisms with substantial intellectual rigor.

I have made a very diligent inquiry into the military hogtie. I have thoroughly researched the medical, legal, military, and martial arts data, have discussed it with many experienced people, and have both applied it to my partners and had it applied to me on many occasions.

Regarding bondage, SM in general, sex in general, and even life in general, the choice is rarely between "safe" and "unsafe," but rather a choice of "what risk level are you comfortable with?" Thus, we increasingly see descriptions of "safer sex" rather than "safe sex."

In this book, I have described three categories of risk: average risk, above-average risk, and extreme risk. While there is no doubt that the military hogtie is riskier than average, my inquiries have led me to the conclusion that it is, when used under the three parameters described in this book, more rationally placed in the "above-average risk" category than in the "extreme risk" category.

BONDAGE AND POSITIONAL ASPHYXIA

"Positional Asphyxia" is a rather scary term. It's also a term every bondage fan should understand, because it's one of the relatively few ways that we can get into serious trouble.

Positional Asphyxia, in its simplest form, simply refers to asphyxiation (suffocation) occurring because someone has been placed in a position where it is impossible for them to breathe adequately.

To properly understand positional asphyxia, it helps to review the basics of breathing.

A given breath consists of an inhalation phase and an exhalation phase. An adult at rest typically breathes between 12 to 20 times per minute, with a typical breath volume being around 500 cubic centimeters, and with the inhalation phase lasting slightly longer than the exhalation phase. In most circumstances, inhalation involves a relatively small amount of active muscle contraction of the thoracic (chest) muscles and diaphragm, while exhalation is an entirely passive process, requiring no muscular effort. (Thus, if someone has to work to exhale, or if their exhalation phase is longer than their inhalation phase, they probably have some sort of problem with their breathing.)

In other words, breathing is an activity that takes muscular work, and there is an upper limit to how much work a given muscle or set of muscles can do in a given amount of time. If this work limit is exceeded, the muscles will eventually fatigue to the point where they fail to function, no matter how desperately the person wants them to continue to function.

In positional asphyxia, the person has been placed in a position where the amount of work they must do in order to breathe adequately is greater than the amount of work their respiratory muscles can do indefinitely. Unless this condition is relieved, the person will die of inadequate breathing due to respiratory muscle exhaustion. Depending upon the severity of the condition, this failure could take anywhere from a few minutes to many hours to occur.

I saw my fair share of respiratory failure cases during my ambulance days. It's my experience that all but the most extremely acute cases typically take at least thirty minutes to develop to the point where they become life-threatening, and most take at least an hour to reach this point. Many take far longer.

Thus, once again, we see the importance of a sympathetic monitor. As long as the person in bondage is even loosely monitored, there should be no significant problems with positional asphyxia. On the other hand, if no such sympathetic monitor is present, such as in a self-bondage situation, the bound person could be facing a slow, painful death.

A few further points.

If a bottom has a medical condition that might make it suddenly more difficult for them to breathe, they should let the top know before allowing themselves to be bound. They should also tell the top what to do if this difficulty in breathing develops. Ideally, of course, this should be covered in pre-play negotiations. Examples of such conditions include asthma and a sudden, severe allergic reaction (particularly allergies to something likely to be in the bedroom or playroom, including dust, scents, cat or dog hair, and so forth).

Also, if the bottom has other respiratory conditions that might make it harder for them to breathe but are relatively unlikely to suddenly become more severe, they should advise the top of this. Examples of such conditions could include emphysema, chronic bronchitis, and chronic congestive heart failure.

(Important Note: people who have chronic congestive heart failure may not be able to lie flat on their back or stomach for any significant length of time, or to have their chest constricted by bondage or by their own weight, without developing a genuinely dangerous degree of respiratory failure. If these people develop problems, they usually breathe better when placed in a sitting position.)

Intoxication can be especially dangerous in these cases. In those cases where positional asphyxia does become a problem, it often takes more than an hour to become life-threatening, and the person will have been in respiratory distress for quite some time before then. Thus, as long as the bound person is aware of their respiratory distress, they can easily communicate this to their top and correction can be accomplished with a great deal of time to spare. However, the bottom must, of course, be aware that they are finding it increasingly difficult to breathe. Therefore, it's important that the bottom not be so drunk and/or stoned that they are unable to recognize or communicate their situation. Intoxication has been an obvious co-factor in many positional asphyxia deaths, and it is very plausible that had the person not been intoxicated they almost undoubtedly would not have died.

One particularly graphic example found in the medical literature involves a drunken man who passed out while kneeling and bending over the edge of his bathtub (possibly to vomit). When he passed out in this position, the pressure of his body weight on the edge of the tub prevented his diaphragm and chest wall from moving adequately, and he died of positional asphyxia complicated by intoxication. ("Positional Asphyxiation in Adults" by Bell et al. *American Journal of Forensic Medicine and Pathology* 13(2): 101-107, 1992.)

Of course, if the top is intoxicated, then the hapless bottom (even if they are not intoxicated) may not be able to communicate their respiratory distress to someone who can do something about it. If both the bottom and the top are significantly intoxicated…

BONDAGE AND BREATHING

In my experience, the four positions most likely to be associated with breathing problems are the hogtie position, what I will call the "fetal" position, the crucifixion position, and the top-sitting-on-bottom position.

The Hogtie Position. A person who has been hogtied in a face-down position may, in some cases, develop some degree of respiratory distress.

Please note that this is highly variable, and that many bottoms can be quite happily hogtied in a face-down position for the two-hour upper limit recommended in this book with no problems whatsoever – other than feeling disappointed when it becomes time for them to be released. ("Aw, do I gotta be untied?")

In general, younger and/or lighter bottoms will have fewer problems than older and/or heavier bottoms. In almost all cases, unless the person is some combination of intoxicated, enraged, obese, terrified, and violently struggling, any respiratory distress that might develop tends to develop very gradually, and can usually be remedied by a sympathetic monitor long before it becomes dangerous. In most cases, this distress is fairly simply remedied by having the bottom roll onto their side (many bottoms will figure this out on their own) or by rolling them into that position if they are unable to do this for themselves. Note that if the bottom is in a military hogtie, they may be better positioned by placing them on their back rather than on their side.

The fetal position. This term refers to a wide range of positions in which the bottom is bent forward at the waist with their knees brought into relatively close proximity to their shoulders. In such a position, the ability of the chest wall to expand, and of the diaphragm to move downward, may be limited to a dangerous degree. This can be done with the bottom standing or sitting and bending forward, with the bottom lying on their side, or with the bottom kneeling and tied over something like a log or ottoman. However, probably the most common position is with the bottom lying on their back with their knees drawn up towards their chest. As with the hogtie, any respiratory distress that may develop – again, it won't develop in every case – will typically develop relatively slowly and thus can be easily corrected by a sympathetic monitor with plenty of time to spare.

The crucifixion position. This position is a bit outside the stated scope of this book, but it is close enough, and important enough, that I decided to include a brief mention of it anyway, particularly given that its mechanism is somewhat different.

In such cases, a significant portion of the bottom's body weight hangs from their arms, such as might happen if their hands are fastened above their head while they are in an upright position. (I have heard of no problems with this position if the bottom's body was relatively horizontal.) This weight can force their chest to expand into a sort of "permanent inhalation" position, making them expend muscular effort to exhale. Given that exhalation is normally a passive process, this increased extra workload may, over time, become more than the bottom can sustain and they will slowly go into respiratory failure due to exhaustion of their breathing muscles. Again, a sympathetic monitor can usually remedy this long before it becomes genuinely dangerous.

For more information, see "On the Physical Death of Jesus Christ" by Gabel and Hosmer, *Journal of the American Medical Association*, 1986;255:1455-63.

In inverted suspension, in which the bottom is head-down to a significant degree, the chest also may be forced to expand into a sort of permanent inhalation position. This condition may be further worsened by the pressure of the bottom's intestines and other abdominal organs pressing on the underside of their diaphragm, thus making it harder for the bottom to inhale as well as exhale. Once again, these difficulties generally develop gradually and can usually be easily remedied by a sympathetic monitor. For more information, see "An Unusual Accidental Death from Reverse Suspension" by Purdue, *American Journal of Forensic Medicine and Pathology*, 13(2); 108-111, 1992.

"You tie your ankles, then I'll tie your wrists."

Footnote: Inverted suspension also has the potential to increase blood pressure in the brain, thus possibly increasing the chances of a stroke due to a ruptured blood vessel. This could happen with no warning signs. (Any bottom who develops a sudden headache while being placed in inverted suspension should be taken down immediately.) Presumably, older bottoms and/or bottoms with a history of high blood pressure would be at increased risk for such an incident, although to what extent the risk increases with age and/or high blood pressure is difficult to estimate.

Top-sitting-on-bottom position. The top-sitting-on-bottom position has a number of variants. What these variants all have in common is that the bottom has to endure having some or even all of the top's body weight while the top sits, kneels, or squats on the bottom's chest, abdomen, or back in a dominant manner. Obviously, this extra weight will force the bottom to increase the amount of work they must do to breathe. As with the other positions, this can be relieved by a sympathetic monitor long before it becomes life-threatening.

Footnote: There is obviously some risk that the bottom might sustain injury to their ribs, spine or internal organs if the top puts some of their body weight on the bottom's chest, abdomen, or back. Obviously, the degree of risk will vary greatly depending upon a number of factors, including the relative sizes of the top and bottom. For example, a very small top might be able to happily perch on the chest or abdomen of a very large bottom for up to the two-hour upper limit recommended in this book without the bottom's condition becoming serious. On the other hand, if a large top were to try to sit on a small bottom, the risk of immediate injury might be very high indeed.

It should be kept in mind, particularly when sitting on the bottom's chest, that older bottoms have less flexible rib cages than younger bottoms have, and thus the risk of a rib fracture increases accordingly. While no sharp dividing line can be drawn, I urge tops to be particularly careful regarding bottoms who are more than forty years old.

It should also be kept very clearly in mind that sudden increases (or decreases) in chest or abdominal pressure may be much more likely to cause injury than a more gradual increase or decrease in pressure. Thus, the top should both get on and get off slowly, and should not move around in any sudden ways while in position.

However, as with the other positions, as long as a sympathetic monitor is present, there should not be any major problems – particularly if the top does not make any sudden moves while upon the bottom.

In conclusion. We come back again and again to how important it is for the top to stay in the here and now as the scene progresses, to observe what is and what isn't working, and to play both the role of "captor" and the role of "sympathetic monitor."

HOGTIE REFERENCES

"Restraint Position and Positional Asphyxia" by Chan, Vilke, Neuman, and Clausen. <u>Annals of Emergency Medicine</u>, *November 1997, 30:5 [key article showing no intrinsic problem with hog-tie position]*

"Restraint Asphyxiation: Letter to the Editor" by Hirsch. <u>American Journal of Forensic Medicine and Pathology</u>, *15(3): 266-267, 1994*

"The Perils of Investigating and Certifying Deaths in Police Custody" by Luke and Reay. <u>American Journal of Forensic Medicine and Pathology</u>, *13(2): 98-100, 1992*

"An Unusual Accidental Death From Reverse Suspension" by Purdue. <u>American Journal of Forensic Medicine and Pathology</u>, *13(2): 108-111, 1992*

"Positional Asphyxia During Law Enforcement Transport" by D.T. Reay et al. <u>American Journal of Forensic Medicine and Pathology</u>, *13(2): 90-97, 1992.*

"Restraint Asphyxiation in Excited Delirium" by O'Halloran and Lewman. <u>American Journal of Forensic Medicine and Pathology</u>, *14(4): 289-295, 1993.*

"Sudden Death in Individuals in Hobble Restraints During Paramedic Transport" by Stratton et al. <u>Annals of Emergency Medicine</u> *25:5, May 1995*

"Effects of Positional Restraint on Oxygen Saturation and Heart Rate Following Exercise" by Reay et al. <u>American Journal of Forensic Medicine and Pathology</u>, *(9)1: 16-18, 1988*

"Positional Asphyxia in Adults" by Bell et al. <u>American Journal of Forensic Medicine and Pathology</u>, *13(2): 101-107, 1992*

"A Case of Death by Physical Restraints: New Lessons from a Photograph" by Miles. <u>Journal of the American Geriatrics Society</u>, *March 1996-Vol.44 # 3*

"Deaths Caused by Physical Restraints" by Miles and Irvine. <u>The Gerontologist</u>, *Vol. 32, No. 6, 762-766*

"Positional Asphyxia during Law Enforcement Transport – letter to the Editor" by Laposata. <u>American Journal of Forensic Medicine and Pathology</u>, *Vol. 14, No. 1, 1993*

"Death by Reverse Suspension – letter to the Editor" by Lawler. <u>American Journal of Forensic Medicine and Pathology</u>, *Vol. 13, No. 1, 1992.*

BONDAGE EQUIPMENT

NON-METAL RESTRAINTS. Restraints can be logically grouped into two categories: those made of metal and those made of other materials. Let's look first at one of the most popular items of bondage gear: non-metal restraints.

OK, if they're not made out of metal, what are they made of? Leather is, of course, a very common material. Other popular materials include heavy-duty cloth, nylon webbing, polypropylene – and, of course, rope.

Most such restraints are, of course, wrist or ankle cuffs; however, there are also some interesting variants, such as "bondage mittens."

Going a bit further, there are two categories of non-metal restraints: those made for industrial use, such as within hospitals, and those made specifically for SM use.

Industrial restraints. These types of restraints are made for use in hospitals, on ambulances, and in psychiatric wards.

Probably the most heavy-duty restraints made for industrial uses are made by a company called Humane Restraint. (Their catalog makes for fascinating reading.) This company makes a wide variety of restraints, but are probably best known for their heavy-duty, lockable restraints made of sturdy, light brown leather. These excellent restraints have a number of unique features, including a flap that locks on top of a post on each cuff that requires a special type of key to unlock. (This key is so distinctive that, like handcuff keys, "civilians" have no legitimate purpose for having one. Thus, if you wear or carry such a key in a visible way, you may get some knowing looks, and maybe even some knowing smiles.)

I was given a Christmas present a few years ago that consisted of a set of two wrist cuffs, two ankle cuffs, and four four-foot straps, all made of heavy leather with locking buckles, and all made by Humane Restraint. The end result is something of a "bondage erector set" whose possibilities I'm still happily exploring.

Another major manufacturer of industrial restraints is the Posey Company. (Their catalog also makes for fascinating reading.) Most of their restraints are made of heavy-duty cloth or webbing and are washable. Their lockable restraints use a different type of key, more similar to a handcuff key. (My personal key ring contains a handcuff key, a Humane Restraint key, and a Posey key.) These restraints often come with tails already attached to them and may have built-in padding as well.

"Dedicated" restraints. Restraints made specifically for SM use can range very widely from the very simple to the very ornate. They can come in a wide variety of colors, although black is the most common color, and can have either locking or non-locking buckles. (As you might imagine, I personally prefer the ones with locking buckles.) Some are lined with fur, wool, or softer leather.

All restraints have some means of being attached to a strap, chain, or rope. This is frequently by means of one or more D-rings or something similar. Good-quality restraints will use metal attachment points which are welded, not simply bent into shape.

Almost all restraints have similar advantages. These advantages include:

- *Ease of application.* While learning rope bondage can be challenging, applying restraints is generally fairly simple. Thus, even a relatively inexperienced top can often effectively immobilize a bottom.

- *Speed of application.* Applying rope bondage can be time-consuming. Although there are some rope techniques that can be applied fairly quickly, in general, rope bondage takes longer to put on than restraints take to put on. In situations where time is important, such as professional SM sessions, this can be an important factor.

- *Wider distribution of pressure.* While I recommend that rope bondage wrapping turns be at least half an inch wide, restraints can be substantially wider with no loss of security. My personal leather restraints, for example, are slightly more than two inches wide. This wider distribution can be helpful for bottoms who have problems with their wrists.

- *Greater security.* Restraints can often be significantly harder to escape from. In particular, it can be much harder for a bottom to successfully perform the "cone out" escape maneuver.

In a worst-case situation, restraints could be cut off with EMT scissors if absolutely necessary. This is one situation where the heavy-duty cutting ability of such scissors over more conventional scissors could actually be life-saving.

Safety Note: Cutting through the actual leather cuffs may be possible with the EMT scissors, whereas it may not be possible with more conventional scissors – but it will still take considerable time. In a time-critical situation, it would probably be better to cut through the straps to which the cuffs are attached, rather than the cuffs themselves. Given that cuffs vary in their construction, a certain amount of "mental rehearsal" could be very important here. A top should always have a credible backup plan for getting cuffs off quickly.

Widely shared disadvantages of restraints include:

- *A certain lack of precision in their adjustability.* Many restraint buckles can be tightened only at half-inch intervals, which may miss the "baby bear" point by a significant degree. This is one area in which rope or metal restraints may have a significant advantage.

- *Restraints can be much more expensive* than rope, and significantly more expensive than metal restraints. However, given that they may last for years, the satisfaction of using good-quality cuffs will far outlast the slightly painful memory of how much you paid for them.

Specialized cuffs. There are two specialized types of cuffs with which bondage fans should be at least somewhat familiar: bondage mittens and suspension cuffs.

A bondage mitten is applied like a conventional mitten and encloses the bottom's entire hand. It often locks shut at the wrist and has an attachment point such as a D-ring out at the end of the fingertips. Among other things, the use of bondage mittens can make it possible to secure a larger person's wrists behind their back. Furthermore, because of the relative flatness of these cuffs, it is sometimes easier for such bottoms to lie on their back while wearing them. When properly applied, bondage mittens can be essentially impossible to escape from.

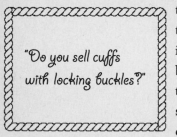

"Do you sell cuffs with locking buckles?"

Suspension cuffs are designed to be used on the wrists of a bottom who is in a standing position with their hands held overhead, as they frequently are when the bottom is being whipped or flogged. Conventional cuffs in such a situation are often pulled too far toward the bottom's hands, resulting in undue pressure on their nerves, blood vessels, and other tissues. Suspension cuffs can also be used on bottoms who are lying face-down or face-up and tied spread-eagled to a bed.

There are various designs of suspension cuffs; most have some sort of feature that allows the bottom to grasp them and thus take the pressure off their wrists.

In summary, a good quality pair of non-metal cuffs, particularly wrist cuffs, can be one of your most frequently used items of bondage gear.

METAL RESTRAINTS

Many bondage fans feel drawn to experiment with handcuffs and other forms of metal restraints. For one thing, using such "for real" restraints can often add a delicious intensity and atmosphere to the bondage play. For another, using such restraints can make it very easy (sometimes all too easy) for a relative novice to put someone in very secure, essentially inescapable, bondage. Among other things, their tightness can be adjusted with a high degree of precision, making it possible to get the bondage "baby bear" tight to a very exact degree.

Note: because metal cuffs cannot be cut off or otherwise be very quickly removed in the event of an emergency, understand that the decision to play with any type of locking metal cuff is automatically the decision to choose to play at an increased level of risk.

There are a wide variety of metal restraints available to the bondage fan, including replicas of ancient "leg irons" and similar devices. Indeed, some SM stores make something of a specialty in selling such items. However, those devices are beyond the scope of this book and thus I will concern myself with more conventional metal restraints such as handcuffs, thumbcuffs, and leg shackles.

Legal note: The possession of such devices may be a violation of your local laws. Be sure to check on this.

Handcuffs. Handcuffs come in what can seem to be a surprisingly large variety of styles and types (and costs). However, in essence, there are two basic types: the poorly made handcuffs and the better-made handcuffs.

Poorly made handcuffs can often be spotted at a glance. These types of cuffs are typically sold in places such as novelty shops and adult bookstores. (Unfortunately, some erotic boutiques and even some SM supply stores also sell them.) They may come lined with inexpensive bits of (fake or real) fur. Such cuffs typically have three chain links running in between the two cuffs, whereas the better-made cuffs almost always have either only two such links or a hinge type of device instead of links. Also, poorly made handcuffs are often "identical twins" of each other, which means that they cannot be applied symmetrically. This makes both applying and removing them more cumbersome. Better-made handcuffs will be "mirror images" of each other, allowing a smoother, more symmetrical application and removal.

Furthermore, poorly made cuffs often have an unreliable "double lock" mechanism (a safety feature that prevents the cuffs from being further tightened after they've been applied), or none at all. It's possible for this safety feature to disengage under certain circumstances, or even be intentionally disengaged by the bottom, thus increasing their risk level.

Additionally, the typical poorly made cuff takes a nonstandard key to open whereas the better-made cuffs usually take a more standard, and thus more widely available, key. (One thing that the often relatively ornate nonstandard handcuff key can be used for is as a telltale decoration. I have seen several such keys worn on pointedly visible key rings, or worn as earrings, brooches, necklace adornments, bracelet adornments, and so forth.)

Finally, poorly made handcuffs can often be broken and escaped with relatively little difficulty. For one thing, the chain links running between the cuffs may be of low-quality metal that uses bent-metal links; better-made cuffs typically use a higher-quality metal and welded links. Thus a heavy, or even not-so-heavy, pull may be all that's necessary to separate such links. For another thing, the actual cuff can often be broken by placing your fingers inside the cuff along with your cuffed wrist and applying a strong pull.

All in all, poorly made cuffs, or their keys, may work well as decoration or as a (perhaps not very) subtle signal of your interests, but they usually don't work all that well for serious bondage purposes. If you try to use them for bondage, more experienced bondage fans may get a faint, or not-so-faint, sneer on their faces.

The better made "police quality" cuffs use a good grade of metal, a strong chain or hinge in between the cuffs, and can be both reliably and safely double-locked (in a way that is very difficult or even impossible for the bottom to disengage). Furthermore, such cuffs are not all that much more expensive than the poorly made cuffs. In fact, you might pay more for a pair of poorly made cuffs in an adult bookstore than you would pay for a pair of better-made cuffs in a police equipment store or an SM supply store. Finally, a better-made pair of handcuffs can last for years or even decades before wearing out. All things considered, the bondage fan is usually much better served by buying a better-made pair of handcuffs.

There are four commonly recommended brands of better made handcuffs. One such brand is "Peerless"; others are "Smith and Wesson," "American," and "Hiatts." (Some differ slightly in their double-locking mechanism.) However, there are other perfectly acceptable brands of handcuffs also available, and given that you are not paying for the name brand when you buy them, they are often available at a significantly lower price.

As to where you can buy handcuffs, my first choice would be my local SM supply store or erotic boutique. If you don't already know where these are, they can often be found in the yellow pages under headings such as bookstores, leather stores, lingerie stores, and videos. If you cannot find such a store, try the police supply store or an online vendor.

Care of your handcuffs. Handcuffs, particularly better-made handcuffs, typically require relatively little care. Some people apply a small amount of lubricating fluid such as WD-40 to them to help them go on more smoothly, but that's about it.

It is a good idea to have a few more keys than you think you'll need. While most handcuffs are sold with at least two keys, I recommend that you have a few more around in easy-to-remember locations. (Some manufacturers recommend having a minimum of "one key per locking cuff.") For example, I always carry a handcuff key on my personal key ring – a fact that has led to my occasionally having interesting and fun conversations. It's also common to find keys hanging on small chains worn around the dominant's neck and/or dangling from hooks on the playroom wall. At SM parties, "dungeon monitors" often carry handcuff keys as part of their safety gear.

Extra keys can be purchased from your handcuff vendor, locksmith, or police supply store. Some such keys come with larger handles that make both double-locking and unlocking the cuffs considerably easier. In general, in the SM world, keys tend to be lying around all over the place (except where the bottom can reach them). That's a good thing.

A few other random thoughts about handcuffs. One of the nicer features of handcuffs is that, unlike rope, you don't have to get the bottom's wrists to actually cross, or even touch, behind their back in order to secure them. (Many older and/or larger people simply cannot do this.) With handcuffs, as long as you can get their wrists to within a few inches of each other, you can effectively secure them.

As I mentioned, it is essentially always a good idea to "double lock" the cuffs so that they cannot further tighten. This is usually done with a small pin on the back of the handcuff key that is pressed into a small hole on the handcuff. (Some cuffs have a different type of double locking mechanism.)

One good safety tip is to store your handcuffs, and other metal restraints, in the double-locked position. Because you must have a key to open them for use, this fact will therefore serve as something of a safety check that you do indeed have at least one key.

As both a security feature and to facilitate removing the handcuffs, it usually works better if the cuffs are applied so that the keyhole is facing toward the bottom's fingers or toes.

Some larger people have wrists that are so big that they will not fit into conventional-sized handcuffs, even on their widest setting. For such people, it is possible to buy "oversized" handcuffs.

How tightly should handcuffs be applied? One of the major drawbacks of handcuffs is that they are made of rigid material that is formed into very narrow bands. The smaller edge of a typical cuff is only about one-eighth of an inch wide. This means that handcuffs have the potential to exert a great deal of force that can be both painful and damaging.

To prevent such pain and damage, the cuffs should be applied relatively loosely. A good landmark is that the top should apply the cuffs so that they are just barely able to be slipped over the large bony bump on the back of the bottom's wrist at their little-finger side. (This is the lower end of a bone called the ulna.) Also, bottoms should not struggle heavily against metal restraints.

Caution: Because metal cuffs are made of rigid, inflexible material, any pain associated with their tightness should be relieved immediately. Even short-term periods of extreme tightness can seriously damage tissues.

Another caution: Given the inflexibility of handcuffs, bottoms may find it difficult or impossible to lie on their back while their hands are cuffed behind them. Experiment and get feedback as necessary.

Handcuffs, and other metal restraints, were never designed or intended for prolonged contact with skin. Even when applied properly, they will eventually abrade the bottom's skin. Thus, if you want to do longer sessions in which the bottom remains bound with metal restraints, you have a couple of options.

First, you can try applying some padding, such as a washcloth, between the bottom's skin and the metal cuffs. (I personally have not had much success with this, but it's worth a try.)

Second, you can apply sleeves to the cuffs that are made out of fur, cloth, or soft plastic. This may cost you a bit of range of motion, but otherwise can work fairly well.

Third, it's possible to buy wrist and ankle bracelets that consists of two rows of pyramid-shaped studs with a narrow band of leather between them that is just wide enough to allow the placement of a metal cuff. These can work very well.

Fourth, a friend of mine who is very much a fan of metal restraints highly recommends the use of long-sleeved sweatshirts and sweatpants in connection with the use of metal restraints (and other types of bondage). Such garments often allow quite adequate padding between the skin and the cuff without much slippage and also allow excellent access to the bottom's body. As my friend remarked about such loosely fitting garments, "they're easy to reach inside of."

In summary, while there is a certain amount of skill associated with applying and removing handcuffs, this skill is usually acquired fairly readily with practice.

Thumbcuffs. A pair of thumbcuffs can be a fun toy to play with, but like all items of bondage equipment, especially all metal cuffs, they must be used with a bit of caution. In particular, because thumbs are not all that big, it can be difficult to apply thumbcuffs to the point of "baby bear" tightness.

Thumbcuffs can be applied to, of course, thumbs. They can also be applied to big toes. Male bottoms can have them applied to their penis. (Just be careful about how tightly you apply them!) By the way, I've found that, as is true with handcuffs, it usually works better if you apply the thumbcuffs so that the keyhole is facing away from the bottom's wrists or ankles.

Given that thumbcuffs applied to thumbs or big toes could cause great pain or damage if those areas move, I've had better results when such cuffs are used as secondary bondage as opposed to primary bondage. For example, I've found that it usually works better to first secure the bottom's wrists or ankles with more "mainstream" bondage techniques, then apply the thumbcuffs, than it does to apply thumbcuffs to limbs that are otherwise left unbound.

One final note: like regular handcuffs, there are poorly made and better-made thumbcuffs. Poorly made thumbcuffs often take a nonstandard-sized key, thus creating the potential for problems. I suggest that you only use better-made thumbcuffs that take a standard-sized key.

Metal leg restraints. Metal leg restraints are often referred to as "shackles" or "leg irons." They share many of the design features of handcuffs and, like handcuffs and thumbcuffs, come in poorly made and better-made qualities. The poorly made cuffs can often be spotted quickly because they are "identical twins" and not "mirror images" of each other. They may also not take a standard key. As with handcuffs, it is possible to buy oversized metal leg restraints.

Metal leg restraints are often applied by having the bottom kneel and applying the cuffs to their ankles with the keyholes facing away from the bottom. As with other metal cuffs, they should always be double locked. Make sure that the restraints are applied loosely enough that they do not become too tight when the bottom stands up.

Most metal leg restraints have a chain that is about eight inches to ten inches long running between the cuffs. Such a chain mainly prevents the bottom from running or kicking. (Their knees may still be dangerous.) Bottoms wearing metal leg restraints can still do things such as walk, climb stairs, and have intercourse.

As with handcuffs, metal leg restraints are hard, inflexible items that can become distinctly uncomfortable after prolonged contact with the bottom's skin. Thus, the bottom may welcome some type of padding. In addition to the padding strategies recommend for handcuffs, the use of socks, stockings, or boots can work well here.

Dealing with failure of release mechanisms. Metal restraints are mechanical devices, and all mechanical devices fail every now and then. Thus, as a responsible bondage fan, you should have a back-up release plan in place in case your key one day simply decides to quit working. Please refer to the "Get Loose Kit" section in the chapter called "On Tying Up and Being Untied."

A final note about metal restraints. Candidly, while some bondage fans absolutely love metal restraints and develop a positive fetish for them, many other bondage fans conclude that metal cuffs often don't work all that well. Metal cuffs were never designed or intended for the type of usage that we often put them to. Handcuffs, and other metal restraints, are hard and inflexible, often uncomfortable, are somewhat cumbersome to remove, and cannot be removed quickly in the event of an emergency. (You have to get the key into the relatively small keyhole, and then turn it, in the proper sequence, under two different conditions. Trying to do this could prove essentially impossible under the often-chaotic conditions of an emergency.)

"Where can I buy a set of wrist cuffs like those?"

Thus, while many bondage fans go through something of a "handcuff craze" in their interests, after a while it's not all that rare for the metal cuffs to end up semi-permanently in the bottom of their toybag, with the ropes and non-metal cuffs actually being used much more frequently.

Still, metal restraints do have a significant number of very devoted fans.

USING TAPE FOR BONDAGE

Nowadays it seems that virtually everyone who is getting tied up in the movies, on television, and in the various books and periodicals is getting wrapped up in duct tape instead of bound with ropes.

In researching this book, I did something of a study regarding the suitability of various types of tape for bondage. (Yeah, I know. I got life rough.) Anyhow, I bought various types of tape from a number of different hardware stores, variety stores, and drug stores. I then went on to spend a fair amount of time both on the inside and on the outside of bondage involving tape. Here's a summary of what I found.

Virtually any type of tape can be used for bondage, but the two general types of tape that seem to work best by far are the various types of medical-grade adhesive tape and that ever-popular "Hollywood" bondage item: duct tape.

I think the biggest advantage of using tape is the atmosphere it can lend to the bondage play. As is true with using "real" restraints such as handcuffs, using tape can lend a sense of authenticity to the bondage play. Furthermore, using tape does have its own energy. There are unique sights, sounds (especially that delicious sound of the tape being peeled off of the roll), textures, and smells associated with using tape for bondage. As the tape is applied to the bottom's body there is often a sort of "spinning the web" quality to what is happening. Also, no knots are needed to secure it in place, thus tape bondage can be harder to escape from than bondage which uses knots. (Bondage novices can often do an excellent job of binding someone if they use tape.)

Also, cinch loops are often not needed when applying tape bondage. The wrapping turns of tape alone often do an excellent job.

Probably the major disadvantage of using tape for bondage is that it is essentially always a "use once then throw away" item. Thus, there is an ongoing expense associated with using it that is not a factor with most other forms of bondage equipment. (Of course, you can always stock up when your local store has a sale.)

Another disadvantage to using tape is that it lacks adjustability. When putting a bottom into tape bondage, the top usually has to decide what position they want the bottom, or some part of the bottom's body, to stay in for the duration of the bondage scene.

Some bottoms are allergic to either a particular brand of tape or to the adhesive used to hold the tape in place. If this happens, you should, of course, spend some time experimenting with different brands until you find on that works, or shield the tape from actually coming into contact with the bottom's skin. If the bottom has sensitive skin, it's probably a good idea to do a test patch on a small out-of-sight place before using a new brand or roll of tape.

Caution: Tape can work quite well to bind wrists, ankles, and so forth, but because it may take some hair, and a few layers of epidermis, with it upon quick removal, I do not (with one exception, listed below) recommend using any sort of tape as a blindfold or gag. (Also, mouth-stuffing cannot be attached to tape: another reason to not use tape as a gag.)

> "If you'd wrap the tape there, I couldn't move my fingers."

A final, major disadvantage of using tape for bondage is that removing it from the bottom's skin can be painful, and sometimes even slightly damaging. (I'll describe some methods of helping to limit this problem later.)

Types of Tape

- *Common silver/gray duct tape:* Widely available. Inexpensive. Fairly strong. Using large rolls can be cumbersome. May leave adhesive on the skin when removed. May take a few layers of epidermis with it upon removal.

- *Ace "Duck" Tape:* Fairly strong. Noticeable solvent smell. Available in a number of colors. Not too sticky upon removal. Leaves a slight residue. Overall, works pretty well.

- *Scotch Plastic Tape.* Not too strong. Stretchy. Strong solvent smell. Available in a variety of colors. Noticeably sticky upon removal. No noticeable residue. Overall, doesn't work very well.

- *Scotch Cloth Tape.* Fairly strong. Will hold against strong pressure if you use three or four wrapping turns. Solvent smell not too apparent. Available in a variety of colors. Not too sticky or painful upon removal. Small roll is relatively easy to work with. Widely available. No obvious residue. Rated best overall.

- *"Gauztape" brand self-sticking banding gauze.* Says on box "Sticks only to itself, not skin or hair." Easy to apply. Generally does not stick to skin or hair. (Does stick to pubic hair, but not to head hair or eyebrows.) Can be wrapped around a penis and later removed without much difficulty. Fairly easily breakable, so doesn't work well for binding wrists, ankles, etc., but can work well for genital bondage and as a blindfold.

- *Medical adhesive tape:* Available in a wide variety of widths and materials. Can be somewhat expensive. Some types will leave glue behind on skin when removed.

Dealing with tape-related problems. Most tape is, well, sticky. It addition to sticking to itself, it can stick very strongly to skin, hair, and so forth. This can make the tape both difficult and painful to remove, with a few layers of epidermis and/or some hair frequently accompanying the tape as it is removed. (Thus leaving a very telltale reddened patch of skin on the bottom's body.) Very few people seem to find this type of pain erotic, and a number of strategies have been developed to deal with it. For example...

Many tops apply the tape, particularly the stickier types of tape, to something other than their bottom's skin. Instead, the tape is applied to some type of clothing that conforms closely to the bottom's skin. Examples of this include boots, socks, gloves, sweat pants, and so forth. Applying a layer of plastic wrap to the bottom's skin and applying the tape over that layer can work very well.

The extent to which tape sticks to skin can be limited to a significant degree by first applying a light coating of baby oil or something similar to the skin before applying the tape. Talcum powder can also be helpful in this regard. (Just don't apply them to the same area of skin at the same time.)

Tape bondage is commonly removed from skin by cutting it off. This can be an excellent opportunity for the top to get some practice with their EMT scissors. Be advised that any glue residue that is left on the scissors can be removed with a substance called "Goo Gone" that can be purchased from hardware stores. (Goo Gone should not be used to remove glue residue from skin. Try using vinegar or nail polish remover instead.)

A few words about benzoin. Benzoin is sold in places such as drugstores. It has several uses, one of which is to apply to skin in order to make tape stick more firmly. Such usage is common in the athletic world.

Let me tell you a very brief story, entirely in dialogue:

Jay removing tape that has been applied to his skin: "Ouch."

Jay removing tape that has been applied to a hairy portion of his skin: "Ouch!"

Jay removing tape that has been applied to a hairy portion of his skin that also had benzoin applied before the tape was put on: "Ouch! Ouch! Ouch! Ouch! Ouch!"

CHAINS

When people think of SM, the phrase "whips and chains" tends to be mentioned. Well, this book doesn't deal with whips (see "SM 101" for more info about them) but it does deal with chains, so let's take a closer look at them.

There are two basic types of chains: welded link and bent-metal link. While both types may serve adequate for our purposes, I generally prefer and recommend welded-link chain. (Note: bent-metal-link chain should not be used for suspension or other vertical-load-bearing purposes.)

For ordinary bondage purposes, even very light chain often works quite well – and the heavier chains can prove to be cumbersome. Chain usually does not work well as a "primary" bondage device, although I suppose that very light, flexible chain could possibly be used in this way. Rather, chain is usually used to attach some sort of wrist or ankle cuff, or some other bondage item.

Given that it can be difficult to either lengthen or shorten a particular length of chain, it's wise to have a fairly specific idea of what you wish a particular length of chain to do. You can then have the hardware store clerk cut the chain to the length you desire.

Chain can be "clanky." Some chain aficionados deal with this by applying an outer sleeve of cloth, plastic, or something similar to the chain. Others simply enjoy the sound of the clanking.

Caution: As is true with metal restraints, chain cannot be quickly cut off. Thus is you play with chains, you should have a "get loose kit" consisting of a pair of bolt cutters, a hacksaw with at least half a dozen proper blades, and a vise or pair of vise grips. See the "metal restraints" section for more info.

There are several "chain accessories" that bondage fans should know about:

Locks. While ropes can be knotted, chains will generally need to be held in place with some sort of lock – particularly in places that the bottom can reach.

There are two basic types of locks on the market: combination locks and keyed locks.

Combination locks can be fun to use in bondage play. In particular, you can leave a bottom in chain bondage secured in place with a combination lock and give them a certain amount of time to get loose. However, combination locks cannot be released quickly in the event of an emergency (imagine trying to dial a combination during an earthquake or a fire), so if you use them you should have some sort of quick-release back-up plan.

Keyed locks can be released much more quickly, and generally offer greater security, so I prefer them over combination locks.

Probably the major drawback to using keyed locks is that (well, duh) they require a key to open. (Have a back-up "get loose" kit available.) Requiring a key is often not a problem in and of itself, but what do you do if your bondage involves using several different locks? The easy, basic solution to this is to use locks that are all "keyed alike" – i.e., all open with the same key. You can accomplish this by taking your locks (they should all be of the same brand) to a locksmith. You may also be able to accomplish this by simply buying locks that are all keyed alike. For example, I have seen four-packs of such locks for sale in hardware stores. Also, some brands of locks come with only a small variety of keys, so if you do a little close comparison shopping you may be able to solve the problem that way.

The panic snap. A panic snap is a device used to release a chain that is under tension. Basically, it is a "quick-release" chain link. There are various types of panic snaps on the market. (In the boating world, they're often called "snap shackles.")

As time goes on, I have become less and less impressed with panic snaps as a safety device. For one thing, the typical type of panic snap seems to be made of not especially high grade metal. I have received several reports of unwanted breakages of such devices, including metal failure and hinge failure. However, I have never heard of a failure of a marine-quality snap shackle. Thus I am more and more inclined to recommend that only such snaps be used in critical applications.

Also, I am increasingly of the belief that the use of any sort of panic snap in a vertical chain under tension may be a Very Bad Idea. Even if it doesn't break or otherwise fail, such an item is at best an "all or nothing" device, and while a top may be able to release a bottom with such a device, doing so may send the bottom plummeting towards the floor. I have received credible reports of tops being seriously injured when they tried to hold up a bottom under these circumstances. This being the case, I no longer recommend the use of panic snaps as a safety device under vertical load conditions. I recommend instead the use of some type of block-and-tackle device. Such a device can allow even a very small top to lower a very large bottom safely and in a controlled manner.

The double snap. The double snap is sold in places such as hardware stores and often works well for joining two items together. However, the metal in such devices is often not of high quality, so I do not recommend the use of a double snap in load-bearing situations.

Double snaps are very low-security devices. While they can sometimes be used to link ankle cuffs together, or to attach an ankle cuff to an eyebolt, if a bottom can reach a double snap with their fingers they can be out of it in an instant.

Carabiners. These are links which can usually be quickly opened and shut. They are very frequently used in mountain climbing types of situations. There are many different types of carabiners on the market. (A visit to your local outdoor supply store can be very educational.) Carabiners can be used a quick attachment points, but they can often be opened very readily by a hand. Furthermore, if the wrong kind of pressure is exerted on them, they can pop open spontaneously. (Mountain climbers learn how to avoid applying "the wrong kind" of pressure.) Locking carabiners offer a bit more safety than carabiners that are simply held shut with a spring. In summary, these devices can be fun, but you need to learn more than I can go into in this book before you trust a bottom's well-being to them.

Eyebolts and screw eyes. These are commonly confused items and bondage fans should know the difference.

Basically, an eyebolt is just that – a bolt. It has a large "eye" on one end and it secures in place with a nut (and maybe a washer). Screw eyes are basically screws with a large eye on one end. They are inserted in the same way that more conventional screws are inserted.

Major caution: A very, very common cause of bondage equipment failure is a screw eye pulling loose, frequently from a ceiling or other overhead attachment point. The result is that the bottom falls, and an instant later the bondage gear falls on top of them. The most frequent scenario in which I have heard of this is when the pull on the screw eye is in the same axis that the screw eye was inserted with – for example, a straight downward pull on a screw eye that was inserted vertically upwards into a wooden beam.

On the other hand, I cannot recall hearing a similar report of an eyebolt pulling loose. (There are occasional reports of mishaps like the collapse of the beam into which the eyebolt was drilled.)

I should note that all the screw eyes and eyebolts that are currently being sold in my local hardware stores come in plastic packets that have "not for overhead use" printed on them. It seems that if you want to find devices rated for overhead use, you'll have to go to your local boating supply store or climbing supply store.

Quick links. I have, in this case, sort of "saved the best for last." I have used quick links quite a bit and really like them.

A quick link is basically a link of chain with a side section that can be screwed open and shut. Quick links are available in several different sizes.

While quick links can work if they are simply closed "finger tight" (and that will work just fine if the bottom cannot reach them) they can be made much more secure by simply using a small wrench to tighten them a bit more. This allows the quick links to be tightened more tightly than the mere fingers of a bottom will ever be able to loosen. The top should be sure to keep the wrench within easy reach, possibly in a pocket or on a belt.

SPREADER BARS, ETC.

The term "spreader bar" is typically given to rods made of wood, metal, very sturdy plastic, or some similar rigid material that is incorporated into the bondage to help make some part of the bottom's body more immobile and/or more accessible.

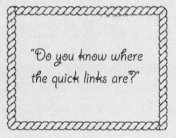

"Do you know where the quick links are?"

Spreader bars range considerably in material and sophistication. I've seen everything from a sawed-off and sanded-down broomstick (very effective, by the way), to elaborate, machined metal bars whose length could be adjusted and locked into place.

Some spreader bars come with screw eyes or eye bolts attached to them (typically one at each end and often one in the middle as well, the latter often used for connection to the bottom's genitals) and/or with holes drilled into them at various strategic intervals. Typically, these bars are cylinder-shaped, but relatively long, narrow, flat pieces of wood, metal, or similar material can also be used.

Probably the most common use of spreaders bars is to keep the bottom's legs spread apart. This is usually accomplished by spreading their ankles widely apart and securing them to the spreader bar; however, sometimes spreader bars are attached to the bottom's widely spread knees instead. One occasionally sees spreader bars used at both locations, but this can border on overkill.

As to how to attach the bottom's ankles (or knees) to the spreader bar, there are, as usual, a number of options.

If the bottom is wearing some type of ankle cuff and the spreader bar comes with screw eyes or something similar, it is usually a very straightforward matter to attach the ankle cuffs to the spreader bar by the use of quick links, double snaps, carabiners, rope, or something similar.

If the bottom is not wearing some type of ankle cuff, the top can tie the bottom's ankles to the spreader bar. This is usually done by placing the bar behind the bottom's widely spread ankles and tying the ankles in place. It's a good idea to run the ropes for these knots through the eyebolts at the end of the bar, or the bottom may be able to pull their legs together by sliding the ropes along the bar. The top can also run a rope from one end of the spreader bar under the bed and up to the other end of the bar for even greater security. Many of the single-limb and double-limb bondage techniques presented earlier in this book work very well for this, although the techniques for tying the ankles into the perpendicular position may work best. Note: tying the bottom's ankles to the bar often immobilizes them more effectively than merely securing the ankle cuff to the bar.

Using a bar to immobilize the bottom's hips. One of the more interesting uses of a spreader bar is to immobilize the bottom's hips. This can be done by bringing their legs together and placing the midpoint of the bar on the back of the bottom's legs just at the junction of their upper legs and their buttocks. (If the bottom is male, be sure to lift his testicles before bringing his legs together.)

A twelve-foot length of rope works well here. Place the midpoint of the rope between their upper thighs and run each end out to the bar, then run the tails under the bar in a feet-to-head direction. Bring the tails back up to the midpoint, pull them snug, then run the tails again over the bottom's upper legs (just below the bottom's testicles, if he's male) and run the tail under the bar in a head-to-foot direction. Repeat this pattern until you run out of rope and tie the tails together. If this is applied snugly, the bottom will be unable to rock their hips from side to side, thus immobilizing them to a significant degree.

This technique can be modified a bit to work effectively if the bottom's legs are spread apart. In this case, each upper thigh may be lashed to the bar individually.

Strong Caution: Given that the center of a bed tends to "sink in" more than the edges of the bed, significant pressure could be exerted on the midsection of the spreader bar when it is used this way. This pressure may be increased even further if the spreader bar is run under the midpoint of the bottom's buttocks. The pressure may be dramatically further increased if the top were to sit on this portion of the bottom's body while they are tied in this way (for example, if a female top were to sit on a male bottom's penis for intercourse). In such situations, there is a very real possibility that a bar made of relatively rigid material, such as wood or brittle metal, might break. The cracked portions could produce sharp pointed ends which could injure the bottom (or, if the bottom is on a waterbed, puncture the bag), plus their skin could end up being pinched between the fragments to a painful, injury-producing degree.

There are a number of steps that can be taken to reduce the risk of such injuries. Probably the most important step is to choose your spreader bar wisely. Bars made out of hardwood, steel, and similar materials will be sturdier and less likely to break. Also, most bars do not break without giving some kind of warning. In situations I have been involved in where the bar broke, invariably at least a few "warning creaks" were heard well before the bar actually broke. Additionally, a towel or some other type of relatively heavy cloth can be placed between the bottom's body and the bar to provide them with at least some protection in the event that the bar breaks. (If the bottom is on a waterbed, the top would be well-advised to place some padding in between the bar and the bed as well.) Finally, the risk of such a break can be almost entirely eliminated by placing the bottom on a lightly padded section of floor instead of on the bed.

If the bottom is lying face-up on the bed with their ankles tied together in the anti-parallel position, the top can add a bit of spice to the tie by placing a spreader bar so that it's behind the bottom's knees and tying it in place there. This is especially useful for those sessions in which the top intends to devote a significant amount of attention to the bottom's genitals.

THE STICK

This very immobilizing bondage technique involves using either a strong rod or a long, relatively narrow (2"-4") piece of sturdy wood – thus, "the stick" – to bind the bottom lying face-up with their legs together and their arms held firmly by their sides. Such a stick is typically long enough to run from the base of the bottom's neck down their back to at least their mid-calf area. It usually takes a bit of "tweaking" to apply a stick properly to a particular bottom, but once the top gets the fit right, the bottom will find themselves well and truly bound. Also, while it may be a bit time-consuming to apply this bondage technique the first time, the ropes may be secured in place so that applying it on subsequent occasions can be done fairly rapidly.

This technique will typically need at least six lengths of rope. (One or two supplementary lengths of twelve-foot rope may be added as well.) It's probably best to start with three twelve-foot lengths and three six-foot lengths. The three twelve-foot lengths will be used to secure the bottom's upper chest, lower waist area, and lower-thigh area to the stick. Two of the three six-foot lengths will be used to bind the bottom's wrists closely to their sides, and the final length will be used to bind their ankles to one another, but not necessarily to the stick.

To prepare the stick for use, have the bottom lie face-up on the ground with their hands close by their sides and their ankles together. Place the stick on the ground beside them with one end just at the top of their shoulders. Note the location of their armpit area, lower waist area, wrist area, and lower-thigh area. Also note the approximate distance from the midline of their body to their wrists.

Fold each twelve-foot length in half (bight the rope) and wrap the midpoint of each bighted rope around the stick at the three approximate locations mentioned. (It usually works better if the rope is wrapped around the stick so that the tails end up on the underside of the stick.)

Now use two of the six-foot ropes to create prefab Lark's Head cuffs (as described in the "single-limb bondage" chapter). Attach these cuffs to the stick as you would attach them to a bedpost, leaving enough free so that the cuffs will just barely be beside the bottom's body.

To apply the basic tie, lay the stick down on the floor and have the bottom lie on top of it so that the top of the stick is just at the base of their neck and the various ropes are placed about where they need to be. Given that the stick may be pressing directly against bony parts of their body such as their spine and tailbone, it will often be necessary to place a folded towel or something similar between the stick and the bottom's skin, especially if the bottom is naked. If may also be necessary to add additional padding in locations such as the small of the bottom's back and under their knees. (Get feedback as indicated.) This padding should not normally affect the security of the bondage.

Once the bottom is lying face-up on top of a properly padded stick, the top can begin tying them in place. I usually do this by working in a head-to-toe direction.

To immobilize their upper body area, the top can run the tails of the first twelve-foot rope either over both the bottom's chest and upper arms, or just over their chest (under their arms). Given that some bottoms may be able to "shrug off" this rope if it's tied over their arms, some tops may prefer to tie this rope over just the bottom's chest. Because the purpose of this rope is to prevent movement of the bottom's upper torso, it should be tied in place as high up on the body as possible. The final knot can be a Square knot or Surgeon's knot. Some bondage fans like to use a Trucker's Hitch here.

Next, have the bottom bring their wrists to their sides and tie them closely in place there with the prefab Lark's Head cuffs.

To immobilize the bottom's lower torso area, wrap the tails of the second twelve-foot rope over their forearms and lower abdomen, preferably over the bottom's pelvic bone. Secure this rope in place very snugly and tie off with a Square knot, Surgeon's knot, or Trucker's Hitch. Make sure that the final knot and the tails are placed so that the bottom cannot possibly reach them.

To immobilize the bottom's upper legs, wrap the tails of the lowermost twelve-foot rope over the bottom's lower thighs, just above their knees. Secure this final rope very snugly and tie off as you did with the others.

Finally, bind the bottom's ankles together using the six-foot rope and any of the double-limb bondage techniques.

Supplemental ropes may be applied over the bottom's lower chest, just above their elbows, to help immobilize their arms and to the bottom's mid-calf area to help immobilize their lower legs. Caution: The rope wound around the bottom's mid-calf area could press painfully into their shins. Adjust or pad as necessary.

> "She asked me about the handcuff key on my keychain."

At this point, the tie is basically complete, and the bottom is highly immobilized.

A couple of final points:

As with using a bar horizontally across the bottom's hips, there is some danger of breakage if this technique is used on a bed or in some similar manner.

While this technique is very immobilizing, it is possible for some bottoms to rock back and forth until they turn over. This can be prevented by running a second, perhaps shorter, stick under their upper thighs, lower back, or similar location to prevent such side-to-side rocking.

THE LONG STICK

The long stick is another very immobilizing variant of the basic stick tie. The main difference is that in this bondage technique a much longer stick is used – anywhere from seven to ten feet in length – and the bottom's wrists are tied to the upper end of it. Due to the exceptional length of this stick, this position almost always requires that it be done on the floor.

Caution: In addition to possible "bad pain" developing in the usual locations such as the small of the bottom's back and under their knees, some bottoms will develop "bad pain" in their shoulder area from having their hands tied over their head in this position. As always, get feedback and correct as necessary.

SPECIAL TECHNIQUES

WRISTS-**B**EHIND-THE-**B**ACK **T**IE **for larger bottoms.** Many bottoms are so large that they cannot bring their wrists together behind their back, yet they would very much like to be tied in this position. There are several ways to deal with this problem.

One solution is to use handcuffs. This can work reasonably well; however, a frequent problem with this approach is that the bottom is often not able to lie comfortably on their back if their wrists are in metal cuffs. An interesting variant on this approach is that two or more pairs of handcuffs can be linked together if a single pair does not provide enough reach. On a recent TV broadcast, it was mentioned that five pairs of cuffs needed such linking to secure the wrists on one especially large suspect.

Another solution is the use of leather cuffs, particularly locking leather cuffs such as the Humane Restraints. This approach, which often solves the problem very well indeed, can work better than using handcuffs. The wrist cuffs are usually wide enough, and clear enough of sharp points or edges, that the bottom can lie comfortably on their back if their wrists are cuffed behind them with these devices. (They may need some extra padding over the cuffs and, as is true with essentially every bottom who is lying on their back with their wrists secured behind them, they may need pillows or towels under their buttocks and/or back to take their body weight off their wrists.) The cuffs can be joined together by a series of quick-links, or by a short length of chain – perhaps with quick-links at each end. Such an arrangement allows for the bondage to be adjusted with a good degree of flexibility.

The bottom's wrists can also be secured behind their back with rope, but a somewhat unorthodox approach is often needed. The technique I will describe calls for two six- to 12-foot lengths of rope, and possibly for a third six-foot to 12-foot length as well.

To apply the basic tie, take one of the bottom's wrists and apply one of the single-limb bondage cuffs to it. While different rope cuffs can be used here, I recommend the basic obi knot cuff. Apply the cuff to the bottom's left wrist, then bring their arm back behind their back, bending their elbow as far upwards as they can reasonably tolerate. Separate the two tails, then run one tail over the bottom's right shoulder and the other under their right armpit. Dress the tails and tie them together. Repeat this process for the bottom's right wrist. This completes the basic tie.

This tie often works very well in its "basic" version; however, a number of refinements are possible. For example, to prevent the bottom from "shrugging" the wrist cuffs from their shoulders, you can tie the free tails of one cuff to the shoulder-loop of the other cuff. (I recommend using a Finishing Lark's Head knot for this.) This can usually be done in a way that puts no pressure at all on any part of the bottom's neck.

If that is still not enough, the top can use the third rope to help limit the motion of the bottom's arms. This is done by looping the midpoint of the rope through both cuffs and drawing the cuffs as closely together as the bottom can tolerate. Then tie the tails together and finish by running

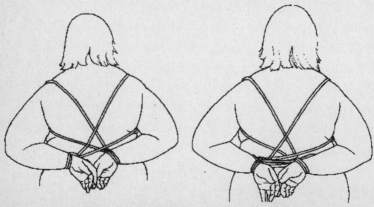

large-bottom arm tie & variation

the rope around the bottom's sides and securing it in place at the front of their waist.

When this tie is employed, it may be possible for the bottom to reach the cuff on one hand with the fingers of their other hand. However, if the cuff has been properly tied they will usually not be able to loosen it. This can be particularly true if a few extra tucks were done when the cuff was applied.

HIP CONTROL ROPE

This is a very simple but often very powerful and effective bondage technique. It typically calls for a six-foot length of rope, and wider rope or tubular webbing often works better than narrower rope for this purpose.

This technique is used during doggie-style intercourse and similar rear-entry positions. The top simply bights the rope, and perhaps ties the ends together. They then pass the rope in front of the bottom's hips and grasp the "handles" thus created in either hand, usually with either handle protruding from the bottom of their fist. This very simple technique can allow the top a powerful degree of control over the bottom's hips.

LEG ELEVATION AID

This bondage technique is used when the bottom is lying on their back and they need to keep their legs elevated for a prolonged period of time. It can be of real assistance when the top desires access to the bottom's genital and/or anal area. Depending on the size of the bottom and the desired position, either a six-foot length or a twelve-foot length of rope can be used. (The twelve-foot length typically works better.) As with the Hip Control Rope, wider rope or tubular webbing often works better.

In a very simple example of this tie, the bottom is lying on their back with their knees closely drawn up to the sides of their chest. The rope is bighted

leg elevation aid

and the midpoint is looped over the bottom's left lower thigh, just above their knee joint. Both ends are then passed under the bottom (this process may be assisted by having the bottom first roll slightly to their right, and then to their left) and then looped just above the bottom's right knee joint and tied in place.

Caution: This can result in a fairly strong pressure being applied to the back of the bottom's upper legs. Pad as necessary.

There are a number of variants possible with this technique.

One variant is to simply tie more wrapping turns around the bottom's lower thighs. This can distribute the pressure and make the tie more comfortable. Taking measures to prevent wrapping constriction can also be useful here. In such a case, the top might use the "wrap, tie, and tuck" cuff knot for the first thigh and the "pre-fab Lark's Head" cuff knot for the second thigh.

Another variant is to pass the tails behind the bottom's neck instead of their back. This approach can help eliminate the possible risk of having the rope slip down the bottom's back, but it can also apply a very strong

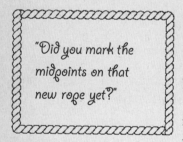

"Did you mark the midpoints on that new rope yet?"

amount of pressure to their neck. This problem can be mitigated by applying the rope as low as possible on the back of their neck and by padding this area. Hint: There's probably a pillow handy.

A third variant of this technique is to run one tail (the "innermost" one) under the bottom's back and the other tail (the "outermost" one) around the lower portion of their neck. The tails are then joined behind the bottom's opposite thigh in the usual manner.

ONE LONG ROPE – STARTING AND STOPPING

Throughout this book, I have pretty much described bondage techniques that start at the midpoint of the rope and work outwards. Truth be told, my experience is that this is the approach that usually works best. Still, just for the sake of completeness, let me describe a method of starting at one end of a rope and working your way out to the other end.

Before I go too much further, let me mention in passing that bondage generally works better when you use several shorter lengths of rope than one long length. Furthermore, the more extensive the bondage, the truer this tends to be.

Still, it can be great fun to use a single, relatively long, length of rope, particularly for double-limb bondage techniques. This can be especially true when applying the various types of hogties or other bondage that involves arm harnesses and/or leg harnesses. There is a sort of "spinning the web" energy associated with applying bondage of this type that can be intense.

Note: As I mentioned, this type of bondage often works best for relatively elaborate bondage that involves double-limb techniques. For a single-limb technique, particularly something like a Spread-eagle bondage, I recommend the French Bowline knot with at least two wrapping turns around the limb for use as a single-limb cuff. This can be secured in place by using something like a Round turn with a slipped double half-hitch located someplace where the bottom cannot reach it.

Starting a long rope. Bondage that begins with one end of a rope can be effectively begun by creating what's called a running loop in one end. While there are a number of ways to do this, a simple and quite effective method is as follows: Take one end of the rope and fold back a bight. When using bondage rope of average thickness, folding back about six inches should work fine. Create a loop in the end by tying this bight

end-of-rope loop

into an Overhand knot or a Figure-eight knot. Dress the knot so that only a very little tail is left over. For security purposes, pull this knot fairly tight. (Remember that a Figure-eight knot is usually the easier of the two knots to untie afterwards.)

Now that your loop is created, either thread the free end of the rope through the loop or fold the loop back over the knot and pull the rope through the loop. This latter approach can be particularly useful if you're using a very long rope.

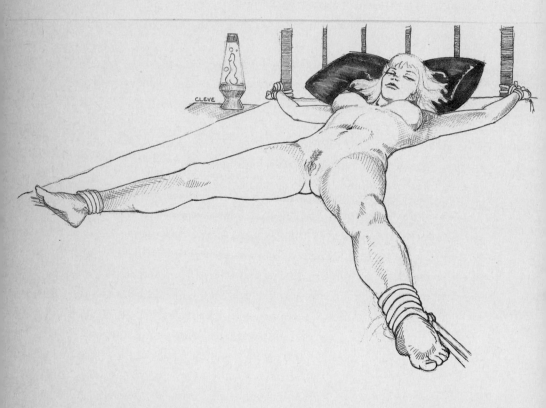

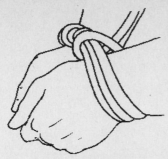

using cinching turns to reduce constriction

Caution: There is a potential hazard regarding cinching constriction when using this technique to apply double-limb bondage, such as when tying two wrists together. This potential hazard can be dealt with relatively simply by merely applying the bondage so that when the cinching turns are applied they reduce the space between the wrists to zero. If for some reason this cannot be done, you can also greatly mitigate the cinching constriction by winding the last cinching turn around only one of the wrapping turns before moving the rope on to tie another body area.

Finishing a Long Rope – The Square knot on a Bight. A very good technique for tying off "the single free end" of a long rope can be called the Square knot on a bight. This knot is often taught as a bandaging technique and works very well for that. It is usually tied as a final knot in the last cinching turns of the bondage.

bighted Square Knot

To apply this knot, you create two opposable ends by bending back the last six inches or so of the rope to form a bight. One good way to do this if you're applying the rope mainly with your right hand is to fold the rope back towards you over your left index finger. You then leave the arch of this bight where you want the finishing knot to be, and fold the remaining few inches of the rope around the area in question. (This will typically be over the cinch loops just created by the rope.) Bring the free end up to the bighted end and tie them together. You can use any of the common finishing knots here, including the Square knot, Granny knot, Surgeon's knot, or Bow knot.

TELL-TALE BONDAGE

This is not a technique so much as it is an idea. The basic idea here is to tie the bottom in some way, or to include something in the bondage, that will indicate that the bottom has moved when they are not supposed to while in a loosely monitored situation.

Examples of telltale bondage include the following:

* Placing the bottom in a face-down hogtie position and then stacking plates on their upper back.

* Placing a glass or cup of water on the part of the bottom's body that the top wants the bottom to keep still.

* Incorporating toilet paper into the bondage, the idea being that the line of toilet paper sheets is not to be broken.

* Having the bottom touch the fingertips of their left hand and of their right hand together, holding a coin in place between each pair of fingertips.

There could obviously be many more variants on this concept. Again, the basic idea is that the bottom is tied in such a way that as long as they hold still, nothing is disturbed, but if they do move something is disturbed in a way that cannot be fixed before the top returns.

In Conclusion

I want to thank you for reading this book. I hope you learned new and valuable information from it, and I hope it gave you a few things to think about.

I hope that you are a better, safer person for having read this book, and that the world is a better, safer place for your having read it.

I want you to regard this book as a starting point, not as an ending point. It would please me a great deal to learn that you went on to learn, explore, and grow in this area of life – and perhaps even made original contributions of your own.

I also want you to regard this book as only one point of view. While I would certainly like to think that it's a balanced, informed point of view, it's definitely not the only point of view that an informed person could come to. By all means seek out the opinions and advice of other informed practitioners.

Also please keep in mind as you seek out other informed practitioners that there is no objective standard of training or expertise in this area, and that people learn and grow at different rates. Thus, while "time in grade" is generally useful, understand that there are people who have been exploring SM for only a few years who possess substantial understanding and insight, and there are also people who have exploring SM for decades who are superficial, clueless, ham-handed blunderers.

Don't automatically accept anybody as an authority. In particular, the possession or lack of formal academic degrees has essentially no predictive value regarding whether or not a given person possesses any significant expertise or insight in this area. Check each authority out carefully for yourself and make up your own mind regarding how much insight they have.

Achieving any significant amount of growth or expertise in this area takes time, honest work, intellectual rigor, dedication, study, trial and error, trustworthiness, an open mind, willingness to learn, willingness to admit that you were wrong if that was indeed the case, and a certain degree of humility. One of the wonderful side-benefits of study in this area is that you will be challenged to develop and improve all of the above qualities in yourself.

I wish you and your companions well in your explorations. I sincerely hope that I have helped to prepare you to embark on your journey into the world of erotic bondage with the knowledge, judgment, skill, and equipment you will need for success. Perhaps we shall even meet as you explore.

Just please remember: take one more precaution than you think you need to.

GLOSSARY

Analingus: Oral stimulation of the anus.

Baby-bear point: Adjusting the tightness of bondage so that it is neither too tight nor too loose but "just right."

BDSM: A relatively new term in the SM vocabulary. Attempts to address the wide variety of viewpoints and styles of SM play. Often understood to stand for "bondage and discipline, dominance and submission, sadism and masochism."

Bend: A name given to a type of knot used to join two ropes together.

Bight: To fold one end of a rope back upon itself.

Bighting the rope: To fold a rope in half.

Bottom: A very general term for the person who takes the submissive and/or masochistic role, and/or the person who gets tied up, during SM play. The precise definition of this term is the subject of never-ending debate within the SM community.

Capillary refill test: One of several tests done in an attempt to evaluate how well blood is flowing into and out of a limb. Typically performed by slightly pressing down on a fingernail or toenail until it becomes pale, and then quickly releasing the pressure. A normal capillary refill time is typically less than two seconds.

Cinch loops: Loops that are run over wrapping turns and in between bound limbs. A very effective means of increasing the security of the bondage and regulating the tightness to a very precise degree.

Close monitoring: Paying close attention to a bottom, especially a bottom in bondage. In a close monitoring situation, the top can typically both see and hear the bottom and can return to them within a very few seconds without running.

"Cone out": A bondage escape technique in which the fingers and thumb of a bound hand are narrowed by pressing them tightly together into a cone-like shape, followed by an attempt to pull the bound hand free from the bondage.

CSM: Circulation, Sensation, and Movement – criteria for judging how well a limb is tolerating bondage.

D&S: Stands for "domination and submission" – in general terms, a form of SM play in which one person is willingly obedient to the commands of another.

Dressing (the rope): Fine-tuning the location of the rope prior to securing it in place.

"Do Me Queen": A somewhat pejorative term for an overly selfish or greedy bottom. A bottom much more interested in how the top can please them than in how they can please the top.

Eel: A slang term for someone who attempts to escape from their bondage. Many eels are smart, knowledgeable, creative, flexible, and determined.

Edge Play: A general term for SM play in which both the risks and the intensity are increased to an extreme degree.

Finishing knot: A knot used to tie the two tails together at the end of the bondage technique. Common examples of such knots include a Square knot, a Granny knot, a Surgeon's knot, a Surgical Granny, or their slipped variants.

Flat webbing: Nylon webbing, such as seat-belt webbing that has no hollow inner space. Flat webbing is, in general, not much used for bondage. However, a form of it known as "mule tape" often found at places like army surplus stores can work excellently.

Frapping turns: A more formal "ropespeak" term for cinching turns. Used to adjust the tightness to a very precise degree.

Gonad thinking: Basically, thinking with one's gonads instead of with one's brains (sometimes known as "thinking with the little head"). Rushing into an erotic situation, or significantly increasing its intensity, without adequately thinking about it first.

Good pain/bad pain: Good pain is typically caused by relatively non-damaging activities that add to the erotic intensity of the play; a typical example would be the pain caused by skillfully pinching a nipple. Bad pain is typically caused by activities that might be damaging and that usually do not add to the erotic intensity of the play. An example would be pain caused in a bottom's neck by making them strain to hold an awkward position.

Good tight/bad tight: "Good tight" bondage is bondage which is tight enough to do its job without causing significant harm or pain. "Bad tight" bondage is typically bondage that has been applied so tightly that it may cause significant harm or pain.

Hitch: a name given to a knot used to attach a rope to a non-rope item such as a bedpost. A common example would be the Double half hitch.

Load: A rope that has tension on it. For example, a rope that is being used to raise a 50-pound weight can be said to be "under load."

Load spreading: The (usually unwanted) separating of a knot typically produced when some portion of it is placed under load. Commonly seen in Square knots.

Loop: coiling a portion of a rope without wrapping it around an object.

Loose monitoring: Staying close enough to the bottom that the top can hear them if they yell for help and return within a maximum of thirty seconds without running. Comparable to how close one would stay to a sleeping infant. Visually checking the bottom about every 15 minutes. Sometimes supplemented with electronic monitoring devices such as a nursery monitor.

Lunge Distance: A degree of proximity close enough to your bottom that you can reach them with a lunge. This is typically a maximum of 20 feet.

Perineum: The portion of the bottom's body between their anus and their genitals.

Positional asphyxia: Difficulty in breathing, caused by being placed in a particular position, that has progressed to the point of becoming dangerous.

Predicament bondage: A form of bondage in which a bottom can ease one aspect of their bondage only by making another aspect of it worse.

Queening: Sometimes called "face sitting." Sitting or squatting over the bottom's face so that the top's anal or genital area is pressed against the bottom's face. A popular form of female-dominant play.

Rope Salad: An unorganized tangle of ropes stuffed into a nightstand drawer, toy bag, or similar location. Often a somewhat ominous sign of carelessness or cluelessness.

Round turn (540 turn): A wrapping turn of rope that goes one and a half times around an object.

Rule of finger: measure a part on your finger or thumb that is about one-half inch long or one inch long.

Sensation Play: SM play that concentrates on the sensations created by spanking, whipping, and other activities, usually without much in the way of emotional domination and submission (D&S play). The degree of bondage used can vary.

Setting (the knot): The final act of pulling a knot tight.

Silent Alarm/Safe Call: A standard BDSM safety practice in which someone, when playing with a relatively new play partner in private, first tells a trusted friend where they will be and who they will be with. If the person does not check in by an agreed-upon time (and often in an agreed-upon way) the trusted friend is to assume that the person is in trouble, probably due to nonconsensual behavior on the part of the new play partner, and to take action. Silent alarms are primarily for the protection of bottoms, but they can also be useful for tops. They are mainly used for play dates, but some very cautious players use them for social meetings as well, particularly when they are meeting someone that they might play with.

Slippery knot: A knot that has been tied in such a way that it can be quickly released even if it is under tension. Common examples of such knots include the Bow knot and the Half-Bow knot.

Slipped variants: Knots tied in such a way that they are now "slippery."

Slipped Square Knot: another name for a Half-bow knot.

Squeeze test: Test for capillary refill of the palms.

Suspension bondage: A form of bondage in which the bottom is either partially or entirely suspended off of the ground. A high-risk practice that takes special equipment, training, and knowledge.

Switch: A person who, under the right circumstances and with the right person, enjoys taking either the top or bottom role. The author is a switch.

Tails (of a rope): The tips of a rope.

Tantric Sex: A highly spiritual form of sexuality, with roots in India, that teaches techniques for forming a very strong sense of connection with one's partner. (Tantra comes from the word meaning "to connect" or "to weave.")

Tooth (of a rope): A rough estimate of how rough or smooth the outer surface of a rope is.

Top: A very general term for the person who takes the dominant and/or sadistic role, and/or the person who does the tying, during SM play. The precise definition of this term is also the subject of never-ending debate within the SM community.

Toy Bag: A container in which SM "toys" are kept. Examples include briefcases, softball bags, violin cases, gym bags, and guitar cases.

Turn: Wrapping a rope around an object such as a wrist, ankle, or bedpost.

Tubular Webbing: A form of flat nylon webbing that contains a hollow inner space. Tubular webbing is strong, low stretch, washable, and available in many colors. It is very popular for bondage.

Unmonitored bondage: A form of bondage in which the bound person is highly immobilized in bondage that is either very difficult or impossible to escape from and there is no other person readily summonable to quickly come to the bound person's assistance. The form of bondage by far associated with most bondage-related fatalities.

Wrapping constriction: Bondage tightening to an unwanted and possibly dangerous degree when tension is applied to wrapping turns.

Wrapping Turn: A coil of rope or similar material wrapped around a wrist, ankle, bedpost, etc.

Yelling Distance: The area around a bound person from which an individual can be summoned by a yell from the bottom, and can respond within 30 seconds without running. A slang term for loosely monitored bondage.

Yabyum position: A very popular sexual intercourse position associated with Tantric sex. In the classic yabyum position, the male sits cross-legged while the female sits in his lap facing him with his penis in her vagina as they embrace each other.

BIBLIOGRAPHY

General knot and non-erotic bondage information:

"The Ashley Book of Knots" by Clifford W. Ashley. Doubleday, 1944.

"The Essential Knot Book" by Colin Jarman. International Marine, 1986. 0-87742-221-4.

"The Handbook of Knots: A Step-by-Step Guide to Tying and Using More Than 100 Knots" by Des Pawson. DK Publishing, 1998. 0-7894-2395-2

"Hojo Jitsu: Samurai Tying-Arts" and "Hojo Jitsu II: Samurai Tying-Arts" Both Copyright 1998 by Dragon Video Library.

"Kill or Get Killed" by Rex Applegate. Paladin Press. 0-873640-84-5.

"The Klutz Book of Knots" by John Cassidy. Klutz Press, 1985. 0-932595-10-4.

"Knots for Climbers" by Craig Luebbben. Falcon Press, 1985. 0-934641-58-7.

"Knots and How To Tie Them" by Boy Scouts of America. Copyright 1978. 0-8395-3170-2.

"The Morrow Guide to Knots" by Mario Bigon and Guido Regazzoni. Quill Press, 1981. 0-688-01226-4.

"On Rope" by Allen Padgett and Bruce Smith. National Speleological Society, 1987. 0-961-5093-2-5.

BDSM information:

Unfortunately, many of these excellent books have fallen out of print. They are worth looking for.

"The Bottoming Book: Or, How to Get Terrible Things Done to You By Wonderful People," by Dossie Easton & Catherine A. Liszt. Greenery Press, 1992. 0-9639763-1-1.

"Come Hither: A Commonsense Guide to Kinky Sex" by Gloria G. Brame. Fireside, 2000. 0-684854-62-7.

"Consensual Sadomasochism: How to Talk About It and How to Do It Safely," by William A. Henkin, Ph.D., and Sybil Holiday. Daedalus Publishing, 1996. 1-881943-12-7.

"Different Loving: The World of Sexual Dominance and Submission," by Gloria G. Brame, Will Brame, Jon Jacobs. Villard Books, 1996. 0-679769-56-0.

"Health Care Without Shame: A Handbook for the Sexually Diverse and Their Caregivers," by Charles Moser, Ph.D., M.D. Greenery Press, 1999. 1-890159-01-8.

"KinkyCrafts: 99 Do-It-Yourself S/M Toys for the Kinky Handyperson," edited by Lady Green with Jaymes Easton. Greenery Press, 1997. 0-9639763-7-0.

"Learning the Ropes: A Basic Guide to Safe and Fun S/M Lovemaking," by Race Bannon. Daedalus Publishing, 1993. 1-881943-07-0.

"The Leatherman's Handbook II," by Larry Townsend. Jiffy Fulfillment, Inc., 1995. 0-503099-99-6.

"The Lesbian S/M Safety Manual: Basic Health and Safety for Woman-To-Woman S/M," edited by Pat Califia. 0-917597-12-5.

"The Loving Dominant," by John Warren, Ph.D. Greenery Press, 2000.

"The Master's Manual: A Handbook of Erotic Dominance," by Jack Rinella. Daedalus Publishg, 1994. 1-881943-03-8.

"The Mistress Manual: A Good Girl's Guide to Female Dominance," by Mistress Lorelei. Greenery Press, 2000. 1-890159-19-0.

"Screw the Roses, Send Me the Thorns: The Romance and Sexual Sorcery of Sadomasochism," by Philip Miller and Molly Devon. Mystic Rose Books, 1995. 0-964596-00-8.

"Sensuous Magic: A Guide for Adventurous Couples," by Pat Califia. Masquerade Books, 1998. 1-563336-10-3.

"SM 101: A Realistic Introduction," by Jay Wiseman. Greenery Press, 1996. 0-9639763-8-9.

"Ties That Bind: The SM/Leather/Fetish Erotic Style: Issues, Commentaries and Advice," by Guy Baldwin. Daedalus Publishing, 1993. 1-881943-09-7.

"The Topping Book: Or, Getting Good At Being Bad," by Dossie Easton and Catherine A. Liszt. Greenery Press, 1994. 1-8901059-15-8.

Other Books from Greenery Press